mud sweat & GEARS

CYCLING FROM LAND'S END TO JOHN O'GROATS (VIA THE PUB)

LAND'S END

Ellie Bennett

MUD, SWEAT AND GEARS

Summersdale Publishers Ltd
46 West Street
Chichester
West Sussex
PO19 1RP
UK

www.summersdale.com

Printed and bound by CPI Group (UK) Ltd, Croydon

ISBN: 978-1-84953-220-4

Substantial discounts on bulk quantities of Summersdale books are available to corporations, professional associations and other organisations. For details contact Summersdale Publishers by telephone: +44 (0) 1243 771107, fax: +44 (0) 1243 786300 or email: nicky@summersdale.com.

For Mum and Dad, who met at a cycling club circa 1949 and who loved cycling (or at least they did until Dad bought a motorbike); and for Anne, with love

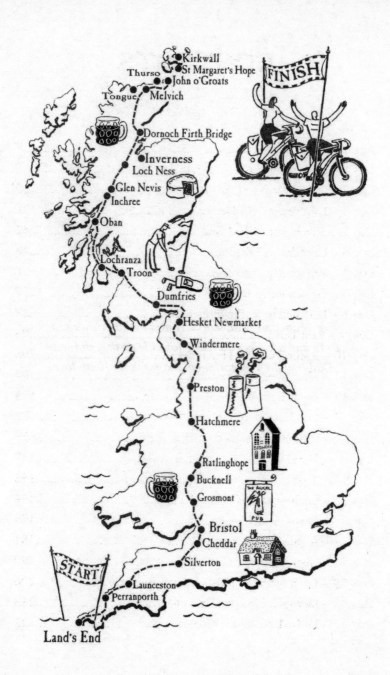

Kirkwall
St Margaret's Hope
Thurso
John o'Groats
Tongue
Melvich
Dornoch Firth Bridge
Inverness
Loch Ness
Glen Nevis
Inchree
Oban
Lochranza
Troon
Dumfries
Hesket Newmarket
Windermere
Preston
Hatchmere
Ratlinghope
Bucknell
Grosmont
Bristol
Cheddar
Silverton
Launceston
Perranporth
START
FINISH
THE ANGEL PUB

Land's End

CONTENTS

ABOUT THE AUTHOR

Ellie Bennett is a recent convert to long-distance cycling but has been exploring the real-ale pubs in her home town of Bristol for many years. After her epic End-to-End ride she decided it was time for a good sit down, so she turned her hand to writing – this is her first book.

LAND'S END

>>>>>>>>>>>>>>>>>>>>> TO >>>>>>>>>>>>>>>>>>>>>>>

PERRANPORTH

'One more wouldn't hurt,' said Mick.

I looked at him doubtfully. 'I'm not sure. It's gone three already. What time does it get dark in Cornwall at this time of year?'

'Not for ages,' said Mick, waving his hand dismissively. 'One more and then we'll get on.' He headed back to the bar with our empty beer glasses.

It was a lovely pub, to be sure, and goodness knows when we would be passing this way again. But I was having serious doubts about our ability to cycle over 800 miles if we had managed to get waylaid so easily after only 16. Any competent cyclist would have got to Launceston by now – or at least Liskeard or Lostwithiel. We were not even in St Ives. *And* we had been four hours late setting off from Land's End. We should have been there ready to go at nine that morning but we had overslept. By the time we had stopped for a full English breakfast and Mick had done some last-minute shopping, it was one o'clock before the van containing us and our bikes had finally pulled into the Land's End car park.

The plan had originally been to get the train down to Penzance. However, when I attempted to book tickets for the journey, I quickly discovered that travelling by train in this country is not at all straightforward when accompanied by a bike. It proved impossible to book two people and two bikes on one train. One company said we could reserve places for our bicycles but they could not guarantee that they would be able to travel with us when we arrived at the station. What were we supposed to do? Tell the bikes to follow us down later and we would meet them in the pub?

Rail travel is also not cheap – unless you book six months in advance and travel at five o'clock in the morning. I couldn't find anything under £200 on the Internet so I trudged to my local station in the vain hope that speaking to someone in person would elicit more information. After queuing for an age, I finally found myself in front of the ticket window and asked whether I could purchase some saver fares to Penzance.

'They're not available,' said the woman behind the counter.

'When will they go on sale?' I asked.

The woman in the ticket office shrugged in a manner that clearly indicated she was not remotely interested in either me or my train enquiry.

'No idea,' she said. She handed me a leaflet. 'There's a phone number on there – ring that,' she said.

When I got home and phoned the number on the leaflet it connected me to an offshore call centre and the conversation went like this:

'Can you please tell me when the saver tickets for Bristol to Penzance become available for travel at the end of April?'

'I'm sorry, those tickets have all gone.'

'But when were they sold? I was told at the station they are not yet available.'

'Those tickets are not yet on sale.'

'But you just said they have sold out.'

'Yes, those tickets have all sold out.'

'When did they sell? I thought they were not yet available?'

'That is correct, they are not yet available.'

'So how can they be sold out?'

'Those tickets have all gone.'

'Do you know what tickets I am asking about?'

'No, Madam.'

'Can I just check, are you reading from a script?'

'Yes, Madam.'

'I thought so. OK, I'll leave it.'

At this point I had given up and had called my friend Frank, who had kindly agreed to drive us down to Land's End in his van.

Avoiding the shops and other attractions, we walked through the complex to the headland and gazed out across the Atlantic. Below us we could hear the sea crashing onto the granite rocks. Clad in T-shirts, with the springtime sunshine warming our skin, it was hard to believe that after the Isles of Scilly the next landfall was Canada, and that Land's End is on the same latitude as Newfoundland and Labrador. Typical temperatures in the winter in Labrador fall between -10 and $-15°C$. Thank goodness for the North Atlantic Drift! If the Gulf Stream does shift, or switch off altogether as some scientists predict, then it might be prudent to invest in a few pairs of thermal pants.

How many less than sensible ideas have been cooked in the pub after one too many beers? This one was no exception. I had been out on an enjoyable bike ride with my good friend Mick a couple of months previously and we were relaxing with a couple of well-earned pints. (Years ago Mick and I had dated for a couple of disastrous months, after which we gave up, agreeing that we weren't each other's type. This immediately took the pressure off and we subsequently found we got along rather well. We had fallen into the habit of going for walks and bike rides together once or twice a month and had shared quite a few holidays. Whether our friendship would survive this particular jaunt remained to be seen.)

'I think we should cycle End-to-End,' he had announced, after the third pint.

I looked at him blankly. How did one cycle end-to-end? Did he mean single file?

'End-to-End!' he said, impatiently. 'From Land's End to John o'Groats!'

'Are you mad?' I had protested. Neither of us was experienced at cycling long distances. We had once cycled the length of Hadrian's Wall and back – a ride that had taken over a week, averaging about 25 miles a day – and it had nearly killed us. We were hopelessly slow and had even given up going out with the local cycling group because we kept getting left behind. 'We can't manage that! We're rubbish,' I said.

'No we're not,' replied Mick. 'You just think we are because you keep comparing yourself to cyclists who are faster than you.'

'Well, yes, that's pretty much everyone,' I retorted.

'But don't you see? We don't have to go fast. We just have to keep going.'

'Yes Mick, we have to keep going for miles and miles, thousands of miles.'

'Ha – less than a thousand,' he said triumphantly. 'It's only 874 miles, I looked it up.'

'Only!' I muttered.

Mick was clearly determined and after another beer or two I began to share his enthusiasm. Maybe we could manage it. After all, how hard could it be? Mick was right; it was simply a case of 'keep pedalling'.

'OK,' I said. 'We'll do it.'

Now, as we tried not to look at the remembrance plaques for cyclists who had died en route, my enthusiasm was slightly less pronounced.

'What the hell was I thinking of, agreeing to this?' I wondered.

I was still not sure what had made me do it. Maybe it was because I was charging towards yet another birthday, which now seemed to be rushing at me faster than a TGV en route to Paris. In my twenties and thirties there had seemed to be all the time in the world to do the things one idealistically hopes to achieve in life. The world was full of possibilities. Plenty of time to get rich, have a career, climb Everest, drive around the world in a beaten-up old bus – the usual things. I was now more than halfway through my forties and had managed none of them. I was running out of time; so maybe it was that. Or maybe I was just a complete idiot. My nerves were getting the better of me and I felt slightly sick. I was hopelessly unprepared. All I had to back me up were a handful of training rides and a lot of bravado. It was too late to back out now though. Mick, ridiculously, seemed unconcerned and was thoroughly enjoying himself.

We headed back towards the start line outside the entrance to the Land's End complex. Confusingly, right next to the white line painted across the road with 'start' on one side and 'finish' on the other, was a no-entry sign for the road ahead. We pondered this for a while before deciding to ignore the sign and, in true cycling tradition, started our epic journey from Land's End to John o'Groats by heading off in the wrong direction up a one-way street.

This was it. We were off! I turned to wave to Frank as we headed out of sight. I was not used to cycling on a heavily loaded bike and the front wheel wobbled alarmingly. I stopped waving and hastily grabbed the handlebars.

Three minutes later, on the very first gradient, my chain fell off. I looked at it ruefully. Maybe I should have treated myself to a decent bicycle instead of relying on my old Dawes, which I had been riding around for years, and which had really seen better days. I had not been very kind to it; maintenance involved chucking some oil on the chain every twelve months or so and grudgingly changing the brake blocks when I noticed that after careering down hills, there was a marked reluctance on the part of the bike to come to a halt at the bottom. I pulled the chain back onto the chainring. I did not, of course, have anything as useful as some disposable gloves in my panniers, so after replacing the chain I wiped my oily hands on some grass. This simply added green smears to the black ones already adorning my palms. Great. Mick, who was riding a brand new Cannondale touring bike, which he had purchased especially for the trip, tried not to look smug but failed.

Once back on the road we followed the coast road north. The first few miles were fairly gentle and I began to feel better. Thick yellow gorse lined the road as we coasted through small Cornish villages and past the chimneys of disused tin mines. Near Pendeen we passed Geevor Tin Mine Museum. Tin mining was once big business here but the mines have long since closed. Many Cornish miners headed off to the mines of South America,

Australia and the USA among other places, taking their famous Cornish pasties with them. This explains why every year in June the mining town of Calumet, Michigan, holds a Pasty Fest, which includes a pasty parade and a pasty bake-off, and why *pastes* are also a local delicacy in Pachuca, Mexico – although they are usually filled with un-Cornish ingredients such as chicken tinga, or lamb and poblano chilli peppers. We stopped at a local shop for one and my pasty, although peppery, did not contain poblano chilli peppers, for which I was grateful. I am not good with spicy food; I can barely manage a ginger nut biscuit without waving my hand up and down in front of my mouth and going 'Ooh, it's hot isn't it?'

'I predict,' said Mick, as we cycled along, 'that we won't get more than four days of wet weather on the whole trip.' About thirty seconds later, the sun disappeared and Atlantic rain came rolling in towards us from the coast. We hastily donned our raincoats and popped our blue, plastic £1.99 capes over the top as an extra layer of weather protection. Mick commented, rather unkindly in my opinion, that swathed in blue plastic I resembled a condom. He had obviously not looked in the mirror, he was not exactly a picture of sartorial elegance himself. However, the capes were effective in keeping the rain off, although it was annoying when the hood kept falling over my eyes, casting a bluish hue on the landscape and making Cornwall look like Atlantis. The rain was still coming down when we reached the Tinners Arms at Zennor – a thirteenth-century stone building nestled off the road – and the temptation was too much to resist. With its open fire, flagstone floors, low ceilings and hard wooden benches, it's the sort of place you would like to take friends visiting from abroad, as they would go crazy for it.

D. H. Lawrence stayed at the pub in 1916 before renting a cottage just down the road – and it was while living in Zennor that he wrote *Women in Love*. When Lawrence arrived at Zennor he loved it, writing enthusiastically that he felt as if he was 'coming to the Promised Land'.

Sadly, the dream soon turned sour. It was the middle of World War One and the local people were suspicious of Lawrence's German wife, Frieda. Frieda had a habit of wandering the paths across the top of the cliffs singing German songs, and she also managed to arrange for a German newspaper to be delivered to the cottage every week. As time went by, in the highly charged and suspicious atmosphere of the war, rumours spread that she was a spy. When Frieda hung out her sheets on the washing line, local villagers suspected her of signalling to enemy U-boats. To make matters worse, Frieda had a cousin, a pilot named Baron Manfred von Richthofen. By the spring of 1917, von Richthofen had become infamous in Britain, better known by his nickname, the Red Baron. The couple also used to have fearsome arguments. There is some speculation that Lawrence was having an affair with a local farmer, so perhaps that's what the arguments were about. In any event, in October 1917 the authorities ordered them to leave the county under the Defence of the Realm Act of 1914. They moved to Hermitage in Berkshire and at the end of the war they left Britain and never came back.

We were drinking Tinners (what else?), an ale brewed by St Austell Brewery, and it was going down exceedingly well, but after the second pint I put my foot down.

'No more or we shall never get there,' I said firmly.

We had pre-booked the youth hostel at Perranporth 30 miles further on. After that we intended to find places as we went along, as we were not sure how far we would manage to get each day. Now I wondered whether even booking one night's accommodation had been a good idea. Mick reluctantly followed me out to our bikes and we set off once more. We scooted through St Ives – by now it was past five o'clock. At least the weather had started to improve and the late-afternoon sun shone warmly. After St Ives the terrain began to get hillier, up and down, up and down, and I began to have an inkling of the enormity of the task in front of us. This journey was going to be rather hard work.

At last, as it was getting dark, we wearily reached Perranporth and followed the signs for the youth hostel, which was perched on cliffs overlooking the beach. The building, constructed in the 1950s, was once a coastguard listening station and there were some interesting displays on the wall showing the hostel's history. It opened as a hostel in 1982 and is now a favourite haunt for surfers, as well as walkers and cyclists, enjoying this fabulous, if somewhat hilly, section of Cornish coastline. The warden made us a cup of tea as soon as we arrived, which was jolly nice of him, and we sat for a while gazing out of the window as the sun went down. Eventually we heaved ourselves up and went to unpack.

We were booked into separate dormitories so I went off to my dorm, not realising Mick had managed to get his room number wrong. When I went to find him, he was busy assuring a very attractive young Korean woman he would be sharing her room for the night, much to her evident consternation. I corrected him and pulled him out, apologising on his behalf. In fact, he was sharing a dorm with a group of male ramblers from Wolverhampton. His attempt at hiding his disappointment was truly pathetic to witness. The next day he told me he had hardly slept a wink for all the farting and snoring.

Once unpacked, we wandered down into the town to see what was happening which, in early April, did not appear to be very much. We stepped into a fairly deserted pub with much-too-bright lighting and supped a couple of pints of Doom Bar from Sharp's Brewery. The beer takes its name from an infamous sandbank at the mouth of the Camel Estuary, where over the centuries countless ships have come to grief on the shifting sands. It was said that ships would rather take their chances in a storm at sea, than risk entering Padstow Harbour across the dreaded Doom Bar. The drink itself is a reasonable session beer but is now mass-produced and fairly ubiquitous. I find it a little bland by real ale standards – although it's a million miles ahead of keg beer – and at least it was local.

By now we could barely keep our eyes open, so we retired to the hostel to cook supper. Preparing two Pot Noodles didn't require a lot of effort, but it was all we could manage in our weary state before falling into bed – and that was after only 45 miles. For a brief moment I wondered how on earth we would manage the next 900 or so, before falling sound asleep.

Stats
Miles: 47
Total miles: 47
Pints of beer (each): 3
Hills pushed: 14
Laggardly cyclists: 2

PERRANPORTH TO LAUNCESTON

The next morning the weather was glorious. The view from the hostel wasn't bad either. Below us the golden sand of Perranporth beach stretched away to the sea. Farther out at the western horizon was a large ship, seemingly motionless, at the point where the aqua blue sea met the cloudless azure sky. Gulls swooped and wheeled on the cliff faces, calling insistently to each other. Waves crashed rhythmically onto the rocks below and then lapped gently onto the beach. The smell of salt blew off the sea.

We sat in the tiny garden on the cliff top, sipping a cup of tea and playing 'fetch the twig' (we couldn't find a stick) with Roxy, the hostel's resident Jack Russell. Every time we threw the twig she charged after it at top speed, usually overshooting it by a few feet before skidding to a halt, wheeling about and then returning it triumphantly to our feet. She would then run about in small circles, beside herself with excitement, until the exercise was repeated. I loved her exuberance; Roxy was a creature that knew the only thing to do with life was to grab it by the scruff of the neck and give it a good shake. When we, somewhat regretfully and stiffly, mounted our bikes and set off, Roxy came down to the gate and gave her bottom a good wiggle in farewell. We waved her goodbye and headed off up the coast towards Newquay.

After agreeing to embark on this journey, I had quickly realised that I would have to undertake the route planning if we were going to get any done at all. Mick seems to think planning a route is completely unnecessary. I suspect he views it as some kind of personal failing, verging on cheating, if he has to consult a map during the course of a journey. His 'method' is to decide on a destination, head off in that general direction and hope he ends up roughly where he intended.

I had discovered this while walking with him in the Lake District. I foolishly assumed that, as Mick had been there many times before and I had not, he would be equipped with maps for the walks we were going to do. Not so. Too late, I discovered he had not brought one map with us. Instead he would start each walk by climbing the nearest hill, then look about, decide on the direction of the intended destination and then strike out, often ignoring footpaths altogether. On one memorable occasion, a mist descended and we spent many miserable hours walking around in circles under the towering bulk of Scafell Pike, before finally working out the way back to the campsite. As someone who can barely go to the shops without a map for reassurance, I found this very disconcerting.

'Don't you ever get bored of looking at maps?' Mick asked one day when I had spent an hour studying a new purchase, a 1:25,000 map of the Mendip Hills.

'No, I can look at them for hours,' I replied, 'and when I've finished I can turn them upside down and look at it all again!'

I knew that if we were going to have any chance of navigating the country without accidentally finding ourselves on the M5, I would be the one who would have to do it.

We had already agreed on the first major criterion: we wanted to avoid main roads if we could possibly help it. Cycling on main roads is horrible, especially for cyclists as inexperienced as us. For most of the country this would not be a problem; but the only obvious and direct route out of Cornwall was the A30 and this is the route many End-to-Enders take, particularly if time is a consideration. As we did not want to tackle the main road, and as we had up to a month to complete the trip, the other choices were meandering routes up the centre of Cornwall or the coast road up to Padstow, and then an inland route to Launceston. I opted for the scenic coast road. However, I underestimated how 'lumpy' this road would prove to be.

Yesterday's hills were mere pimples compared with the ups and downs we encountered on the 15 miles between Newquay and Padstow. This section of the Cornish coast is like a roller coaster. I switched onto the 'granny wheel', the lowest gear, but to no avail; these hills were far too steep for either of us to stay on our bikes. Time and again we wearily pushed the bikes to the summit, remounted and rolled gingerly down the other side, clutching the brakes for all we were worth, rounding a small cove speckled with surfers only to be confronted with another fearsome gradient on the other side. The beauty of the scenery, with rolling hills and the blue Atlantic beyond, made it worthwhile, however, and despite the agony it was better than cycling up the dreaded A30. Well, that's what I told Mick every time he complained anyway. By the time we reached Padstow, 30 miles along the coast from Perranporth, we were definitely in need of a rest.

Rick Stein's presence is everywhere in Padstow. No wonder it has been nicknamed 'Padstein'. Not only will you find his famous seafood school here, but there are four Rick Stein restaurants, catering for every budget, plus a delicatessen, a patisserie, a gift shop and a smart hotel offering bed and breakfast accommodation. Unsurprisingly, there is some resentment among local residents, who blame him for attracting smart city types to the town, hiking up the prices and making houses unaffordable for local people. On the other hand, there is no doubt his presence has increased the number of tourists who visit the town, bringing their purses and wallets with them. Eschewing any Stein establishment, we opted for tubs of cockles and whelks from the fish stall by the jetty, which were delicious and which we enjoyed whilst sitting on the harbour wall in the sunshine. After our seafood, we then repaired to the Shipwrights Inn, where we both had a wonderful pint of Proper Job from the St Austell brewery, an excellent IPA (India Pale Ale, a type of beer originally developed for export in the eighteenth century) which went down a treat; so well, in fact, that we felt compelled to have a second pint.

By now we both had a fairly strong desire for respite from hills, so we decided to turn inland and ride the half a dozen miles along the Camel Trail to Wadebridge. It proved to be a good choice. The Camel Estuary sparkled in the sunshine alongside the cycle track and the cycling was flat and easy going. It was great to see it busy with so many families out for a jaunt. We were enjoying it so much we were almost disappointed to reach Wadebridge, where we left the path and crossed the bridge that gives the town its name. According to the sign on the bridge, it was originally built in 1468 by the Vicar of Egloshayle, the Reverend Thomas Lovibond, which I thought a fantastic name. It was known as the 'Bridge on Wool' from a local legend that it was founded on sacks of wool, which seems to me to be an odd choice of material to stand a bridge on. Wouldn't it get all soggy? Maybe there was nothing else suitable to hand...

Leaving Wadebridge, a steep climb out of the town ensued. We decided to break our rule of avoiding main roads for a short spell and headed straight down the A39 for a dozen miles to Camelford – as on checking the map I noticed the road followed the line of the River Allen and was therefore likely to be flatter than the minor roads on either side. Mercifully, I was right. Although the route was undulating, there were no major shocks until just before Camelford, when the road began the climb up to Bodmin Moor. At a pub somewhere near Camelford we refuelled with another pint of Proper Job. Mick thought the pub was reminiscent of the Slaughtered Lamb from the film *An American Werewolf in London*. Someone was eating a roast dinner with their bare hands and few of the patrons appeared to be familiar with toothpaste.

We were now in the Cornish interior, well away from the coast, and the scenery was very different. Cornwall is like a chocolate-covered Brazil nut. It's sweet and gooey around the outside but has a harder, grittier centre. We pressed on, hoping to find a country pub and B & B further along the road. Neither appeared and we eventually found ourselves peddling wearily into Launceston. From the Camelford road, the entry into Launceston was an unbelievably steep hill down, followed by an unbelievably steep hill up. The town straggled messily up the hill, and as we wearily pushed the bikes up it I became determined not to return the same way, no matter what. We spotted a local man, swaying gently as he climbed the hill, and stopped to ask for directions.

'Excuse me, good sir, do you know of any fine bed and breakfast establishments in the vicinity?' we enquired.

'Aaaarhghh urrggghhh ssshhhhwwwrrrrrrdddddd,' he offered in reply.

Gosh the accent was strong hereabouts.

We tried again.

'Are you aware of any hostelries nearby where we may rest our weary heads?'

'Uuuggghhhhhsssshhhhwwwrrrrrddddddaaaarrrrrggghhhh!!!!!!'

As he finished uttering these sounds he took several steps backwards and staggered into a wall. We took his response to be a negative, thanked him anyway and continued toiling up the hill. By now it was seven o'clock and we began to wonder whether we would be able to find anywhere at all to stay. We wandered around what we presumed was the centre of town, but we couldn't see any signs offering accommodation. Finally, Mick spotted a Salvation Army building and we wondered whether we might be able to get a bed for the night there. No need – one of the officers kindly walked us to the top of the town and pointed us towards Glencoe Villa Bed & Breakfast. We gratefully thanked him and knocked on the door. The proprietors were a kindly couple in their sixties and helpfully allowed us to put the bikes in their garage before booking us in. They asked whether we wanted single rooms or a double and we told them that we didn't mind – Mick and I have spent enough time camping in tiny tents and cramped camper vans to be quite comfortable in each other's company. We were given a room at the top of the house and were delighted to find the adjoining bathroom was huge, and furnished with every kind of bubble bath, oil, soap and other washroom accoutrements you can imagine. We were both desperate to soak our aching limbs; we had a brief fight for first use of the bath and discovered we would not both fit through the doorway at the same time. I lost the battle and in desperation tried to use the 'if you were a gentleman' – card which failed completely.

'I'm no gentleman,' crowed Mick triumphantly, locking the door behind him.

After we had both enjoyed a hot bath, we hit the town. This was not a pleasant experience. I cannot recommend Launceston for a night out; it lacks class, even by my unexacting standards. Groups of youngsters hung around the streets drinking super-strength lager or sped about in small cars with enormous spoilers, making as much noise as their twin-bore exhausts and sub-woofers would allow. A police car cruised the streets and an ambulance sat on standby in the main square. We spotted what were clearly a couple of tourists who had strayed here by mistake – they soon scuttled off looking rather scared. We ate a mediocre Chinese takeaway, sitting on a bench near the ambulance, and then supped an even more mediocre pint of beer in a dreadful pub. As far as we could tell, all the pubs in Launceston were dreadful. After that we called it a day and headed back to the B & B, taking care to avoid the boy racers on the way.

Stats
Miles: 56
Total miles: 103
Pints of beer (each): 2
Hills pushed: More than I can remember – loads
Instances of disgraceful ungentlemanly conduct: 1

DAY
3

LAUNCESTON
>>>>>>>>>>>>>>>>>>>>>> TO >>>>>>>>>>>>>>>>>>>>>>
SILVERTON

We were late leaving the next morning for a number of reasons. Firstly: the breakfast. When we later compiled our stats – best B & B, best beer, etc. – the accolade for best cooked breakfast went to Glencoe Villa. What a shame it was in Launceston, as we thought it unlikely we would stay there again. Fantastic pork sausages with no fat, eggs with bright-yellow yolks, cooked to perfection, and mountains of buttered toast. Secondly: the stories our landlady told us. Her husband had worked in the Diplomatic Service and, as she chatted to us about her life in Soviet Russia under Brezhnev, and in Burma and India, the minutes slipped away. Once again, our lack of urgency was getting the better of us. Finally, I dragged Mick away, as I feared we would still be there at teatime.

We had a quick scout around Launceston before heading off. In the daylight the town didn't seem so bad and I wondered whether our judgement of the previous evening had been unfair. Is it ever possible to form an objective opinion of a place based on a few hours visit when one is utterly exhausted and cheesed off? But I can only describe things as they felt at the time and I cannot say I left Launceston with any feeling of regret.

Coasting down the hill, we almost immediately cycled out of Cornwall and into the county of Devon.

Devonshire hills are different to Cornish ones. The short, sharp shocks of the Cornish 'curtseys' are replaced by long, sweeping climbs up and long rallies down. Unlike the Cornish hills, these were far too long to get off and push, so we had no choice but to switch into a low gear and keep pedalling. Hah – sounds so easy, doesn't it? It wasn't. After a few yards of uphill cycling, there was nothing I wanted more than to get off and have a lie down on the grass verge by the side of the road. I knew if I did there was a good chance I wouldn't get back on again, so I developed my own method of getting up hills, which served me pretty well most of the time. This is my technique:

- Engage the lowest gear possible.
- Stay sitting in the saddle.
- Fix your gaze on the tarmac, roughly 12 inches beyond the front wheel. Never, ever look up to see how much farther up the hill there is to go, this will result in immediate discouragement and a possible refusal.
- Count from one to ten in elephants, thus: one elephant, two elephants, three elephants and so on.
- Control your breathing to coincide with an in and out breath on each elephant.
- At ten, repeat as often as is necessary to propel yourself to the top of the hill.
- If things get desperate and the ability to count deserts you, switch to expletive mode: fuck this, fuck this, fuck this.

There is something about the way you spit out the F-word that keeps you going. Strange, but true. Try it!

- If however all has failed and disaster befalls you then safely pull over, indicating your intentions if you still have the strength to do so. Indulge in a good blub and, if possible, eat something for energy. A banana is ideal, but anything you have with you will do. Then recommence.

Mick prefers to honk uphill. I don't mean he throws up, although he has come pretty close on occasion, especially after a skinful the night before. To 'honk' is to ascend a hill by standing up on the pedals out of the saddle. This does appear to be more effective in getting up the hill quickly if you can do it, but I can't, not with loaded panniers anyway. The back wheel starts wobbling in an alarming way and I don't get anywhere. I suppose it's a matter of preference or capability and Devon certainly gave us plenty of opportunity to practise our individual methods.

Luckily, the road was very quiet from Launceston to Okehampton and after a while the hills evened out. We were cycling up the old A30, which has now been declassified, with the traffic being carried by the new, fast A30 slightly farther west. For the next 15 miles we therefore pretty much had this 'old' road to ourselves. As we neared Okehampton we were pleased to have Phil Horsley's little guide book with us – *Land's End to John o'Groats: The Great British Bike Adventure*. Instead of turning left and linking up with the busy main road into Okehampton, we followed his advice and took a right turn towards Sourton, where it is possible to get onto the Granite Way – a fantastic cycle path into town. Like the Camel Trail in Cornwall, this was another ex-railway track, and the path is now part of NCN (National Cycle Network) 27.

Soon we came across the very impressive Meldon Viaduct. Constructed of wrought and cast iron, it is a 'scheduled' ancient monument, built in 1874 for the London and South Western Railway main line between Waterloo and Plymouth. It is a beautiful structure and has now been fully refurbished. It was constructed as a single line, but just four years later it was decided a two-way line was needed. A second viaduct was built next to the first and the two were lashed together in an effort to reduce sway when a train crossed the line. This would seem to me to indicate a lack of foresight but, hey, what do I know?

We continued on, soon accompanied by that rare sight in modern Britain, a functioning railway line, and the two of us rode pretty much side by side into Okehampton.

It was time for a cuppa, and we sought out a cafe in the centre of the town. While supping our drinks, a news piece on the TV in the corner caught my attention. It was about potholes in the road and some numpty parish council somewhere around Essex. Apparently the council was claiming it would not be filling in holes in the road as they acted as a 'traffic calming measure'. I stared at the TV in disbelief. Maybe I had misheard? It was fortunate Mick returned from a visit to the toilet just in time to hear this piece of claptrap, or I may have been forced to conclude I had been dreaming. Potholes are a menace to cyclists and one has to be constantly vigilant. On a poor road it sometimes takes a swerve manoeuvre to avoid the hazard, which is dangerous and annoys the cars behind; I fail to see how leaving big holes in the road would calm anybody.

Since we set off I had been keeping a journal of the trip in the form of a blog as I had promised to keep friends and colleagues updated on our progress. I was hoping to upload the latest entries in Okehampton but, to my surprise, none of the cafes advertised a Wi-Fi connection. This was Devon after all, not Dar es Salaam. Surely they used the Internet here? I decided to try the library.

'Excuse me, do you have Wi-Fi here?' I enquired.

'Why Fie?' repeated one of the elderly ladies at the enquiry desk, looking mystified.

'I want to upload my blog onto the Internet,' I explained.

At the word 'Internet' she visibly brightened.

'Oh yes, we have the Internet,' she said proudly. 'It's on that machine over there.'

She pointed to a computer that was set apart from the rest.

'Thank you, but I need to use the machine I have with me, as that's where I have everything stored,' I explained. This was proving to be hard work. I tried again. 'In some places you can get onto the Internet without plugging into a connection.'

The ladies were clearly a bit out of their depth with the concept.

'You can use a laptop or a phone to do it,' I added.

'Ooh! What an excellent idea,' said her colleague with enthusiasm.

'Er yes,' I said. 'So… I take it you don't have that here?'

They both shook their heads. 'No dear, we don't have anything like that here. They probably have it in Exeter. More call for it there.'

It's not a hard and fast rule, but computing technology does seem to be a generational thing. I was ahead of the library assistants and my daughter is way ahead of me. She talks in a strange tongue of mysterious processes that mean nothing to me: downloading apps, bluetoothing photos, syncing her iPhone. When I ask her what any of this means she looks at me as if I am a total idiot.

Some years ago I bought my mum a computer, as I thought she would like to use it for surfing the net, finding out useful titbits of information and so on. If things went well, I thought – optimistically as it turned out – she could even email my brother, who worked abroad. The next time I went to visit, the machine had been sent to the naughty corner. It was facing the wall and she had put a towel over the screen.

'It hates me!' she said vehemently when I enquired what the machine had done to warrant such treatment. 'It never does what I want it to and it keeps staring at me!'

In an effort to show her the machine was, in fact, inanimate and not capable of hating anything, and that it could be jolly useful, I plugged it in.

'Come and look Mum,' I said encouragingly, patting the seat next to me. 'You can find all sorts of interesting things on the Internet.'

'Oh yes?' she retorted. 'Like what?'

I pondered. What would impress her? She was quite interested in stars and stuff, and it was not long after the Hubble telescope had started sending back images to Earth. I thought I would find a picture of something from space to show her. I typed 'Venus' into the search engine and called her again.

'Come and look at this!' I said.

'OK love,' she said. 'I'll just make us a cup of tea and then I'll come and look. I still think the damn thing hates me, though.'

While she clattered about in the kitchen I waited expectantly for an impressive picture of our sister planet to appear on the screen. This was long before broadband had been developed, and it took an age for the picture to load, gradually revealing itself, line by line, down the screen. I watched in horror as I realised what image the search engine had found in response to my request. As the woman's nipples came into view, I frantically hit the close button, but nothing happened. Inexorably the picture continued to reveal more and more of the woman's not inconsiderable attributes. I was bashing the keyboard now, to no avail. Finally, as Mum appeared in the doorway with a tray of tea and biscuits, I leaned over and pulled the cable out of the wall.

'Right then love, what have you got to show me that will persuade me this damn thing is worth having?' she said, as she settled herself down next to me.

I looked at the now blank screen.

'No, you're right, Mum,' I said. 'It's pretty rubbish, really. I'll go and get the Scrabble board.'

After the library I gave up trying to find somewhere in Okehampton to upload my blog. Maybe I would find somewhere in Somerset. On the way out of town we stopped at the local supermarket for provisions. I disappeared inside for some sandwiches and was somewhat surprised when I emerged fifteen minutes later to see Mick gamely pushing a number of shopping trolleys across the car park. He told me what had happened. One or two older folk, spotting him standing outside the store in his yellow hi-vis jacket and blue cap, had mistaken him for a trolley attendant. He didn't want to embarrass them by explaining their mistake so took their trolley with a view to parking it in the designated bay. En route, however, other passing shoppers understandably made the same mistake and added their trolleys to the front of the first two. A couple of them were even heard to comment that it was so nice and so unusual to see a trolley boy these days. Soon he was vainly trying to steer half a dozen trolleys, only narrowly missing stationary cars as he inexpertly weaved his way across the car park. Eventually he shuffled them into a bay and we cycled off quickly before anyone else could nab him. However, this was not the last time those bright-yellow jackets would result in a case of mistaken identity.

We were heading for a village called Sticklepath and, when we saw a brown sign for a cycle path to the village, we foolishly took it. It started off promisingly, with a gentle ride along a flat valley. Ten minutes later, however, we were climbing up an enormously steep country lane with a gradient of one in four (or for Europhiles 25 per cent), which resulted in the first tears of the trip. I gave Mick a tissue and told him it would all be OK. Only kidding – it was me who had started blubbing. Mick looked at me, aghast, and then started yelling at me.

'What the hell is wrong?' he shouted. 'It's only a hill; push the bike to the top.'

Through snot and tears I tried to explain that it was not just the hill, it was the fear. Fear that I couldn't do this, that I would find it too difficult; that I would give up. He wasn't getting it so I told him to get lost, which he promptly did, pedalling off out of sight. Left alone, I stood there and gave myself a good pep talk.

'One bad hill, that's all it was,' I told myself. 'One lousy hill; stop snivelling and get back on the bike.'

Finally I caught up with Mick and we carried on along the track in silence. I made a mental note to write a strongly worded letter to Devon County Council about its appalling choice of cycle route, which I suspect was designed more for the benefit of motorists, saving them from being hindered on the main road up the hill out of town by inconvenient cyclists. Later, Mick confessed that seeing me cry frightened him. He, too, was afraid I was about to give up. For some reason he thought yelling would strengthen my resolve.

Rather than dip and dive through any more country lanes with crazy gradients, we decided to stick to main roads until we got to Crediton. We were now in the heart of Devon, or, in the local dialect, *Debn*. At Crediton we stopped for a pint of Otter Ale at the Three Little Pigs, which had a very idiosyncratic decor, although my mother would have said it was trying too hard. It was here that Mick pushed our campaign to be served a full measure a little too far.

For centuries weights and measures acts have made it illegal to give short weights or measures to consumers. A pint of milk must be a pint; a litre of petrol must be a litre. Wine is served in set measures, as are spirits. Yet, legally, a pint of beer is defined as 95 per cent liquid. How can this be right? How many drivers would like it if every time they filled up with a litre of petrol only 95 per cent was dispensed? When we are in the pub, therefore, every time we are served a short measure we ask (nicely) for it to be topped up. No one has ever refused, although the level of courtesy with which it is served does vary enormously. In the Three Little Pigs, however, Mick took a large swig out of his glass before handing it back to me.

'Not a full pint,' he gurgled through a mouthful of beer. 'Ask the barman to top it up will you?' The barman and I both looked at him and simultaneously shook our heads.

From Crediton, we travelled along the leafy back lanes of Devon to Thorverton, before struggling up the hill into Silverton, a village about 8 miles north of Exeter. We were headed there because I had marked the village as having a pub with an entry in CAMRA's

Good Beer Guide. CAMRA, for those who aren't familiar with the term, is the acronym for the Campaign for Real Ale – the organisation that saved British beer drinkers from the horrors of Double Diamond and Watneys Red Barrel. In 1971 four young men from the north-west of England – Michael Hardman, Jim Makin, Bill Mellor and Graham Lees – were on holiday in Ireland. While visiting Kruger's Bar in Dunquin, County Kerry, they got talking about the poor quality of British beer and decided to start a campaign to revive proper ale. Back home, the popularity of the organisation soon grew; evidently lots of people were fed up with drinking rubbish beer and now CAMRA is one of the most successful campaigning organisations in the country. In my book, those four young men deserve medals – and one of them did indeed get one. In 2009 Michael Hardman was given an MBE for services to the brewing industry and never was a gong so richly deserved. Now CAMRA has more than 100,000 members including three Ladies, four Lords, 80 reverends and more than 1,600 doctors.

I was very pleased to discover that at least 1,600 doctors appreciated the wondrous qualities of real ale. It was a pity that Mick's doctor was not one of them, as he very nearly jeopardised the whole journey, or at least threatened to turn it into a beer-free one – which is pretty much the same thing. Mick had made an appointment to see his GP for a minor ailment, but his own doctor was away and a locum was covering the appointment. The locum was a clean-living sort of chap with scrubbed pink cheeks and a checked tweed jacket, who no doubt spent his weekends dragging his hapless family for 20-mile hikes when they would much rather be sat at home watching TV or playing video games.

'How much do you drink, Mr Webster?' he asked.

Mick was slightly mystified – he had come about a spot on his eyelid (he is a bit of a hypochondriac).

'Dunno, it varies – a couple of cups of tea in the morning, coffee at lunchtime... '

'No, no, how much *alcohol* do you drink, Mr Webster?'

'Oh, I see! Well, I would say two to four pints, once or twice a week.'

'Two to four pints? Eight units? In one go?'

Mick was slightly flustered now. 'Um, yes... but not always and not every night. Can't afford it for a start. It depends.'

'Mr Webster you are a binge drinker! I am going to make a note of it on your medical record! No more than two units per day maximum.'

True to his word, he made a note on Mick's medical record that he was a binge drinker, which, these days, is only one step above child molester.

For about a month after that Mick decided he wouldn't drink beer. He sat in the pub nursing his orange juice and lemonade, looking thoroughly miserable, while the rest of us tucked into something deliciously malty and hoppy. I was getting worried; the ride was only a couple of weeks away and the thought of cycling the length of Britain without my beer buddy was too depressing to contemplate. One night, however, it got too much for him. I had drunk a couple of pints of something delightful (I think it was Tunnel Vision from the Box Steam Brewery) and I was feeling thoroughly content. I loved the world and everyone in it – especially my mate Dave, who had just offered to get another round in.

'Same again for you, Mick?' he asked.

For about thirty seconds the internal struggle was etched on Mick's face.

'Yeah, OK,' he said miserably. His dayglo orange drink arrived and he looked at it with hatred. Five minutes later he jumped up.

'Fuck it!' he exclaimed. 'I'm gonna have a beer!'

'Hooray!' we all cheered, rushing to the bar to buy him a pint and welcome him back into the fold after his brief sojourn in the wilderness. He that was lost was found. Amen.

I'm going to stick my neck out here and assert that beer, at least proper real ale, is good for you. This is not just my opinion; there is plenty of research that indicates drinking beer has positive health benefits. Beer is a live substance, full of micro-organisms and packed with B vitamins including B6, which has been shown to protect against heart disease. In another study, the xanthohumol (try saying that after a few!) in hops has been shown to inhibit a group of enzymes that can initiate the cancer process. Beer is packed with iron and antioxidants, and hops also contain phytoestrogens – compounds that help reduce hot flushes and fight osteoporosis in postmenopausal women, which is good news for us female beer lovers. Beer, to quote Tom Hodgkinson, editor of *The Idler*, is 'compost for the soul'. It is also extremely enjoyable. It makes one happy and being happy is very good for your health.

The health puritans hate this sort of thing. In their eyes it gives people the excuse they need to go off and have a jolly good time without any qualms of conscience at all. 'Alcohol is bad for you!' they shriek. 'Two units a day and no more!' What they don't mention is that the safe drink limits were more or less made up. It was a sort of intelligent guess by a committee. Of course, drinking a bottle of vodka a day is not going to do you any good. But I think health professionals would do well to be a little more discerning before labelling someone a 'binge drinker'.

Maybe they should take a look at Hogarth's work. In 1751 William Hogarth produced two prints: *Beer Street* and *Gin Lane*. He printed them in support of the campaign against gin-drinking amongst London's poor which resulted in the Gin Act of 1751. *Gin Lane* depicts a scene of squalor and misery. In the foreground a woman in a stupor drops her baby off the steps, while behind her all is chaos. Another woman has drunk herself to death and a third is feeding gin to her child. No wonder it became known as 'mother's ruin'. The gin addiction that plagued the country, especially in London, had been deliberately encouraged by the government in the late-seventeenth century. The landowning classes, which dominated Parliament, wanted to keep the price of grain up at a time of surplus harvests and by encouraging domestic gin production at rock bottom prices they could do this, while at the same time collecting tax on the gin that was sold. The result was binge drinking of epidemic proportions. By the 1720s, Londoners were drinking, on average, a pint of gin per person per week. By the 1740s the amount of gin being produced in the capital had almost quadrupled again, from 2.2 million gallons in the 1720s to 8 million gallons in the 1740s. There was also no control over the quality; gin was frequently adulterated with other substances, particularly turpentine, which, quite frankly, must have tasted pretty disgusting. By 1750, one in four of the residences in St Giles, the setting for Hogarth's depiction of Gin Lane, was a gin shop.

Beer Street, by contrast, celebrates the virtues of good old ale. Everyone looks healthy, happy and content. A blacksmith is sitting with a foaming tankard of ale and a huge piece of ham, while builders on the roof above the tavern share a toast to King George II. The drawing is a celebration of England and carries the message that English beer is a Very Good Thing. As Hogarth was pointing out, not all alcohol is the same. Beer beats wine, wine beats lager, lager beats gin and gin beats meths. (Actually, if you're on the meths, then it really is time to consider a prolonged spell of abstinence.) Beer, as Benjamin Franklin famously noted, is 'proof that God loves us and wants us to be happy'.

Silverton turned out to be a quintessential Devonshire village – one of the oldest villages in the country – dating from early Saxon times. Narrow roads, lined with thatched cottages, snaked away from the large central square. Down one of the roads we found the Silverton Inn which offered accommodation, but a local told us the landlord had only that day flown to Sharm el Sheikh for a week in the sun, so it was possible we wouldn't be able to get a room. As it was, we struck a deal with the cover staff at the pub who let us have a room for a discounted price, provided we were willing to forego breakfast.

Although small, the village boasted three pubs and, as I couldn't remember which one was in the *Good Beer Guide*, we decided to try them all. We started downstairs with a fine pint of Red Rock from the small Red Rock Brewery – a nice straightforward best bitter. After that we wandered down to the Lamb where we had a pint of Dobs Best Bitter, from Exe Valley Brewery based in Silverton itself. We also had an excellent meal for a price that was so reasonable I twice protested it was not enough. The landlord assured me it was correct, so I decided not to argue a third time.

'Where are you going?' asked one of the locals, seeing us securing our bikes at the pub.

'Land's End to John o'Groats,' we replied proudly.

'What are you doing here, then?' he asked. 'Are you lost?'

I laughed. 'We're taking the scenic route,' I said.

We then repaired to the Three Tuns, another fine pub with a huge resident cat that was stretched out on the bar. It reminded me of the Cheshire Cat in *Alice in Wonderland*, and I half expected it to disappear, leaving only its grin behind. Here we tucked into a pint of Yellowhammer by O'Hanlon's: a golden beer with a distinctive, zesty flavour. There had been a darts match in progress at the Lamb and, curiously, there was also a match in progress when we arrived at the Three Tuns. On our return to the Silverton Inn, there was a darts match in progress here as well. At every pub we visited, the darts team was already there, mid-way through a game. It began to feel a bit surreal. Perhaps we had unknowingly stumbled upon Silverton Darts Festival? We made some enquiries and it turned out a team from a nearby village was catching up on some matches missed during the icy weather earlier in the year. To save time they had decided to get them all done in one evening. We were mightily impressed with Silverton. It was a small village yet it had three decent pubs and a fine array of very local beer. We gave it top marks as we bade goodnight to the darts teams and wearily climbed the stairs to our room in the hotel.

Stats
Miles: 50
Total miles: 153
Pints of beer (each): Mick 5, Ellie 4¼,
as I tipped the rest over in the Lamb
Times someone said 'Are you lost?': 4
Blubs: 1

SILVERTON
>>>>>>>>>>>>>>>>>>>>>>>> TO >>>>>>>>>>>>>>>>>>>>>>>>

CHEDDAR

'I've got a tip for 'ee,' a chap in one of the pubs last night had said. 'If thee just go up to the top of the hill behind the village on the Old Butterleigh Road, the view is magnificent. Bit of a climb like, but it's worth it.'

There spake a man who had never cycled the length of Devon, let alone the length of Britain. We were learning to be very wary of the advice of anyone who was not on a bicycle. We resisted the urge to ask him if he had ever traversed to the top of the hill without the benefit of an engine and instead nodded politely.

'Maybe we will,' we said. The next morning we decided that, however magnificent the view from the top of the hill, it would most definitely not be worth it. Instead we opted for the northbound A396 to Tiverton, which followed the river and was flat all the way. Before setting off, however, we called in to the butchers in the square and bought a couple of Scotch eggs. We are both fond of Scotch eggs: not supermarket ones which are dry and flavourless, but proper home-made ones like my mum used to make. Scotch eggs are not Scottish, by the way. They were invented by the fancy London store Fortnum & Mason in 1738. I have never tried theirs but I bet they would be hard pressed to improve on the Scotch eggs produced by D. J. Haggett in Silverton, which were superb.

At Tiverton we followed the signs for the Grand Western Canal. We were slightly miffed when we realised the canal was at the top of a hill, but when we got there it was fabulous and a lovely flat ride to the Somerset border. Opened in 1814, with the section from Lowdwells to Taunton finally completed in 1838, it was originally envisaged the canal would form part of a much longer route from Bristol to Topsham near Exeter, thus avoiding the long sea journey around Land's End. The ambitious route included no less than seven boat lifts and, although the section from Tiverton to Taunton functioned for a few years, problems with the design of the boat lifts and then the advent of the railway meant the rest of the canal was never completed. By the mid-twentieth century the canal was derelict and, unbelievably, plans were put forward to turn it into a linear landfill site. Thankfully, after protests, in 1971 Devon County Council took control of the 11-mile section of canal from Tiverton to Lowdwells, near Wellington, on the Somerset border. The canal was restored and transformed into a country park – and very wonderful it is, too.

The towpath was peaceful and it definitely beat cycling on the main road. At Lowdwells, however, the canal stopped (the Somerset section is still derelict) and so we rejoined the road. As the back roads were very winding, we took the A38 past

Wellington on to Taunton. One fast road, a hundred heavy lorries, two very stressed cyclists. We grimly stuck it out for an hour until Taunton when, with some relief, we switched to our second canal of the day: the Bridgewater & Taunton. Opened in 1827, the Bridgewater & Taunton Canal similarly suffered from competition from the railway and closed for traffic in the early-twentieth century. To start with the going was rough, as the path had been laid with scalpings, which were much too coarse for comfortable cycling, and pains shot up through my arms as we bumped along. I worried about getting a flat tyre, but the investment we had made in puncture-resistant Kevlar tyres for the trip paid off. Thankfully, the path eventually evened out and the rest of the ride to Bridgewater was lovely, albeit not particularly fast.

While on the towpath, we met a couple cycling the other way. Noticing our laden panniers, they asked where we were going. When we said 'John O'Groats', their first reaction was disbelief.

'What are you doing here?' the man asked. 'Are you lost?'

We smiled. 'We're taking the scenic route,' we explained.

He said he was sixty-five (he most definitely didn't look it) and that it had always been a dream of his to cycle the End-to-End.

'Do it,' we encouraged him. 'You won't regret it. If we can do it anyone can.'

I nodded to emphasise our point. 'We're rubbish,' I told him. 'I expect you're a proper cyclist. You would definitely be able to do it.'

As Mick chatted to him about bike specifications and so forth, I chatted to his wife.

'He's always going on about it,' she confided, 'but I'm not sure whether I am fit enough to go with him.'

I assured her again that if we could do it then, with a bit of determination, anyone could. I wished I felt as confident as I sounded. This was only day four after all. We left them feeling inspired, though, and I really hope they do fulfil their dream of completing the journey.

At Bridgwater the canal abruptly entered a deep and rather forbidding cutting, before emerging in the middle of the town amid a throng of noise, traffic and pollution. We weaved our way across the busy lanes of cars before finding the A39 out of town. This road was heavily used by lorries and we didn't like it at all – they hurtled past us, terrifyingly close. It was rush hour and at every junction queues of cars with impatient drivers were waiting to join the main road.

'THIS IS SHIT!' I had to yell at the top of my voice to make myself heard.

Mick nodded grimly. Shortly afterwards, a cart sped past loaded up with dirt, some of which shot off the back and straight into Mick's eye. For some reason he hadn't been wearing his sunglasses, which are worn by cyclists for protection from detritus off the road, stray flies and other hazards, as much as to protect one from the glare of the sun. We decided to take the next turning off the main road and hang where it took us. As it happened, it took us straight onto the Somerset Levels and Moors. Immediately, we felt like we were in another land. The landscape was pan flat and there was not a car in sight. All was quiet. Instantly we began to relax.

We gently bowled along narrow roads lined with ancient trees, while drainage ditches criss-crossed the fields on either side. This was more like it. This flat, peaty land is properly known as the Moors. The Levels are the clay ridges that run along the coast, helping to protect the area from sea flooding along with the ditches or *rhynes* (pronounced *reenes*), which humans have built over the centuries to channel the water and allow the land to be farmed. More commonly, the whole area is simply referred to as the Somerset Levels, or to locals just the Levels. The area is of world-class importance as a wetland haven for wildlife.

Once upon a time, the sea flooded the area on a regular basis, particularly in the winter months, leaving only islands of higher outcrops. The area was difficult to access during these months and tended to be used only in the summer. Hence, the area became known as 'Sumorsaete', meaning 'land of the summer people'. Even in the summer, the sea would encroach on the land. To cross the flooded moors, Neolithic people constructed wooden walkways of planks, held in place with wooden pegs, which linked the areas of higher ground to one another. In 1970, Ray Sweet, a local peat cutter, uncovered one of these ancient walkways. Inevitably it became known as the Sweet Track, although it is perhaps serendipitous that Ray had such an attractive last name. (Other Somerset surnames are Bugg, Greedy, Squibb and Urch.) Amazingly, thanks to the science of dendrochronology (tree-ring dating), it is possible to pinpoint the exact date the trees that were used to build the Sweet Track were felled: 3807/3806 BC. It is now known that the Sweet Track is built along the route of an even older track, known as the Post Track, dating from 3838 BC. Until recently it was the oldest known wooden trackway in Europe; then, in August 2009, an even more ancient trackway was discovered alongside HMP Belmarsh in Plumstead, dating from 4000 BC.

Unsurprisingly, as they are so flat, the Levels and Moors are great for cycling on. Birds are plentiful here, too; we saw teal and snipe, as well as a couple of peregrine falcons as we made our way along. Well, Mick claims he spotted them. I am rubbish at identifying birds – seagulls and pigeons being pretty much the limit of my ornithological expertise. He could have been making it all up; I would have been none the wiser. Despite the terrain being so flat, however, we were both starting to feel quite weary and I realised we had foolishly not had a proper meal today. Our entire day's calorie intake had consisted of the Silverton Scotch egg, one banana, two crumpets and a Kit-Kat each. We had cycled 60 miles since Silverton and this was not nearly enough sustenance to keep us going; we had succumbed to 'the bonk'. Wobbly legs and total exhaustion had set in due to our inadequate refuelling and as we needed to stop for a rest, the pub seemed the perfect place to do it.

At Wedmore Mick got lots of brownie points for thinking to look around the corner rather than just head for the big coaching inn on the main road. He discovered the New Inn, a little gem of a place, a proper traditional pub where we enjoyed a wonderful couple of pints of Summerset from Yeovil Ales. Like Proper Job, this was a blonde beer. It tasted deliciously fresh and fruity, and went down a treat, accompanied by several packets of crisps and peanuts to fortify us until we could get something more substantial inside us.

From Wedmore it was a straightforward 5-mile ride to Cheddar. There was no way we could summon the energy for the last 25 miles to our homes in Bristol, so we decided to check into the youth hostel for the night. The hostel had been recently refurbished and we liked the building very much. The staff, however, were spectacularly unfriendly. After dumping our stuff we went into the lounge to watch TV. No sooner had we settled down in front of the news, than a member of staff came in and, without saying a word, switched the channel over to *Home and Away*, then plonked herself in one of the armchairs. Being British, we gritted our teeth and said nothing, deciding instead to go to the local pub for a pint of Gorge Best Bitter from Cheddar Ales, a favourite of mine. As we left we bade good evening to the woman sat on the desk in reception – she made no reply and continued with her knitting. She reminded me of Madame Defarge in *A Tale of Two Cities*. Maybe she was knitting our coded names into the mohair jumper she was fashioning. On the way back from the pub we bumped into some friends who live in Cheddar and who were rather surprised to see us. We showed them some photos of our trip to try and convince them we had been cycling for the past five days and not boozing it up somewhere – or at least that we had been cycling for the past five days as well as boozing it up somewhere. On returning to the hostel we completely overcompensated for the lack of food that day, and cooked and ate enough pasta to feed the whole British Cycling Team, after which we both fell asleep, thoroughly exhausted.

>>>>>>>>>>>>>>>>>>>>>>>>>>>>

Stats
Miles: 66
Total miles: 219
Pints of beer: 3 each
Hills pushed: 0 (woo hoo!)

>>>>>>>>>>>>>>>>>>>>>>>>>>>>

CHEDDAR

>>>>>>>>>>>>>>>>>>>>>>>>> **TO** >>>>>>>>>>>>>>>>>>>>>>>>>>

BRISTOL

Don't believe what you read about Cheddar being ruined by tourists and gift shops. It's true that both are present in abundance, especially in the summer months, but Cheddar is still an amazing place – and not just for cheese. Cheddar Gorge is Britain's largest gorge and the road that snakes up through it is spectacular; sheer rock towering above with rooks and kestrels wheeling around the cliff faces, as well as a pair of peregrine falcons which have been breeding there for many years. At the top there allegedly nestles one of Britain's rarest flowers, the Cheddar pink. The plant is unique to Cheddar Gorge.

At the foot of the Gorge are the magnificent Cheddar caves: the two 'show caves' are Gough's Cave and Cox's Cave, and both are packed with exquisite limestone formations. Beneath the show cave in Gough's Cave, a climb down a narrow fissure leads to Lloyd Hall, a huge underwater cavern. I went on a trip here once with a local caving club, and remember well the eerie, still green water, glimmering in the light of our lamps. The water disappeared under the rocks at the end of the pool, beyond which only those strange creatures known as 'cave divers' can venture. Being underground in a place like that feels primeval and timeless.

Today we only had 25 miles to get under our belt, so we took a short detour up the gorge, although Mick put his foot down when I suggested going on a quick visit to the caves as well. We then turned about and headed along the road to Axbridge. Axbridge is a Somerset town with 2,000 inhabitants, while Cheddar, although it has three times as large a population, is a village, demonstrating the changing fortunes of both places. Axbridge was a major cloth-producing town in the Tudor era but the town stultified as the cloth industry declined. Today it is picturesque, with a large central square dominated by the magnificent early Tudor wool merchant's house known as King John's Hunting Lodge.

We headed out of the village up the High Street, which runs alongside the lodge. As I stopped to take a photo on the way out, a woman opened the door on one of the houses on the main street and put a board outside listing various films with dates. Intrigued, I stopped to have a look. She introduced herself as the owner and told me she and her husband had bought the house, which had once been a pub, the Axbridge Lion. Unsure of what to do with the room that had been the public bar, they decided to convert it into an art deco cinema (as you do). The seats were scrounged from the Colston Hall in Bristol, after a neighbour saw them being thrown into a skip when the venue was being refurbished, and a National Lottery grant had helped to pay for some of the other work. It is now the Roxy, a not-for-profit cinema run by Axbridge Film Society. She kindly invited me in to take a look and I had a very enjoyable time nosing around. Mick was waiting at the top of the road, wondering where on earth I had disappeared. He looked slightly disbelieving when I said I had just been to the cinema.

At the top of the village we joined the Strawberry Line cycle path to Yatton. The path gets its name from the famous Cheddar strawberries, which used to be carried along this section of the Great Western Railway, until it was closed in 1965 – a victim of the infamous Beeching Axe. In the early 1960s, Dr Richard Beeching was the author of an influential report on Britain's transport system, *The Reshaping of British Railways*. He did not believe railways should be run as a public service and recommended wholesale closure of 6,000 miles of branch and cross-country lines – a colossal third of the total network. Beeching has rightly gone down in history as being responsible for decimating the rail network. Curiously, however, despite his unpopularity at the time, almost no one remembers Ernest Marples who, in my view, should stand alongside Beeching, shouldering as least as much of the blame.

Ernest Marples was the Conservative minister for transport who, in 1963, appointed Beeching to conduct his review. Marples was co-owner of a construction company, Marples Ridgeway, which had turned its attention to road building and was remarkably successful at winning road-building contracts in the early 1960s. During his stint as transport secretary, Marples also introduced yellow lines, parking meters and traffic wardens. Unsurprisingly he was not universally popular; a huge piece of graffiti appeared on a motorway bridge, which said 'Marples Must Go', and car transfers with the same slogan became very popular. In 1975 Baron Marples of Wallasey (he had, by this time, been made a life peer, although hopefully not for services to the railway) fled to Monaco to avoid paying thirty years' overdue tax. Although not all the cuts recommended by Beeching were carried out, many were and the railways in this country have never recovered. Beeching later stated his only regret was that his recommendations had not been carried out in full. On the plus side, however, we now have some lovely traffic-free cycle routes, and cycling the Strawberry Line is much easier than going over the top of the Mendip Hills.

We left the track at Yatton where we had a brief argument about nothing in particular (we were both very tired), before heading down the busy A370 to Bristol. By 2 p.m. we were sat outside a pub in the city centre enjoying a pint of Brigstow Bitter, exactly 96 hours after we had set off from Land's End. We thought we had done rather well. That evening we met some friends for a celebratory drink. They didn't say so, but I had the feeling they were surprised, nay amazed, that we had managed to get this far.

I feel I should say something about Bristol, but it's hard to be objective about one's home town. It's rather like trying to be objective about a member of your family; you spend the whole time slagging them off to your close friends, but if anyone else criticises them then you get all defensive and suggest they step outside for a fight. However, in an attempt at objectivity here is a list of the top five things I like and dislike about Bristol:

LIKE

1. The Docks, as we locals say; also variously called Bristol Harbour, the Floating Harbour or Harbourside. Before

1805 the tides of the Avon and Severn, with a differential of 30 feet between low and high tide, caused endless problems for shipping. Bristol was fast losing trade to its rival Liverpool, so a scheme was put forward to construct a harbour free of tidal fluctuations with a lock at each end. At the time, although this solved the tidal issue, it caused another huge problem, as it did not occur to anyone that the sewage, which at that time was discharged directly into the river, wouldn't have anywhere to go. For some years afterwards the centre of Bristol stank to high heaven. Now, thankfully, the sewage is carried off underground and the Floating Harbour is much more pleasant. In the summer it's a great place to wander around, with its cafes, art galleries, museums and, of course, boats of every shape, size and age.

2. Clifton Suspension Bridge and the SS *Great Britain* – two of Brunel's masterpieces. I can still remember standing in a huge crowd waiting for the SS *Great Britain* to be brought back to Bristol. It was 1970 and I was seven years old. I couldn't see much, but I could sense the excitement my parents and the rest of the crowd felt. There had been huge media coverage of the ship's limp home from the Falklands, where it had lain abandoned for decades, and it struck a chord with Bristolians. The previous year the good old planners at Bristol City Council had announced plans to fill in the harbour to make way for a road system and the people of Bristol had been fighting a campaign all year to stop it going ahead. A turnout of 100,000 people cheering Brunel's ship into the harbour scuppered that outrageous plan once and for all.

3. Sustrans and the Bristol to Bath cycle path. In 1977 a group of environmentally minded cyclists formed a group called Cyclebag (Cycle Bristol Action Group). Within two years, thanks in large part to the efforts of one of the founder members, the indefatigable John Grimshaw, permission was granted to allow volunteers to convert the old Midland Railway line into a cycle path from Bath to Bitton, with work continuing west to Staple Hill tunnel on the edge of the Bristol City Council boundary. The path was formally opened along the entire length in August 1985. I can remember in particular the section through Staple Hill tunnel. In the early days the path through the tunnel was not tarmac, but stony track, and there were no lights. Making one's way through, lit only by a feeble bicycle light and listening to the drips from the tunnel roof was slightly unnerving. Now it is tarmacked and lit throughout, which makes travelling through it easier, if less exciting.

   Cyclebag reformed as Sustrans (Sustainable Transport), when it formed itself into a charitable trust, and over the next ten years or so, with Grimshaw as chief executive, went on to build many more paths. Sustrans is now responsible for the National Cycle Network – more than 10,000 miles of cycle routes. Although not all the paths are without criticism, cycling in the UK is definitely a far better experience thanks to them.

4. Banksy. I always thought he was overhyped until I went to his exhibition at the Bristol Museum, which I thought was just brilliant. The image of Metropolitan Police in riot gear skipping though a field of daisies is one that will stay with

me for a long time. Practically everyone in Bristol knows someone who knows someone who knows Banksy. He's not popular with the people at the Keep Britain Tidy campaign, though, who claim he is just another vandal. Rather misses the point of street art, I think.

5. The accent – 'Alreet me luvverrr? Grrt lush! Cider I up landlord!' There is now even a T-shirt company doing a roaring trade in Bristol phrases such as 'Theyz me daps, mind!' (Excuse me, those are my plimsolls) and 'Coz ize wurf it.'

DISLIKE

1. Bristol's shameful history – with most of the city's wealth being based on the slave trade. From 1698 until abolition in 1807, an average of twenty ships a year left Bristol on slaving voyages. Bristol merchants made huge profits from the trade and huge numbers of Bristolians were employed either directly or indirectly in trades related to slavery. Bristol still suffers from a feeling of collective guilt about its history.

2. A hopeless and ludicrously expensive public transport system. Thanks, First Bus!

3. Killer hills (Bristol has a street which claims to be the steepest residential street in Europe). Bristol is supposed to have been built on seven hills. Any local cyclist will tell you it is many more than that.

4. Kingswood. A nondescript and uninteresting area to the east of Bristol where the BNP tends to do well.

5. Scrumpy. Proper scrumpy I mean, not the namby-pamby stuff. I used to like it. As a teenager we would go down to one of the Somerset farms clutching containers to fill with scrumpy from the cider mill on the farm. The liquid had the appearance of cloudy urine with bits of apple floating in it. We would go off camping and spend the night looking at the stars and getting out of our heads on two or three pints of the stuff. That's the thing about scrumpy. After one pint you feel fantastic – you have never felt happier in your life and the world is filled with a rosy glow. After two pints the world feels slightly lopsided. And after three you stand up and realise your legs have lost all feeling and you crumple gently into a heap. One evening at a party I drank too much of the stuff. I spent the evening throwing up into the sink – lumps and all. That was thirty years ago and, sadly, I have not been able to touch it since.

Stats
Miles: 28
Total miles: 247
Pints of beer (each): 2
Pints of scrumpy: 0
Pointless arguments: 1

BRISTOL

≫≫≫≫≫≫≫≫≫≫≫ TO ≫≫≫≫≫≫≫≫≫≫≫

GROSMONT

It had been suggested to us that going home during the course of the ride was not a very good idea. We had, of course, ignored this advice, and now wished we hadn't. Going home was not a good idea. We were both weary and apprehensive of the many miles ahead of us. Setting off from home seemed like starting out all over again, but this time we had more of an idea of what we were letting ourselves in for. It wasn't a happy thought. So, instead of simply packing and leaving, I started doing some housework, then, ridiculously, I set about tidying the shed. Mick, understandably, got rather cross and when I started hosing down old overalls he said that he had had enough, he was leaving and if I didn't want to come along then that was up to me. Reluctantly, I threw everything back in the shed and began loading up the bike.

Our loads were even heavier now as we were also carrying a tent. We planned to stay in hostels or bed and breakfasts on occasion, depending on the weather, but as we were intending to be away for a month, we decided that camping some of the time would keep costs down and would ensure we always had somewhere to stay. We also had sleeping mats, sleeping bags and travel pillows. We had decided against taking cooking gear as the additional load would outweigh the benefit in money saved; instead we would eat cold food or dine out as the mood took us.

Weight is very important when cycling. When we had cycled coast-to-coast from Bowness-on-Solway to Whitley Bay and back the previous year, we were pretty clueless about what to carry, or – more accurately – what to leave behind. I had taken a full make-up bag, a family bottle of shampoo and (I swear this is true) a hairdryer. Not even a lightweight travel one either. Mick was equally clueless: he had packed a couple of spare pairs of trainers and an extra coat in case he fancied a change. We simply had no idea how crucial it was to keep weight to a minimum. Our complete naivety on that trip is illustrated by the story of the Brampton wine.

On the first night, after leaving Bowness-on-Solway, we stopped at a bed and breakfast in the small town of Brampton. Fancying some wine, we had bought a bottle from the supermarket opposite. However, by the time we had settled down for the evening we were too tired to open it and so we packed it in our bags and took it with us. Each evening we did not feel like drinking it. So we carried on lugging it with us, right across country to the North Sea and then back again, for 250 miles. We finally opened the bottle eight days later, on our penultimate night, in the very same B & B in Brampton, not 10 yards away from where we had bought it. It had been a particularly hard ride that day (although to us every day was a hard ride) and, after pouring out a glass each, we both fell asleep without touching a drop. To make matters worse, Mick was still clutching his glass when he slipped into unconsciousness. When we awoke we discovered he had spilt it all over the crisp white bed linen. After fruitlessly trying to wash it out in the basin, we were forced to confess our crime to the proprietor who, thankfully, was quite relaxed about it. Well, she didn't add the cost of the laundry to our bill anyway. We threw the rest of the wine away. This time, conscious of the importance of weight, we put much more thought into deciding which items we would carry with us. This is a list of the kit we had when we set off from Bristol – and we were pretty sure we had pared it down to the absolute bare minimum:

EQUIPMENT

- Two-man tent
- One lightweight compact sleeping bag each
- One self-inflating bed mat each, plus bedrolls and inflatable pillow
- One compass
- One small guidebook – Phil Horsley's *Land's End to John o'Groats: The Great British Bike Adventure*
- Pages torn from atlas for route finding
- Marker pen and biro
- Plastic bags/stuff sacks
- Bicycle pump and two spare inner tubes
- Two pieces of tyre (on advice, but not sure what we would do with them)
- Bike tools – one multi-tool, tyre levers, chain-removing thingy
- Mini bottles/sachets of soap, shampoo, conditioner, hand cream, shaving foam, wet wipes, suncream (optimism), nappy cream (realism)
- Razors and comb

- One travel towel each
- Travel pegs and length of twine
- One lightweight digital camera, charger and lead
- One computer notebook, power lead and charger (my luxury item)
- One Swiss army knife (because every camper has to have one of these)

CLOTHING (EACH)

- One pair of Lycra cycling shorts
- One pair of long cycling trousers
- One pair of lightweight casual trousers
- Two short-sleeved lightweight T-shirts
- One long-sleeved T-shirt
- Cycling jersey
- One sweatshirt
- Underwear, plus lightweight pyjamas
- One pair of cycling shoes (ones which look like trainers for evening use as well)
- One pair of plastic shoes
- One neck scarf (me)
- One pair of sunglasses
- One cap
- One cycling jacket
- One plastic cape
- One pair of gloves

We had shown our kit list to friends in the pub the previous evening and it had caused a great deal of merriment. Crestfallen, we realised we were still pretty clueless, although I pointed out, in my defence, that I had left the hairdryer and make-up behind. Nevertheless, we decided we could not manage without anything on our list, so this was the gear we had loaded on our bikes as we wobbled our way down the drive and off on the next leg of our journey north.

Mick had suggested writing 'Land's End to John o'Groats in aid of BRACE' on our hi-vis jackets. (BRACE is an acronym for Bristol Research into Alzheimer's and Care of the Elderly.) When we had initially planned the trip we hadn't considered doing it as a sponsored event, but so many people asked us whether we were doing the ride for charity that in the end we decided it was rather a waste not to raise money on the way. As my mum had suffered from the effects of Alzheimer's disease for many years, we decided to raise money for a local organisation that was researching Alzheimer's and other related illnesses. I have to admit to a small amount of self-interest here, as there is some evidence of genetic factors being at least partially responsible, and I am hoping a miracle cure can be found before my brain begins to shrink to the size of a walnut. Mick rather unkindly said he doubted many people would notice the difference in my case. Anyway, we decided it would help to advertise the cause and Mick also hoped it would prevent him being mistaken for a trolley boy when he called in at supermarkets.

We headed out through Filton, a suburb in northern Bristol. Mick was in favour of stopping at the Jolly Fryer for a Super Scooby burger to set him up for the ride. The Super Scooby lays claim to being Britain's biggest burger. It consists of a teetering column of four burgers, eight rashers of bacon, eight slices of cheese, twelve onion rings, salad, mayonnaise, barbecue sauce and relish, sandwiched between two bread rolls, and comes with a side portion of chips. The meal clocks in at a terrifying 2,645 calories. Nick Lomvardos, the proprietor who invented this salt-and-fat-fest, offers a free can of Coke to anyone who can finish the meal in one sitting. He says he doesn't give many cans away. Mick argued that this would be the only chance he would get to eat one without feeling guilty, as he could burn off the damage during the rest of the ride. I sensed disaster. For one, there was a fair chance that after eating a Super Scooby we would exceed the maximum weight permitted on the Severn Bridge. Secondly, I was reluctant to carry all the extra gallons of water we would undoubtedly need after consuming our own bodyweight in salt. I said no. Instead we pressed on towards Almondsbury, a quiet and unassuming village on the outskirts of Bristol.

In 1817 this small village was at the centre of a hoax that enthralled the entire country. On 3 April of that year, a young woman was found wandering the streets of the village by a local cobbler. She had thick dark hair, dark eyes and was wearing a turban. She seemed dazed and confused but no one could understand the strange language she spoke. The cobbler took her to the overseer of the poor, whom in those days was responsible for dealing with vagabonds and beggars, usually by imprisonment or the poorhouse. The overseer however, realising this woman was unusual, took her to Knole Park House, the home of Mr and Mrs Worrall, the county magistrate and his wife, who decided to take her in. Over the next few weeks she became the centre of attraction and was visited by a steady stream of travellers, language experts and curious members of the local gentry. One traveller, a Portuguese chap called Manuel Eynesso, claimed he understood the strange language she spoke. He translated for her, explaining that she was called Princess Cariboo and she came from the island of Javasu in the Indian Ocean. He said she told him she had been abducted by pirates but had managed to escape into the Bristol Channel. (What pirates were doing in the Bristol Channel remains unclear.) After this information was revealed, her fame grew and newspapers were full of descriptions of the exotic visitor. She would climb trees to pray to 'Allah Tallah', all the while continuing to speak only in her strange language. She excelled at fencing, was proficient with a bow and arrow, and was partial to 'exotic dancing' and swimming naked in the lake. No wonder she was an attraction.

Unfortunately for Princess Cariboo, one of the readers of the newspaper reports was a woman called Mrs Neale who ran a guest house in Bristol. She recognised the princess as the same young woman who had lodged with her a few months previously, and who had entertained her children by talking to them in a made-up language. Mrs Neale also reported that when the young woman had left the house for the last time she had been wearing a turban. Unsurprisingly, this clinched it. When confronted with this information, Princess Cariboo broke down and admitted that she was in fact Mary Baker from Witheridge in Devon.

The Worralls, embarrassed at having been fooled, dispatched Mary to Philadelphia in the care of three religious ladies charged with keeping an eye on her. To start with she got quite a lot of attention and gave performances as the princess, but after a while she disappeared from public view and little is known about the rest of her time in America, save that she seemed to have moved from Philadelphia to New York. She left America in the 1820s and spent some time travelling Europe, before finally settling down back in Bedminster, Bristol, where she made a living by selling leeches to Bristol Royal Infirmary. She died in 1864, aged seventy-five. When interviewed after the exposure of the hoax, her father said that Mary had always found it difficult to settle down, and had grown restless every spring and autumn. He thought her 'not quite right in the head' and attributed this to her contracting rheumatic fever at the age of fifteen. 'That,' he said, 'was when all the trouble had started.'

From Almondsbury we headed up towards the Severn Bridge. At the village of Olveston we chanced upon the Olveston Stores, which has a community coffee morning from 10 a.m.–12 noon every Thursday. It happened to be a Thursday and the time was 11.45 a.m., so we pulled in. We were locking up our bikes when a woman crossed the road and pressed a fiver into my hand.

'I know about BRACE,' she said. 'My mum has Alzheimer's. Good luck.'

The cafe was packed with customers, although we were the only ones under sixty-five. While we waited to be served, one of the old ladies began waving me over. I looked around to check it wasn't someone behind me, but she nodded vigorously.

'Yes, yes, can I have a word?' she asked impatiently. I went over to the table where she was sitting.

'I just think you should know,' she said, 'I have seen a car parked at the end of the village with a young man in, I don't recognise either the car or the young man; he seems to be waiting for someone.'

'OK...' I responded, wondering where on earth this was going. 'And um, why do you think he is there then?'

'Drugs, of course,' she said in an exasperated tone. 'Heroin I expect. Or cocaine. What I want to know is, what are you going to do about it?'

This had me nonplussed.

'The thing is,' I demurred, 'we are on a bit of a schedule. Why don't you tell that police officer over there.' (A young female PCSO was stood at the counter buying a Mars Bar.)

'Aren't *you* the police?' she asked.

Then it dawned on me. It was that darn yellow hi-vis jacket again! She had mistaken me for an officer of the law. I wondered whether the young man ended up being questioned. He was probably only waiting for his mum to finish getting her hair done.

Once that misunderstanding had been cleared up, however, everyone was very generous with their donations, and it was with a light heart and a renewed sense of optimism that we left the cafe and continued on our journey. Maybe it wouldn't be so difficult after all. Everyone we met was so friendly and to cap it all, the sun was shining. Yes, this was going to be a magnificent trip. Our wheels whizzing round, we sped along quiet country lanes until we reached Aust, a few miles up the road on the edge of the River Severn. This was once a quiet village until the M4 motorway came and trampled through it, now it is surrounded by rushing traffic despite the M4 being re-designated the M48, with the M4 being routed over the new bridge farther south.

We pedalled past Severn View Services. The naming of the services must, I think, have been given to someone with a fine sense of irony, as this new services no longer has a view of the Severn, only a slightly pathetic garden, while the now defunct old

Aust Services had a huge restaurant with panoramic views over the river.

The Severn is a magnificent river. Magnificent by British standards anyway. Stretching 220 miles in length, it is the longest river in the country. The water that passes here starts its journey at Plynlimon massif, the highest point of the Cambrian Mountains, and the birthplace of the Wye and the Rheidol as well as the Severn. A trickle of water seeps out of a peat bog 2,000 feet above sea level on the slopes of the Welsh mountain. It chases down the mountain and through Hafren Forest, before swinging north and meandering casually around the Welsh Marches, and heading down through Shropshire, Worcestershire and Gloucestershire. Along the way other rivers and brooks rush to join in, like the Pied Piper collecting children. By the time the water has reached Aust, nineteen tributaries have swollen the river, the Wye meeting us just across the water. Farther south, the Severn is joined by the Bristol Avon and finally the River Usk, spreading ever wider, before finally meeting the Bristol Channel at the mouth of the river near Brean Down in Somerset.

Here at Aust the river is about 2 miles wide and prior to the first Severn Bridge opening in 1966, unless one wanted to take a 60-mile detour via Gloucester, it was necessary to cross the Severn using the Aust Ferry. Or if departing from the opposite bank, the Beachley Ferry. For centuries this ferry crossing was the main connection between the south-west of England and Wales. Daniel Defoe, when he visited the area in the 1720s as part of his grand tour around the country, was not too keen on the arrangement:

> *There is also a little farther, an ugly, dangerous, and*
> *very inconvenient ferry over the Severn, to the Mouth*

of Wye; namely, at Aust; the badness of the weather, and the sorry boats, at which, deterr'd us from crossing there.

When we came to Aust, the hither side of the Passage, the sea was so broad, the fame of the Bore of the tide so formidable, the wind also made the water so rough, and which was worse, the boats to carry over both man and horse appear'd (as I have said above) so very mean, that in short none of us car'd to venture: So we came back, and resolv'd to keep on the road to Gloucester.

Mr Defoe was obviously not as intrepid as his fictional Robinson Crusoe. Maybe he feared getting shipwrecked on Steep Holm.

It is likely that my great-great-grandfather, who in 1870 left his home town of South Petherton in Somerset, travelled by way of this ferry. He was one of many West Country inhabitants who crossed the border looking for work in the coal mines and other heavy industries of South Wales which roared into life at the end of the nineteenth century. He found work as a labourer in the tin works of Abertillery. Twenty years later, his son, my great-grandfather, was already working in the pits as a coal miner at the age of fifteen, alongside his thirteen-year-old brother.

Aust Ferry's other claim to fame (aside from possibly carrying my ancestors across the river and Defoe's refusal to use it) is that it featured on the album cover of the soundtrack for Martin Scorsese's film about Bob Dylan, *No Direction Home*. The photograph by Barry Feinstein shows Dylan stood in front of the ticket office; taken on 11 May 1966, he was on his way to South Wales having played a gig in Bristol. Six months later the bridge was opened and the ferry was no more. Although Dylan, judging by the moodiness of the photograph, was probably jolly glad he would no longer have to stand around in tedious traffic queues with the rain lashing off the Bristol Channel.

We cycled along the path on the northern side of the bridge. As we crossed the midpoint we stopped for a snack break and enjoyed great views of the Severn Estuary and the newer bridge to the south, known as the Second Severn Crossing. I like the new bridge; it is a structure of great beauty and elegance. It opened thirty years after the first Severn crossing and, unlike the older bridge, the new one starts in England and finishes in Wales proper. On this older bridge the foot/cycle path is lower than the traffic lanes, however, and it was slightly off-putting to eat our sandwiches with our noses exactly level with the exhaust pipe of a 36-ton lorry.

Leaving the bridge, we skipped Chepstow and carried on up the hill to St Arvans and Chepstow Racecourse. Beneath the racecourse is a wonderful cave – Otter Hole. It can be accessed at low tide, although it is gated and can only be entered with a guide, for reasons that will soon be obvious. At high tide, just inside the entrance, the rising river level causes the cave to 'sump' or completely fill with water. Missing the deadline to depart entails another six-hour wait before the level is once more low enough to exit the cave. Inside the cave the Hall of the Thirty contains huge calcite bosses on a scale unknown anywhere else in the UK, and with a great variety of colours, from pure white, to yellow, ochre red and jet black, caused by the different minerals in the rock. For those who would like to see the cave without getting covered from head-to-toe in gloopy river mud, the Piercefield pub at St Arvans, directly above the cave, has some impressive photographs in the bar.

At the fork in the road just beyond the pub is a magnificent iron fountain. The Sun Foundry in Glasgow made the fountain in 1893 at a cost of £30. Two cherubs stand on top of the huge bowl and fish tails are entwined around the main stem. It is a grand structure for such a small place. Although it has recently been restored, it was, of course, not working. I cannot think of many public fountains that still function, which is a great shame. Not only are some of the structures quite beautiful, but there is surely a health and environmental benefit in having water freely available rather than having to buy the stuff in plastic bottles when you are out. Did you know (at the time of writing) the bottled water market in Britain is worth £2 billion? We even import bottled water from Fiji! What a triumph of marketing over common sense that is. We live in a country where we are lucky enough to have water on tap, which is perfectly clean and healthy, and yet we spend our money on buying bottled stuff imported from all over the world. Even the bottled water companies themselves do not claim that their water is any healthier than the stuff that comes out of the tap – and yet people drink bottled water in preference to tap water 'for health reasons'. In Bristol there is now an organisation called Turn Me On, which is campaigning to bring back public drinking fountains for citizens to use. This seems to me an eminently sensible idea and one that will hopefully be taken up nationally. Maybe one day the fountain at St Arvans will once more supply travellers with a plentiful supply of fresh drinking water. In the meantime we asked the barman in the pub to fill our water bottles for us.

From the racecourse we followed the road into the Wye Valley. For a while the road felt almost alpine, as it twisted and turned along the side of the steep cliffs of the gorge, before dropping down into the valley and Tintern Abbey. (Mick said: ''Tis an Abbey. Tint-Ern Abbey? Oh never mind!') The Abbey ruins are very dramatic in the beautiful setting alongside the River Wye, although they have not always met with universal approval. The eighteenth-century essayist William Gilpin took a tour of the Wye Valley and was evidently not overly impressed by the Abbey, feeling it to be too complete and not in a sufficient state of ruin to be picturesque. He had a real issue with things being picturesque. He suggested bashing the Abbey about a bit with a mallet to make it look a bit more ruinous and attractive.

The Wye Valley is designated as an Area of Outstanding Natural Beauty and it was easy to see Wye (sorry, couldn't resist). It was at its springtime best: bluebells, celandine and primroses adorned the hedgerows along the route, and the weather was perfect for cycling, with April sunshine dappling the woodland floor. For 16 miles from Chepstow to Monmouth the river is half English and half Welsh, forming the border between the two countries. At Bigsweir Bridge we crossed back into England for a while before re-entering Wales. Plenty of work for sign makers around here – I was particularly amused by one junction as we re-entered England which had nine signs informing us that:

1. Monmouth was straight on via the A466.
2. Redbrook was in the same direction.
3. We should take a right if we wished to visit Mork (¾ mile), St Briavels (1 ¾ miles), Stowe (2 miles) or Coleford (5 miles).
4. We should also head right for Clearwell, which offered a bed and some food, or at least some cutlery.
5. Clearwell Caves also required a right turn.

6. We should however *not* take a right turn if travelling in a vehicle weighing more than 17 tons...
7. ... unless we required access in which case more than 17 tons was OK.
8. We were welcomed into the county of Gloucester.
9. We were also welcomed to the Forest of Dean District, which apparently is 'A place to be proud of'.

It was a good job we were travelling by bicycle and had time to stop and take all this in. If we had been travelling in a car at 50 mph I don't see how we could possibly have absorbed all this useful information in the couple of seconds it would have taken to pass the junction.

The ability to stop is one of the great advantages of travelling by bicycle. Travelling in a car, if you pass something interesting and someone says, 'Ooh, what's that, shall we stop?', by the time the thought has translated from the speaker's brain into verbal speech, and the driver has processed the request and thought about a response, the car has travelled another half a mile down the road. Another car is a few inches behind yours, so close that you can see the glazed and psychopathic whites of the driver's eyes, and there is nowhere obvious to pull in.

'What?' says the driver, temporarily thrown from the immediate task of controlling a moving lump of metal at the unnatural speed of 60 mph.

'No, it's too late now and there's nowhere to turn around. Let's keep going.'

And the moment is gone. On a bicycle, however, it is easy. One simply glides to a halt, yelling to one's companion that the intention is to pull over, slings the bike on the fence or verge and then a happy few moments (or more if you like) can be spent looking at whatever it is that has caught your attention.

Having digested all the information on the signpost we decided to continue along the A466 and soon found ourselves coasting over the River Wye and into Monmouth. Monmouth has a good solid market town feel to it – well-off but not show-off with a pleasant network of narrow streets and pedestrianised areas. We decided to stop for tea and cake at a cafe in a little square. I am not sure whether it was my Bristol accent, but we ordered two cream teas and an orange squash, and got two coffees and an orange juice. Ho hum. The waitress apologised and said she had just got back from her holiday. Once we had sorted out the drinks it was very pleasant, sitting there in the spring sunshine, reading the papers.

Refreshed, we detoured to the bottom of the town and had a look at the Monnow Bridge – a well-preserved medieval bridge with a gatehouse on it. The bridge has a defensive gate with a portcullis, a ditch and a rampart. These were clearly of little practical use, however. During the Civil War the attackers simply waded across the shallow River Monnow and surrounded the bridge from behind. Oops.

We headed back through the town and onto the Hereford Road for a few yards, before turning left onto minor roads heading west, once more criss-crossing the border between England and Wales, initially following the course of the River Monnow. Gradually, the road began to climb up and we found ourselves toiling over Coedanghred Hill. Before embarking on this ride I had breezily remarked to a friend that I didn't think it would be too bad, as there were hardly any hills after Cornwall and Devon or if there were, the roads would go round them. A seasoned cyclist himself, he had looked at me askance, but had said nothing. Now, as the terrain became hillier, I recalled this conversation. He must have been thinking something along the lines of: 'Silly cow, what is she talking about? Are there no hills in Wales? Has she never been to Shropshire? Does she think the Lake District is flat? And what about fucking Scotland?' It now struck me that I had, once again, been talking complete and utter bollocks.

By the way, if you find the F-word offensive then be grateful you have not had the pleasure of meeting Effing Gary. Effing Gary was an employee at a company I worked for many years ago, which manufactured car components. Effing Gary had a talent. This was for using the word 'fuck' at every possible opportunity, not with any intention of causing offence; it was simply his mode of language. Effing Gary turned that expletive into an art form. On one occasion I asked him what the problem was with a certain machine. His reply was concise: 'The fucking fucker's fucked.' Which, as a construction of a sentence, is pretty impressive; adjective, noun and verb in one coherent sentence, using just one expletive. In view of his considered opinion of the machine I suggested he take an early tea break. He said he would 'fuck off to the canteen'. The other memory I have of Effing Gary is when he came in one morning enthusing about a documentary he had watched on TV the night before. He said he had watched 'a fucking brilliant programme about the Hanging Baskets of Babylon. That place looks fucking amazing', he said. 'I'd love to take the missus there for a fucking holiday.' I had never met Mrs Effing Gary, but somehow I doubted that central Iraq was top of her must-visit list.

We had a steep coast down the other side of Coedanghred Hill into the village of Skenfrith, where we stopped for a pint of Wye Valley Bitter at the Bell. It was a very nice pub, but quite fancy, with stacks of laundered towels rather than paper ones, potpourri and little pots of hand cream in the toilets. It was awarded Michelin Pub of the Year in 2007 for Great Britain and Ireland, and the food did look delicious. Unfortunately, both the food and the accommodation were well outside our meagre budget, so we decided to press on.

Before leaving the village we took a look at the castle and church. The castle is one of the Trilateral, a triangle of castles built as part of the Norman Conquest, acting as a line of defence along the Welsh Marches – the border area between England and Wales. For the next four days we would travel the Marches, usually just inside the English border but occasionally crossing into Wales, before turning north-east.

The castle is impressive, with much of it still standing. Behind is St Bridget's Church, dating from the early-thirteenth century. I do like to have a nose around old churches – they always smell so nice – and, as luck would have it, it was open, which I was pleased to see (many are closed to visitors these days). Inside the church is the Skenfrith Cope, a velvet embroidered cape dating from the fifteenth century. Apparently it was being used as an altar cloth when, in the mid-nineteenth century, Father Thomas Abbot came up from Monmouth on a visit and spotted it. I imagined the conversation going something like this:

Father Abbot: 'What's that you've got on the altar over there? That needlework looks old.'

Village priest: 'Yes, sorry, it is a bit shabby, the parish is saving up for a new one.'

Father Abbot: 'Gracious me, man, don't you realise that what you are resting your wine-stained chalice on is a fine example of fifteenth-century Opus Anglicanum embroidery?'

Village priest: 'Er, is it? We found it lying about in the vestry so thought we would make use of it. The other altar cloth has a hole in it from when the Bishop of Llandaff dropped the thurible. He'd had a couple of sherries.'

Father Abbot: 'Well get it off immediately and hang it on the wall out of harm's way. Ask the wife if you can use that nice linen tablecloth of hers instead.'

I also liked the font with a wooden lid which was kept locked to prevent people from nicking the water and using it to cast spells. I don't know whether this is still a problem, although I noted that it was very firmly locked. From the helpful information sheet in the church I also discovered that St Bridget is, among other things, the patron saint of chicken farmers.

It was getting late and we had no idea where we were going to stay for the night. We cycled on to the next village of Grosmont, a couple of miles inside Wales. At the foot of the steep hill leading into the village we were elated to see a sign for a campsite, with a phone number. We tried phoning but could get no signal and the gate was locked. Elation was chased out by despair. There was nothing for it but to tackle the hill up into the village. At the end of the day it felt like we were cycling into a brick wall. I could hardly walk up it let alone cycle up, and by the time I reached the brow the sight of the Angel Inn, with its pub sign gently creaking in the breeze, felt nothing short of miraculous. I could practically hear the cherubim and seraphim singing from the heavens as I wearily pushed my bike the final yards to the pub door where Mick stood, grinning, giving me a thumbs up.

The sound of angels singing didn't stop after we entered this fine establishment. The Angel Inn is surely one of the friendliest pubs in the country, and Margie, who had just opened the pub for the evening session, was fantastic. She phoned the campsite and got no reply.

'Probably a bit early in the season,' she said. 'You can camp on the village playing field if you like and there are toilets next to the pub. We'll keep them open all night for you.'

She gave us directions to the playing field, located at the end of the interestingly named Poorscript Lane.

We went up to the field and pitched up in a corner, all the time being offered helpful information by two eleven-year-old boys on bicycles, evidently keen to greet two strangers into the village. They told us all about the village, the castle, the egg hunt (at Easter) the fireworks (on Bonfire Night) and all sorts of other useful titbits.

'Oh, and there,' said one of the lads, pointing to a corner of the field tucked away out of sight of the houses on the other side of the playing field, 'is the toilet if you don't want to walk back to the pub.'

We thanked them for their assistance and they peddled off down the lane.

After setting up our little camp, we repaired to the Angel Inn for the evening. The pub was busy. Everyone was really friendly and made us feel very welcome indeed. They told us how the pub had been set to close a few years previously, so a group of six investors, comprising two surgeons, one nurse, two builders and a venture capitalist, got together and bought it.

'So you see,' said one of the locals, with a twinkle in his eye, 'they're not all bad.'

I assume he meant the venture capitalist rather than the nurse.

The Angel Inn is a cracking success and apparently the music evenings are legendary. The pub has also starred in a movie, becoming 'the Daffodil' for the Damian Lewis film *The Baker*, which was filmed in Grosmont in 2007. When we told the staff we were doing the ride for charity they refused to take any payment for camping and we were bought pints of beer to boot. The choice of brews was good: I tried Cwrw Hâf from Tomos Watkin in Swansea, although there was no chance I was going to try pronouncing it. 'Erm, that one please,' I said, pointing at the pump. It turned out to be a delicious, fresh golden beer, which went down well. Mick went for .410 from Golden Valley Ales in Peterchurch, 10 miles down the road, and then we both tried Butty Bach from Wye Valley Brewery. The food was good, too, and we wandered back to our little tent feeling extremely content. I felt as if we had found a little piece of heaven right there in the Welsh Marches.

〉〉〉〉〉〉〉〉〉〉〉〉〉〉〉〉〉〉〉〉〉〉〉〉〉

Stats
Miles: 48
Total miles: 295
Pints of beer (each): not sure – 5?
Hills pushed: 2
Angelic bar staff: 1

〉〉〉〉〉〉〉〉〉〉〉〉〉〉〉〉〉〉〉〉〉〉〉〉〉

GROSMONT

>>>>>>>>>>>>>>>>>>>>>>>> **TO** >>>>>>>>>>>>>>>>>>>>>>>>

BUCKNELL

It took us longer than we thought to pack away the tent. It was surely nothing to do with the copious amounts of beer consumed the previous night, but figuring out quite what went where seemed to be a trial. I took longer than Mick, as whereas he had a miniature beanbag for a pillow, I had a blow-up one, which I could only get to deflate by rolling on it like a demented seal. But by nine o'clock we had finally stuffed everything messily back into the panniers, whereupon we had a quick look at the very impressive castle, another one of those Trilaterals, and then set off up the hill back into England.

A few miles along the road we reached the Neville Arms at Abbey Dore. We needed some carbs to soak up last night's beer and so, despite having only being on the move for half an hour, we decided to stop. It was not quite 10 a.m. but the owner was about and said we were welcome to come in for a cup of tea and a bacon roll. (We are not quite hardcore enough to drink beer at ten o'clock in the morning.) We sat at the window enjoying the view.

The green Herefordshire hills were dotted with grazing sheep and below us the abbey lay nestled in the valley, while spring sunshine glinted through the trees.

Suddenly, and unbelievably, the air was filled with the crackling of automatic gunfire and the sounds of grenades exploding. Smoke wafted up from the hill opposite the pub and a helicopter whirred above our heads. We jumped up in alarm, spilling our drinks. What the hell was going on? Had Herefordshire been invaded? Had Plaid Cymru gone paramilitary? The landlord and the other early morning patron laughed. It transpired that the SAS have their training ground opposite the village and such events are a regular occurrence.

'I often hear them from our balcony outside our house over there,' said the other customer, who introduced himself as Bill. He had also popped in for some breakfast.

'I sometimes get the urge to wander over with a plate of the wife's freshly baked scones and say "Hey guys, it doesn't have to be like this, there has to be another way. Let's sit down and talk about it."'

As we left, Mick pointed to some sheep in a field.

'The landlord told me those aren't real sheep,' he said. 'They're fake and have cameras fitted inside them. It's all part of the SAS training.'

I stared at them for a considerable amount of time before concluding they were not very good models and didn't even look realistic. One of them in particular looked a mess with the wool hanging off on one side.

'They are rubbish, I could make a better sheep than that,' I told Mick.

With that, the sheep, evidently disgruntled at being the subject of such criticism, got up and wandered off. Mick had, of course, been winding me up.

We rode through Golden Valley, which was lovely Herefordshire cycling country, with not too many hills. Unbelievably, the weather was still fine. Herefordshire is a fertile and sparsely populated county of spuds and soft fruits, cider and the supremely handsome Hereford cattle. The road was lined with huge fields that stretched away towards the horizon. In the distance, the occasional tractor could be seen, pulling ploughs which were turning over the deep red soil.

A little farther down the road we detoured into the little village of Dorstone, hoping to find a loo so Mick could re-apply some nappy cream (the ride was taking its toll). We found a community coffee lounge called Dorstone's Front Room, operating in the now defunct post office. The staff were very interested in our trip and when I explained we were raising money for Alzheimer's research, one of them disclosed that, like my mum, her husband suffered from the same illness. I was beginning to get an inkling of just what a scourge this disease is. Bless them; they then refused to let us pay for the tea and biscuits we had just consumed. This trip was definitely restoring my faith in human nature.

After finishing our tea and biscuits Mick disappeared to the toilet and came out five minutes later walking like John Wayne.

'Are you alright?' I said, trying not to snigger.

'Yes, I'm fine,' he said. 'I don't want the cream to rub off, that's all.'

We had both, to varying degrees, been suffering from a certain amount of discomfort in the nether regions over the past few days. I had been assiduously and liberally applying nappy cream since day one, so was now fairly free of discomfort. Mick, being more of a life-on-the-edge sort of person, had decided not to bother and was now paying a sore price for it. He gingerly got back on his bike, wincing all the while.

Saddle sores can ruin a ride. I had learnt some basics before this trip on how to keep them to a minimum – mainly from painful experience. Don't wear pants, especially not lace knickers (that goes for you chaps, too) – the fabric chafes horribly. Wear padded cycling shorts and no underwear, with a pantyliner, which should be changed frequently throughout the day. Use a barrier or nappy cream liberally and frequently. Wash straight after a ride – or at least be liberal with the wet wipes. Some people seem more prone than others, and it has nothing to do with experience. The legendary Eddy Merckx suffered from saddle sores throughout his cycling career, causing him on occasion to abandon races and even undergo surgery. Luckily for us, after a few more days the discomfort disappeared and we were pain-free for the rest of the trip.

Heading north, we once more encountered the Wye, as it coursed its way from Plynlimon down through Hereford, when we crossed a solid and attractive brick bridge at Bredwardine. Shortly after the bridge we briefly joined a busier A-road into Eardisley. The village attracts a lot of visitors as it is on the Black and White Village Trail – a circular meander through northern Herefordshire taking in half a dozen towns and villages, with an abundance of medieval buildings with black timbers and white painted walls. During the seventeenth and eighteenth centuries many houses had the beams covered over with plaster, but in the late-nineteenth and early-twentieth centuries it became popular to expose the beams again. Later on someone had the bright idea of painting them black and white. The idea caught on and the effect is very striking

– and also very good for tourism. Fashions change, however, and some houses have now been restored to their original natural wood beams and limewashed panels. The attractiveness of the village was marred, however, by the number of huge lorries that thundered down the main street using the road as a cut-through from the A44 to the A438 Hereford road.

Cycling up through the village we came across the New Strand. At first we thought it was a pub; then we saw people outside drinking tea and decided it must be a cafe. It transpired that the New Strand is all of these things and more. The right-hand room is the pub, on the left is the cafe, and between the two is a second-hand bookshop with an enormous floor-to-ceiling range of stock, a gift shop and a post office. At the back, in the conservatory, you can also buy local organic vegetables. It was an interesting place and we stopped for a spot of lunch.

After leaving the New Strand we turned immediately onto a quieter road through the villages of Upcott and Almeley. Daffodils were the order of the day here; there were masses of them covering the verges. In fact, there was a definite yellow theme, with celandine, dandelion and primroses as well as the daffys lining the road. It was noticeable how many wild flowers there had been along our route; there are definitely more flowers in the countryside and on verges than were evident a few years ago. Much of the news about British wildlife is doom and gloom – songbirds dying out, agribusiness wiping out countless varieties of flowers and bees mysteriously disappearing. Of course these are things we should be concerned about but sometimes, just sometimes, it would be good to hear a bit more about the good news stories. So, in the interests of balance, here are a few good news stories about British wildlife:

1. Cowslips are making a big comeback in the countryside, due to a combination of less intensive grazing and 100 per cent subsidy to farmers who grow it. They are beautiful, delicate little flowers and it's great to see them again. I have seen the flower growing all over the place in the past few years, not only in meadows and fields, but also on roadside verges and even along the sides of motorways. Reduction in pesticide use is also resulting in a comeback in poppies, where flowers whose seeds have lain dormant for fifty years are now bursting through and producing spectacular displays.

2. Otters have made a sustained comeback in our rivers. At one time their numbers were thought to be down to 300 or so, almost wiped out by pesticide use. The offending pesticides were banned in 1984 and since then there has been substantial investment in sewage treatment. According to the Environment Agency, Britain's waterways are probably now in a better state than they have been at any time since the start of the Industrial Revolution. Now otters are thriving all over the country.

3. Once one of our most common birds of prey, the red kite was also driven to the brink of extinction in this country through the use of pesticides. By the 1980s there were less than a hundred pairs left, in the mountains of Wales. Now they can be seen across the entire country and

recent surveys estimate there are at least 1,200 breeding pairs in the UK. Buzzards have also increased, by over 400 per cent since 1994, and now there are 120,000 breeding pairs, so many that in some quarters there are calls for their numbers to be restricted.

4. Large blue butterflies, officially declared extinct in Britain thirty years ago, have made a spectacular return to our countryside; there are now estimated to be at least thirty colonies, with a total population of 20,000, following a concerted effort by the Large Blue Recovery Programme, a partnership of over twenty organisations including English Nature (now Natural England) and the National Trust over the past twenty-five years to reintroduce them into suitable habitats.

These success stories show it is possible to turn things around – and often in a short space of time. So let's keep up the good work and encourage diversity in our countryside. Yes, there is much to do, but let's not forget the good things that are already happening.

It is rather a problem with the media generally. They just love bad news. Good news never gets a look in. Goodness knows we could all do with some these days. They are out there, the good news stories, it's just you have to look for them. Here are a few random ones from the excellent website goodnewsstories.org:

- For men: Prostate cancer risk cut by masturbation.
- For women: German fashion magazine dumps skinny models.
- For kids: Eating chocolate can help improve your maths.

- For animal lovers: Missing dog treks 1,200 miles before being reunited with owner.
- For all of us in the UK: UK heading for Mediterranean summer!

Well OK, we get that last one every year and every year it's wrong. But the point is some good news, rather than incessant doom and gloom, is refreshing. Yes, there are a lot of bad things going on in the world. But there is some good stuff, too. Let's celebrate it a bit more.

Cycling down one of the country lanes beyond Eardisley, we had to stop for a herd of cattle crossing the road. As we pulled up I was amazed to see Ben Fogle sitting on a tractor counting the cows across. It wasn't Ben, of course, but he was a jolly handsome chappie and an uncanny likeness. Mick said it was embarrassing watching me practically lick the tarmac with my tongue. This was not true, of course, although I did indulge in a little daydream about what it would be like to be a farmer's wife. Lots of early mornings I imagine which, it must be admitted, weren't my speciality. Mick asked him whether he was finding things difficult at the moment as he had heard that many farmers were struggling financially. I thought this question was a little impertinent and was about to say so, but Ben chuckled and said: 'I've never been so well off.'

This little snippet made him even more interesting and I sidled a little closer to his tractor. Mick gave me a pitying look. Ben asked where we were heading and when we said John o'Groats he laughed heartily.

'What on earth are you doing here?' he said. 'Are you lost?'

Eventually the cows finished traversing the road and Ben said goodbye as he followed them into the field, looking very manly astride his tractor. Wistfully, I started pedalling off down the road, with Mick following me, shaking his head in mock disgust.

'Pathetic,' he said. 'Totally pathetic.'

After 15 miles or so riding through country lanes, we met the A4116 at a little village called Brampton Bryan. Along the right-hand side of the road was a weird-looking yew hedge atop the wall encircling the church. It undulated its way along the top of the wall, clinging on like a huge green monster. I had never seen anything like it. Aside from the hedge, Brampton Bryan is famed for a siege during the English Civil War. The castle and estate were owned by Robert Harley, a parliamentarian, and in 1643, while he was absent from the castle, a Royalist army attacked it. Harley's wife, Lady Brilliana, was evidently not a woman to be messed with and together with three of her children, and around a hundred local tenants, she held the castle, while it was under siege, for seven weeks. In her diary she complained about the foul language of the soldiers more than the bombardments. Not content with holding the castle she also sent a party to attack nearby Knighton, held by the Royalists. Shortly after the siege she succumbed to 'a very great cold' (more likely pneumonia) and died. Brilliana was a prodigious letter writer and more than 375 of her letters, written to her husband and sons, were smuggled out of the castle, and still survive today. Her story certainly put my moans about aching knees into perspective.

A few hundred yards along the road we crossed into Shropshire and turned right towards Bucknell. We knew (courtesy of 'Ben') that we would find a pub there and we hoped they would be able to tell us whether there was a campsite or bed and breakfast nearby. As it turned out, the Baron at Bucknell had a camping field at the back of the pub. It also served a reasonable pint of

Twisted Spire from the Hobsons Brewery in south Shropshire, a nice golden ale and not too strong (I'm not a fan of very strong beer). The pub also served pretty good food and offered Wi-Fi so we had a relaxing couple of hours, Mick reading the paper and me getting up to date with my blog. The field had no facilities at all, but by now we had become used to peeing in the open air, so that wasn't so much of a problem, although the quantity of beer we drank did mean the nearby hedge got regularly watered during the night.

〉〉〉〉〉〉〉〉〉〉〉〉〉〉〉〉〉〉〉〉〉〉〉〉〉〉〉

Stats
Miles: 52
Total miles: 347
Pints of beer (each): 4
Unrequited love affairs: 1

〉〉〉〉〉〉〉〉〉〉〉〉〉〉〉〉〉〉〉〉〉〉〉〉〉〉〉

DAY
8

BUCKNELL

>>>>>>>>>>>>>>>>>>>>> TO >>>>>>>>>>>>>>>>>>>>>>

RATLINGHOPE

Very early the next morning, as I blearily came round, the first thing that struck me was the noise. Wood pigeons, blackbirds, crows, sheep, cows and even a frog joined in the general cacophony. It is a fallacy to think the countryside is peaceful – it is far noisier than most towns. When a cockerel started crowing, with a decibel level so loud I was convinced it was camping in a tent immediately next to ours, I groaned and gave up trying to sleep. Hauling myself out of bed, I unzipped the front of the tent. It was just as well that I did, I now realised, as I deeply breathed in the fresh, clean air. Last night we had stuffed ourselves with three courses of rich food, washed down with copious amounts of beer, and had hardly been able to waddle back to the tent. This had had serious repercussions for our digestive systems and the resulting methane output during the night was considerable. If it had not been for the cockerel, we would probably have been found days later, asphyxiated by our own farts.

Today was billed as an easy-ish day, only 21 miles to Ratlinghope on the edge of the Long Mynd (Long Mountain), although the last few miles would be uphill. For some reason I had got it into my head that it would be better to cycle up one of the highest hills in Shropshire rather than stay on the valley floor. Ten minutes after leaving the Baron at Bucknell I realised I had set us off on the wrong road, heading west instead of north. Rather than turn around straight away I stubbornly insisted we carry on and so we continued to the interestingly named New Invention. This proved to be my second wrong decision of the day, as from New Invention it was then a steep climb up the busy A488 all the way to Clun. Two bad calls already and it was only half past nine!

We toiled up the hill and then down into Clun. A. E. Housman called this 'the quietest place under the sun'; not at 1.45 p.m. on 2 April 1990 it wasn't. On that day Clun was at the epicentre of an earthquake measuring 5.1 on the Richter scale when, 14 miles under the village, a slip occurred along the line of the Pontesford Linley fault. (Don't you think Pontesford Linley sounds more like a character from a P. G. Wodehouse novel rather than a geographical feature?)

While not massive in worldwide terms, the earthquake was pretty big by British standards, and was felt from Ayrshire to Cornwall. Little damage was caused, however, although a few chimney pots fell over in Shrewsbury and someone in Clun spotted a crack in a nearby wall. On the whole, Britain is lucky in being pretty stable geologically. Although we get around two hundred earthquakes a year, most are tiny 'micro-earthquakes' measuring less than 1.9 on the Richter scale. To put this into context, the largest recorded earthquake occurred in Chile in 1960 and measured 9.5. The Richter scale is logarithmic, so an earthquake of magnitude seven, for example, is ten times stronger than a six, 100 times stronger than a five, and 1,000 times stronger than a four. This was, then, pretty massive. Worldwide there are around 500,000 earthquakes every year, 100,000 of which can be felt. Ninety per cent of them occur around the Pacific Plate in an area known as the Ring of Fire. When they occur in poorer countries the effects are devastating. It's easy to forget, in this green and solid land of ours, that bountiful Mother Earth is at best something of a fidget and quite often more akin to a stroppy adolescent throwing a tantrum.

Clun today, however, was as quiet as Housman predicted. We called into a tea shop for elevenses. On the next table were a couple whom I would guess were in their early sixties, both of them sitting silently, staring into the middle distance. As soon as he saw the inscription on our jackets, however, the man turned to us and began chatting amiably and volubly about pushbikes and cycling and we shared some stories about the journey so far.

'I'm more of a motorbike man myself,' he commented. 'Aren't I, Irene?'

He turned to the woman who had thus far not uttered a single word. She made no response. He was obviously used to this and carried on chattering away about Norton and BSA motorbikes. His wife (as I took her to be) silently sipped her tea. Eventually we explained we had to get on.

'Oh of course, of course,' he said, slapping Mick on the back. 'Have a good journey!'

I made a point of saying goodbye to his wife and received the merest, briefest of nods in my direction. We went to the counter to pay and as we left the shop we passed them, still sitting there. The man had lapsed back into silence.

From Clun we headed back east, parallel with the road we had travelled an hour earlier. Up until now Mick had been pretty good and had not complained too much. At this stage, however, I did hear him mutter: 'How many sides of that sodding hill are we going to look at?'

It was true that we had managed to almost circumnavigate the large hill between Bucknell and Clun, and I was feeling a bit sheepish. But then we came across the Hundred House Inn, an excellent pub. We spent an enjoyable hour chatting to the locals over a pint (another Hobsons brew – Hobsons Best Bitter this time). I was especially tickled by a sign on the notice board that said, 'Interested in time travel? Meet me here last Thursday.' Time travel may have been useful at this stage as I realised that, once again, we were hopelessly behind schedule. We were, I knew, destined to fall even more behind as we were now approaching the real ale drinker's paradise known as Bishop's Castle. The town has three pubs in the *Good Beer Guide*, two of which brew on the premises, and a beer museum to boot. There was no way we were going to cycle through here without stopping.

We stopped at the Six Bells Brewery & Pub, which for the past ten years or so has been run by Big Nev and his wife Sue.

'Why is he called Big Nev?' Mick asked.

I shrugged. 'Dunno. Maybe cos he's big. And his name's Nev.'

Mick nodded sagely. 'Yes, that could be it.'

The pub had an impressive range of beers, all brewed on site: Goldings BB, Marathon Ale, Cloud Nine and Big Nev's. It's not always the case, but I do generally find beer tastes better when it hasn't moved too far from where it was brewed. We dithered at the bar, unable to decide which beer to have. I commented there was too much choice.

'Well, love, we're living in a post-modernist age,' said the barmaid, who reminded me of Bet Lynch. 'It's all about choice now.'

We decided to share four halves, one of each of them, and had a mini beer-tasting session. They were all excellent, although if pushed, I would declare Cloud Nine to be my favourite. We tucked into a jacket potato before heading up to the Three Tuns Brewery and Inn at the top of the town.

In the 1970s the Three Tuns was one of only four remaining brewpubs in the country before the CAMRA cavalry came over the hill. It is the oldest licensed brewery in the UK, having held a brewing licence since 1642, although the pub has undergone extensive renovations. We stopped for a pint of Solstice before calling it a day, not wanting to fall foul of the law by overdoing it.

It is not an offence, by the way, to drink over the motoring drink-driving limit and then cycle. You can't have points added to your licence and there is also no obligation to submit to a breath test if you don't want to. As long as you are capable of riding your bike without endangering yourself or others then you are within the law. This seems eminently sensible to me. Riding a bicycle is not the same as being in charge of a 2-ton metal box on wheels. There's no point in drinking too much on a bike anyway, as the first thing to go is your sense of balance and you fall off. An impecunious student I once knew was shamefully in the habit of raiding the kitchens in the university halls of residence late at night in search of food to take back to his hovel in town. One night he foolishly rode his bike home after having consumed too many alcoholic beverages in the student bar. He lost his balance and fell off, knocking himself unconscious. When the police and ambulance arrived they discovered, scattered over the road around him, three boxes of frozen fish fingers, a dozen beef burgers and a bag of frozen peas, all stolen earlier that evening and which had fallen out of the pockets of his capacious overcoat. When he came round he had some explaining to do.

Leaving Bishop's Castle it was a short 5-mile ride to the youth hostel at Ratlinghope – or at least it should have been. Somewhere in the lanes I missed a turning and we got lost. For the third time that day we found ourselves toiling up a hill that we should have cycled around. Mick had the temerity to criticise my route finding and I bad-temperedly leant forward to rip the map from the bag on the front of the bike. Unfortunately, the Velcro was stronger than I thought. The map stayed put and I careered into a hawthorn hedge. This spectacle cheered Mick up immensely. Five minutes later, declaring he had had enough of my appalling navigation, he headed off for a mile in the wrong direction and had to cycle all the way back up the hill. This cheered *me* up immensely. However, we were both still tetchy when we arrived at Bridges Youth Hostel, hours later than originally planned. We stood outside arguing for a while before heading for reception where we were told it would be £48 for a room in the hostel. We thought this was a ridiculous price so we opted instead to camp in the grounds. After setting up camp we repaired to the pub next door, the only one for miles around, only to discover there was a very loud Dire Straits tribute band playing, which made conversation impossible. We drank a couple of beers then headed back to our little tent in the grounds of the youth hostel.

Stats
Miles: 29
Total miles: 376
Pints of beer (each): 4
Number of times stopped to pee in a field: 410
Number of times someone said 'You're doing this
the wrong way, you're going uphill': 25
Number of times someone said 'John o'Groats?
What are you doing here, are you lost?': 54

REST DAY

>>>>>>>>>>>>>>>>>>>>>>>>>>>>>>>>>

We had really been looking forward to this rest day and we were also expecting to be joined by my daughter and other assorted family members who were driving up for the day to cheer us on. The camping fee included use of the facilities, so we were planning to do some washing, and to shower and brush up before they arrived.

The hostel itself was pretty full – a group of Hash House Harriers were staying for the weekend. The previous night they had been partying hard and we were impressed to see them all at breakfast ready for another run to a pub. Hash House Harriers, also known as HHH, H3 or simply 'hashers', indulge in a pastime which involves running from pub to pub, with a few pubs thrown in on the way, all done in a non-competitive, let's-have-some-fun sort of way. The original Hash House was the Selangor Club in Kuala Lumpur, so nicknamed for the allegedly tedious and unimaginative food they served there.

In 1938 a group of British Colonials, including one 'Torch' Bennett (I don't think we are related), formed a running club based on hare-and-hound chases, as a means of clearing the weekend's hangover. After World War Two the club was revived and in the 1960s and 1970s 'hashing' began to spread worldwide. There are now thousands of clubs all over the world. Styling themselves as 'the drinking club with a running problem', this sounded like the sort of running club I could get involved in.

There have been occasional hiccups, however. Like the hashing club in New Haven, Connecticut, that sprinkled flour across the car park of their IKEA store and inadvertently sparked a terrorist scare when a customer saw two people throwing white stuff on the floor and then running away.

The hashers at the hostel were a friendly group, although we suspected the warden did not entirely approve of the barrel of beer with a line across the kitchen to a makeshift hand pump. We, on the other hand, were quite impressed with the arrangement. The hashers were also gratifyingly impressed with our journey. However, I began to feel like something of an imposter. These people evidently thought we were really fit, athletic types, when in fact we were simply bumbling along on what had now turned into a 1,000-mile pub crawl. I was also slightly embarrassed, as I was not sure which one of them had been getting out of her car just as I had shouted 'You wanker!' at Mick as we cycled into the car park last night.

By half past ten the hashers had all gone off on their run, and Mick excitedly got his towel and dashed off for his first shower since leaving Bristol. He emerged in high dudgeon – the water was stone cold. To make matters worse, the warden informed us that we were to be chucked out of the hostel until five o'clock in the afternoon. Mick did not help our case by informing her this was not so much a youth hostel as a borstal, upon which we duly left the building, vowing to write a strongly worded letter to head office.

There was no sign of the family yet, so we sat forlornly by the road. After an hour and a half they eventually arrived, gratifyingly impressed at the distance we had covered since Thursday. Lunch cheered us up no end. The pub, the Horseshoe Inn, had transformed itself since last night: there were no signs of any musicians and the food was fabulous – we feasted on huge plates of steak and ale pie with lashings of gravy. (Mick enjoyed his pie so much he was still going on about it when we reached Scotland.) The beer was Mojo from Monty's Brewery in Montgomery, Powys. The label said 'amber toasty marmalade' which I thought intriguing. I couldn't really taste any toast but it was a nice brew all the same.

After lunch, still banned from entering the hostel, we all sat in the grounds shivering in the April breeze. We were about 900 feet above sea level here, perched at the foot of the Long Mynd, and it showed in the temperature. My daughter and her cousin played on the swings for a while. I saw the warden striding over the lawn towards us and I wondered whether she would ask them to get off as they were not residents. Mick gave her a steely stare and, if that was the case she evidently thought better of it, turning abruptly and returning to the hostel, locking the door behind her. I wondered, if we had been quicker, whether we could have rushed her, stormed the sitting room and staged a sit-in.

The family bade us farewell and good luck and at five o'clock we stood waiting outside the hostel with our towels. When we were finally admitted, the showers, if not hot, were at least warm this time. We also did our laundry in the sink – no washing machine or indeed any other mod cons here. That's the trouble with the Youth Hostel Association: while some hostels are excellent, too many of them seem to think they are running some kind of boy scout/girl guide outfit from the 1950s. When you arrive you get given a little pack of linen and you have to make your own bed, frequently a bunk bed, an item of furniture I have not used since reaching the age of ten. The mattresses are always thin and hard, the pillows appear to be stuffed with gravel, and the blankets are thin and measly. You get kicked out of the hostel from ten in the morning until five in the afternoon. And at the end of your stay you have to strip the bed as well! Many hostels are now closing and I believe a radical rethink is needed if more are not to follow.

Later that evening we sat back and relaxed in the ancient sitting room with a bottle of wine the hashers had left behind. At least the day off had given our aching legs and sore bottoms some respite, and we didn't feel too bad, not even when the warden poked her head around the door to inform us that the forecast was for rain, heavy rain, all day tomorrow.

'Oh and also,' she said as an afterthought as she left the room, 'it's going to get really cold.'

Was it my imagination or did I see a brief smile flicker across her face as she departed?

>>>>>>>>>>>>>>>>>>>>>>>>>>>>

Stats
Miles: 0
Total miles: 376
Pints of beer (each): 3
Bottles of wine scavenged: 1
Cheery weather forecasts: 0

>>>>>>>>>>>>>>>>>>>>>>>>>>>>

RATLINGHOPE
>>>>>>>>>>>>>>>>>>>>>>> TO >>>>>>>>>>>>>>>>>>>>>>>>>
HATCHMERE

Following a now familiar pattern we were locked out of the hostel again in the morning. We had packed up early to get a good start and standing around waiting for the warden to open the door was, to say the least, irritating. But our teabags and other things were in there and I needed at least one cup before setting off. When we had finally been allowed in and the warden had once more enjoyed telling us how terrible the weather was going to be we departed.

Immediately the narrow road began to climb up the second-highest hill in Shropshire. Part of the reason for this ridiculous detour was I had wanted to see the Stiperstones – jagged pinnacles of quartzite formed some 480 million years ago. I had been reading up on them before our journey and the stones were, by common agreement, quite a spectacular sight. The tallest pinnacle is known as the Devil's Chair and there are numerous legends about this spot. One legend has it that the Devil brought the stones from Ireland by carrying them in an apron. They were intended to fill the nearby Hell's Gutter, but he sat down for a bit of a rest on the top of the hill and as he stood up the string on his apron broke and out fell the rocks. Presumably he couldn't be bothered to pick them up again (typical bloke) and so they lie there still. I don't know about you, but I find the idea of the Devil wearing a pinny somewhat unconvincing. I picture him in one with big flowers and frills around the edge (like my mum used to wear in the 1970s), which he had maybe borrowed from Mrs Devil, who surely would not be best pleased to learn he had been using it to carry muddy old rocks across country. He was probably also in the habit of stripping down old motorbikes in the living room and leaving oily carburettors in the sink.

Sadly, the warden's predictions had been correct; we were now 1,500 feet above sea level, the weather was misty and wet, and we couldn't see anything. I was feeling fed up and disappointed, and my right knee throbbed as I struggled up the hill. For the first time on the trip I was having serious doubts about whether I was capable of finishing the journey. This section of the route had been a big mistake for so many reasons. I vowed that next time, if there ever was one, I would, without doubt, stay in the valley in or around Bishop's Castle, avoiding unnecessary hills, inhospitable hostels and views that were anything but.

At the curiously named Snailbeach we called into the village shop and bought the only items we could find which would serve as breakfast – two tins of chunky soup – which we drank cold from the can. In an effort to get the last dregs from the tin I tipped it right up only to drop lumps of cold potato and tomato on my nose. Soaking wet, freezing cold and with soup dripping off my face, it would be fair to say this was not a high point of the trip. But within minutes the road tipped downwards again, and the north Shropshire and Chester plains lay below us, stretching far into the distance. Flat, flat, flat, followed by flat. Fantastic – bloody fantastic. I cheered up no end at the sight of all that flatness. It would not be until the start of the Lake District, two days and more than 150 miles ahead, that we would have to contend with any more serious climbs.

For the moment, however, I was distracted by concerns of imminent frostbite. My fingerless gloves were not up to the task, and by the time we had coasted down the hill the ends of my fingers were frozen. At the bottom we stood in a bus shelter for ten minutes with me pressing the ends of my fingers under my armpits in an effort to get some feeling back into them. Along the road at Minsterley we stopped at a petrol station that was selling coffee. While I was dispensing the drinks Mick disappeared off and came back with a pair of thick purple household cleaning gloves. I put them on and pulled the fingerless ones over the top of them. They did the trick wonderfully and looked rather natty, I thought. We hung around in the garage for ages, standing under the hot-air blower, drinking coffee and generally getting in everyone's way. It was so deliciously warm in there! Finally, when we were fairly certain losing a digit was not going to be an immediate hazard, we set off once more.

Now we had come off the hills the temperature rose significantly. We cycled through Melverley and, following the advice in our little guidebook, turned down a lane to look at St Peter's Church. Like Herefordshire, Shropshire has a large number of medieval timber buildings. This one, perched on the bank of the River Vyrnwy is a superb example, built in 1406 from local Melverley oak, using pegs throughout. There is not a single nail in the whole building. Inside you can climb up worn wooden steps to a west gallery, where we sat for a while breathing in the aroma of ancient wood, before re-emerging, blinking, into the daylight. A little way down from here the Vyrnwy enters the Severn, immediately doubling it in size as it heads south.

By now the sun was shining and I had forgotten the day's earlier trials. It is strange how we humans live in the moment. When we are warm we forget what it is like to be shivering with cold and when we are cold, it is like we have never been warm in our lives. On hot summer days we cannot imagine the cold dark nights of winter, and on days when it rains incessantly we find it hard to believe the sun will ever shine again. If I am packing to go camping and the sun is shining I don't even bother to pack a raincoat. Conversely, when it rains, the swimming gear gets left behind. I should have learnt by now, but every year it is the same. Which was why I had only thought to pack fingerless gloves for this trip, confident the weather would be as warm as it had been on the day we left Bristol.

Fifteen miles on, just before Ellesmere, we made a last-minute decision to detour via the village of Frankton, to take a quick look at Frankton Junction where the Montgomery Canal meets the Llangollen Canal. The Llangollen had originally been known as the Ellesmere Canal – the initial plan for the canal had proved too ambitious, the only section to be built as intended was the section from the Chester Canal to the Mersey, giving the community that grew up at the entrance to the Mersey its name, Ellesmere Port. Both Mick and I happen to be ex-narrowboat owners and rarely pass a canal without stopping for a peek. Both the Llangollen and the Montgomery are dead ends, so this was pretty much on the western edge of the canal network. But as we stood on the bridge Mick recognised a narrowboat moored on the opposite bank.

It was the boat of someone he vaguely knew through a canal-users forum. He had last seen them at Stourport-on-Severn a year previously. Of all the miles of canal in the country they could have been traversing, they happened to be moored right next to the very bridge at which we happened to stop. We pushed our bikes along the towpath and knocked on the door to say hello. They were very surprised to see us but kindly invited us on board – and so we spent a very pleasant hour on their narrowboat, *Marmaduke*, drinking tea and eating biscuits. It was with some regret that we heaved ourselves up to cycle on.

We headed into Ellesmere, a pleasant enough town, where we lingered long enough to stock up on provisions at an excellent delicatessen called Vermeulens. By now we had covered about 35 miles since the hostel and, thanks to delays shopping and drinking tea, it was gone four o'clock. But we wanted to get a reasonable amount done after our rest day yesterday, so we crossed the border into Wales, traversing the area of land on the east of the Dee known as Maelor Saesneg (English-speaking Maelor). After about 10 miles we crossed back into England and pressed on along country lanes and B-roads through sleepy Cheshire villages. The landscape was pleasant but unexciting – fields, sheep, fields, sheep, village, fields, sheep, fields, village, ooh look a cow! Fields, sheep, village...

There was a marked lack of B & Bs along the route. We began stopping to ask people and called into a couple of pubs to enquire about accommodation. The conversation would go something like this:

Landlord: 'No, sorry, we don't do accommodation. I'll just ask around. Anyone know of a B & B around here? Or, failing that, a campsite?'

Helpful customer at the bar: 'B & B – nooo, don't think so. So and so up the road used to do it but she's stopped now, not much call for it.'

'Well, *I'm* calling for it,' I thought bitterly. 'OK,' trying not to sound desperate, 'not to worry, not a problem; thanks anyway!'

Eventually, after another 25 miles or so, we found ourselves cycling along the edge of Delamere Forest. To our left lay the lake of Hatchmere, which in the evening sun looked delightful. We passed a very organised-looking campsite, but after four nights camping and with the tent still damp, we really wanted to be indoors and hopefully have somewhere to dry our things. We decided to press on for a few miles and if we found nothing we would return to the campsite.

A few miles down the road we stumbled upon a bed and breakfast, and Mick soon got chatting to the owner. Before retiring and opening up the place he had been a builder by trade, and Mick complimented him on his brickwork. Well that was it – they spent the next half an hour discussing pointing, cement and the relative merits of single-skin and double-skin walls, while I tried not to yawn. Once inside, however, I cheered up immediately. We were given, not a room, but an entire flatlet, which was impeccably decorated. It really was fabulous. We were slightly disconcerted when the owner demanded names and addresses before we booked in, declaring that he needed them in case we ran off with the telly.

'Oh yes,' I wanted to say, 'we thought we'd stuff it in the panniers along with the stereo and all the china – after all we haven't got much to carry.'

We were desperate, however, so I judiciously kept my mouth shut and gave him our details – and he did allow us to lay out our wet tent and other belongings in the garage to dry.

We repaired to the Carriers Inn, which our host had described as the 'best pub in England'. Our hopes were high, but when we got there it turned out to be a pub that had reinvented itself as a rather fancy restaurant, as many pubs, both urban and rural, are now doing.

As we all know, pubs are closing down at a phenomenal rate – something like thirty to forty every week. According to the British Beer & Pub Association, we are now down to around 52,000 pubs – a reduction of 17,000 since 1980. Ask why pubs are closing and you will receive a myriad of replies. Cheap supermarket beer, taxation, the smoking ban, lack of local support, breweries making a quick buck from the property boom, expensive prices, tough drink-driving laws, the recession(s), greedy breweries – all have been cited as reasons for the demise of the local boozer.

On the other hand, some pubs continue to thrive and prove that it can be done. Having made it my business to visit a fair few pubs in my lifetime, I would also observe that publicans themselves should shoulder some of the blame for the demise of the traditional pub. For a start there are the opening hours. Time and again we have been disappointed when out for a walk or a cycle ride to discover the pub shuts at two-thirty on a Saturday and Sunday. Why? What is the reasoning?

'Ooh it's a lovely Sunday afternoon, lots of thirsty people will be out taking a walk. I know – I'll shut at half past two!'

I recall one blisteringly hot day when Mick and I had been walking in Herefordshire a couple of years ago. I had (of course) brought my trusty OS map, which showed a tantalising blue jug symbol a mile or so out of our way. We decided to detour down to the pub. It was about three o'clock on a Sunday afternoon when we got there. It was shut. Mick, who had been salivating at the thought of a lovely pint of beer for the past forty-five minutes, lost his temper.

'How the fuck did we ever manage to run an empire?' he ranted. 'We can't even do basic hospitality! I could go anywhere else in what used to be the British Empire – Australia, Singapore, India – and get a beer! Not here! What is the landlord thinking? Oh yes, it's a lovely hot Sunday afternoon, sod the customers, I'm going to close and have a nap in the garden! No wonder they're all closing down!'

We sat on the grass outside, munching on an apple each and supping on the tepid water we had brought with us, before dejectedly trudging back to our campsite.

Even if they are open, some pubs are spectacularly unfriendly. You go in a pub and discover you are the only customers; the landlord is watching Sky TV; he turns with a sigh and asks what you want; you order a beer; he pulls a pint, which is a short measure. You ask for it to be topped up; he sighs again; it is 9.25 p.m. and you ask whether you could have some food.

'No,' he says, without elaboration or apology. 'The kitchen is closed.'

'A sandwich perhaps?' (Chancing it.)

'No.'

'Oh. OK.'

The landlord returns to the game, annoyed because whilst he was serving you he missed a goal. Six months later, when he is closing down, he will blame his customers, the government, the supermarkets, the brewery and anyone else he can think of except himself for the fact he is losing money. Here are my suggestions to publicans who wish to do their bit in halting the demise of the traditional pub:

1. Open all day on Saturday and Sunday. Take Monday and Tuesday off, when everyone else has grumpily gone back to work.
2. If serving food, then do so until 10 p.m. Offer sandwiches or a bowl of chips until twenty minutes before closing.
3. Serve with a smile.
4. Serve a full pint, not a glass 90 per cent full. At three quid a pint, or more, that's surely not unreasonable.
5. Consider the business as a service to the community rather than resenting every single person who enters your establishment.

Just my thoughts. Anyway, we were not that surprised that the Carriers Inn had basically become a restaurant which looks like a pub from the outside. However, the staff were very friendly, which was something, and we enjoyed a huge and beautifully cooked mixed grill, deciding that after the trials of HMP Ratlinghope we deserved some spoiling. The waiter was suitably impressed with our appetites as we demolished everything that was put in front of us.

>>>>>>>>>>>>>>>>>>>>>>>>>

Stats
Miles: 67
Total miles: 443
Pints of beer (each): 3
Fields peed in: 10
Hot showers taken at B & B: 4

>>>>>>>>>>>>>>>>>>>>>>>>>

DAY
11

HATCHMERE
TO
PRESTON

The next morning we indulged in more long, hot showers before packing and taking our leave. A few miles on, Mick commented on the proprietor's approach, bemoaning the fact he had all but accused us of being thieves. I agreed it was unacceptable, before confiding that I had got my own back by nicking the soap. Mick said he would rather I had nicked the telly.

I had originally planned for our route to take in a tour of the Wirral, having never been there, and I was also quite keen on taking a ferry across the Mersey, simply so I could sing the song. Mick, however, had put his foot down and was having none of this route foolishness. He said he was sick of my stupid detours and had no desire to spend a day cycling through the suburbs of Liverpool, and if we did so we would probably never even get to John o'Groats. He had a point. What seems like a smallish detour on a road atlas is, in fact, quite a different prospect when one has already cycled almost 500 miles and has another 500 to go.

Thinking on this, I felt amazed I had even made it this far; to this point, I'd cycled more than twice the distance of my personal best. The previous day, climbing over up the road to the Stiperstones I was really worried I wasn't going to make it. I was afraid that because I had not really trained properly for this journey, an injury would force me to give up. Mind you, I did have form on not training properly; a couple of years ago I had run a half-marathon without having done any training at all. It took me two and a quarter hours and I couldn't walk properly for more than a week. I don't recommend it. Now, as we gently coasted down the road, I was more optimistic. My knee had stopped throbbing and I was feeling refreshed after our good night's sleep. However, I still refused to allow myself to think too much about the journey ahead. Like looking up when climbing a hill, I found it too discouraging to think about how far we had to go. I was taking it one day at a time and metaphorically fixing my gaze at the tarmac rather than the summit.

We had decided to head for the town of Frodsham and then turn right, where we would make a run for it through the conurbations of Runcorn and Warrington.

We soon reached Frodsham, which was only a few miles away from our bed and breakfast. As we entered the main street we were greeted by a distinctive 'farm-yardy' smell. We hoped the smell would be temporary – maybe a lorry carrying pig shit had just passed through. The last time I smelt anything like it was at a wine tasting evening when I sniffed a bottle of very expensive Pinot Noir. Leaving the smell aside, Frodsham is a not-unpleasant market town with a wide central street, although the traffic on it was rather heavy as the central street is also the A56 – the main road from Warrington and Runcorn to Chester – and the rumble of the M56 was only a couple of streets behind the town.

Several of the buildings in Frodsham have a bee plaque on them – the honeybee being the symbol of the town. This is in recognition of the contribution of William Cotton, one-time vicar of Frodsham, to global beekeeping. In the nineteenth century, Cotton was appointed as chaplain to New Zealand's Bishop Selwyn. Cotton had a keen interest in beekeeping and arranged for hives to be shipped over to New Zealand. Although there were native species of bee on the islands, New Zealand had no indigenous honeybee population prior to the 1830s. Cotton was not the first to bring bees to the country (the first bees to be imported were introduced by the appropriately named Mary Bumby of Thirsk in 1839) but he did a huge amount to develop beekeeping in New Zealand amongst both white settlers and Maoris, producing a handbook in English, *A Manual for New Zealand Bee Keepers* in 1848, and the following year a book called *The Bees,* written in Maori, a language he had learned on the crossing from a Maori boy on the ship. Later he was appointed vicar of Frodsham, where he continued his work with bees, before his mental health deteriorated (he suffered from what we now recognise as bipolar disorder) and he was forced to relinquish the parish. New Zealand honey is now some of the most sought after in the world: manuka honey has acquired almost magical status as a wonder food, selling for up to £40 a pot.

Becoming an apiarist would be my idea of the job from hell. I am nervous around bees following an incident a few years ago. I was camping on the Gower in Wales with my husband

and daughter when I was stung by a very large insect. (Actually, I was convinced it was a furry baby elephant that had planted the barb, so large was the creature that flew off over the trees.) I complained a bit about the sting but then thought little of it as I retired to the tent to change into my swimsuit, planning to head for the beach. Emerging from the tent, I suddenly felt very strange, and collapsed in a heap, moaning and feeling extremely unwell with some sort of allergic reaction. A nurse, who happened to be camping nearby, rushed over and, after examining me, said she felt emergency treatment was required. The lanes to the campsite were winding and narrow, so help was summonsed in the form of an air ambulance, which proceeded to land in the middle of the camping field, scattering tents, windbreaks, towels and assorted camping accoutrements to all four corners of the field. As the campers crowded around, curious to see what was happening, I was carried on a stretcher into the helicopter and carted off to Swansea hospital, where I spent six hours lying on a trolley in the corridor with a needle in my arm, still wearing my swimsuit. It was, as my daughter pointed out, totally embarrassing.

From Frodsham there was no real option except to use the main roads. As we entered Runcorn our guidebook advised we look for signs to Shopping City (allegedly known by the locals as 'Shitty City') and then Old Town. We got lost almost immediately in a council housing estate, one of those with alleyways and pathways that never seem to go anywhere. We eventually called into the local fast-food joint for directions. It was 10 a.m. and the place was full of girls of about fifteen with their babies in tow, tucking into a nutritious mid-morning snack of mechanically separated chicken scraps and chips. We followed the directions we were given and soon found ourselves on the 'Expressway', an urban motorway which was terrifying and on which our presence was possibly illegal – and then it started raining.

We got off the Expressway as soon as we could and looked for a sign for a cycle path – any path, just to get us off the horrible roads. Cycle route signage in Runcorn is woefully inadequate; occasionally we would spot a sign for a cycle route, follow it and then find ourselves hopelessly lost again.

Runcorn New Town was built in the late 1960s and early 1970s, alongside what I gather was once quite a pleasant town. I can't comment on the Old Town as we didn't find it, but Runcorn New Town is a dump – it's horrible and depressing. I'm sorry if that sounds harsh but there it is. I was not at all surprised to read recently that it is frequently dubbed 'Scumcorn'. It is the worst example of post-war town planning that I have ever seen, with ugly brutalist concrete architecture that has not stood the test of time, and a huge and hideous shopping centre. The council's website states that 'many architects and town planners from many parts of the world have visited the town', I hope and pray that they come to Runcorn to learn how not to do it, as the thought of Runcorn imitations popping up all over the world is far too depressing to contemplate.

In the end we made a visual fix on the bridge and headed for it, worried that if we didn't we would be forever trapped in this hellhole of a place. We ended up pushing our bicycles along a very narrow pavement alongside railings, against the traffic which was hurtling past us at 70 mph. Suddenly in front of us were two walkers with large rucksacks, one of them was also carrying a guitar while the other one lagged behind, taking photos of the road, the bridge and traffic. Our enquiry confirmed our suspicions: they were indeed also headed for John o'Groats. They said they had been walking through Runcorn for about two hours and they thought they would arrive at John o'Groats in about eight weeks. We jokingly promised to get a beer in for them at the John o'Groats Hotel and I was suddenly very glad that I was doing this by bicycle and not on foot. Mick, however, was by now very grumpy at the thought of cycling through miles and miles of urban conurbations. I had not yet told him that I had a trick up my sleeve, which would hopefully restore my battered navigational reputation.

The Widnes side of the bridge was a complete contrast to the Runcorn side. After cycling down a couple of residential streets we came to the last lock of the Sankey Canal navigation. Sailing boats were moored down the centre of the canal, Widnes Lock giving access to the Mersey below. We crossed over to Spike Island or 'Spikey', an island of land between the canal and the estuary. This was the birthplace of the British chemical industry and was once dominated by factories. In the 1970s it was a real eyesore, with derelict factories and piles of waste blotting the landscape. Since then the local council has got to work and the area has been cleared, cleaned up and reclaimed as a delightful linear park alongside the canal. This path is the start of the Sankey Valley Country Park, which, although not particularly direct, affords a traffic-free green route from Widnes through Warrington and on to Newton-le-Willows. Mick was suitably impressed with my route.

'Cheers, Phil,' I said, patting the little guidebook in my pocket affectionately.

The Sankey Canal was arguably England's first canal, opened in 1757 to carry coal down to the Mersey and Liverpool, although the section here at Widnes was not built until 1832. I say arguably because there is rivalry among local canal enthusiasts – between supporters of the Sankey and those of the nearby Bridgewater Canal. Bridgewater supporters say that one section of the Sankey Canal is in fact Sankey Brook, and that the Bridgewater Canal can therefore lay claim to being the first canal proper. I find it hard to believe this can be the cause of heated debate, but I suppose these things matter to some people. In any event, both canals were a roaring success and their opening marked the start of 'canal mania', a period of frenzied canal building which underpinned the Industrial Revolution until the advent of the railways – which took away the canal trade – often buying up the canals to deliberately allow them to become derelict. Now there are restoration societies all over the country that work to restore some of these waterways for leisure use, and the Sankey Canal is no exception, although we saw later on that this is quite clearly a long-term project.

The next section, past Fiddlers Ferry power station, was not the most scenic, unless you are a fan of coal-fuelled power stations with massive cooling towers dominating the skyline. Here the canal was weeded up and unnavigable. The Mersey flowed on our right, and between the path and the river was a wide area of marshland. The Mersey spreads itself very widely here, after the confines of Runcorn Gap, before narrowing again at Fidlers Ferry where another lock gives access to the Mersey.

We stopped for a cup of tea at a chuck wagon and had a chat to the guy behind the counter. He served us one-handed (he was missing an arm and a leg).

'Motorbike?' asked Mick

He nodded. 'Yeah,' he said. 'Took a bend too fast and came off under the bike.'

'And you didn't let go. Same thing happened to my brother. He lost an arm.'

The guy nodded.

'Damn machines,' he said.

He and his partner had opened the chuck wagon just a week earlier, with some support from a local employment agency. When they realised we were doing the ride for charity they insisted on giving us the tea on the house. Just as we finished it started to drizzle again, so out came the raincoats and capes before we continued on down the path.

We followed the route of the canal through linear parks, while the water disappeared for spells and then reappeared again. Aside from the occasional road to cross, including the M62 (we went under it rather than run across it), it was hard to believe we were in the centre of Warrington. We stuck with paths heading north alongside the Sankey for another 8 miles, until we left the park at Mucky Mountains on the edge of Newton-le-Willows. There was a large information board telling the history of the place and here I learned that the mucky mountains were in fact heaps of chemical waste, a by-product of soda-making from the 1830s. There was quite a lot of it, with 2 tons of waste generated for every ton of soda. Nature had by now begun colonising the area, however, and an information board declared it to be a 'site of community wildlife interest'. I stand to be corrected, but I am fairly sure that this designation is something the local authority has made up, deliberately choosing terms that sound a little bit like 'Site of Special Scientific Interest'. But to be fair, the council is doing its best with what it's got and it certainly sounds better than 'chemical waste dump'. Apparently there is some interesting flora to be found here, including something called 'quaking grass' which I liked the sound of.

The next few miles were not very exciting as we hauled ourselves through industrial estates, car parks and residential streets, at one point dragging the loaded bikes over a footbridge, all the while trying to avoid the M6. At least it was flat. As we cycled through Eccleston, the Original Farmers Arms caught our eye, not least as it was advertising beer on special offer. It was, we decided, time for a break.

A few people were eating – the pub obviously majored in food – and judging by the extensive menu it looked like it did it very well. The bar area was quiet, however, with just three or four chaps sat there supping on pints. As usual our jackets broke the ice for us.

'Heading to John o'Groats, eh?' said one of them conversationally.

I nodded. 'Yes... hopefully', I said.

'Some mates and I did that a couple of years ago,' he said.

'Oh really? How long did it take you?' (By now I had become slightly obsessed by our slow progress and was hoping to find someone even slower than us. After all, this chap didn't look terribly fit.)

'Five days,' he said.

'You cycled Land's End to John o'Groats in *five days*?' I said, incredulously.

He looked at me pityingly. 'No lass, not cycling,' he said. 'On the beezer.'

I looked at him blankly. I had no idea what he was talking about. Mick laughed. 'It's a motorbike, you ninny,' he said. 'A BSA.'

I concentrated on my beer, a pint of Owzat! from Slater's in Staffordshire, a copper-coloured bitter which was very pleasant.

We debated whether to stop for food but time was getting on and we wanted to get Preston under our belt before throwing in the towel for the day. So, after our drink we said goodbye and set off once more.

An hour or so later we coasted into Preston, where we once again got lost and found ourselves on a major busy through route. It was also getting late and we had no idea where we were going to stay. We tentatively knocked on the door of a very scruffy establishment that advertised itself as a B & B – I was relieved when no one answered the door. We asked various people if they knew of anywhere to stay but drew a blank each time. Not that anyone was unfriendly or unhelpful, but they had no concept of distance if it was not in a car.

'You could try so and so,' they would say.

'How far is it?' we would ask warily.

'Only about fifteen minutes or so.'

'Fifteen minutes or so, *how*?' we pressed.

'Well, by car.'

Fifteen minutes by car is at least 10 miles, or an hour cycling and there was no guarantee once we got there we would get a bed for the night. We were feeling very tired by now and I wondered whether we could get away with putting the tent up in a local park. It didn't feel like bandit country, although Preston does have a certain claim to bandit fame. Back in the 1850s there was a couple who lived in Victoria Road, Preston, by the name of Maximilian Parker and Ann Gillies. They were Mormons, followers of the Church of Jesus Christ of Latter-day Saints. In the late-1850s they joined 3,000 other pioneers from Britain and Scandinavia who were moving to the Utah Territories. Once in the US they produced a large family of thirteen children, the eldest of whom was named Robert Leroy Parker. Robert was a bit wild and left home in his early teens. After a spell as a butcher in Wyoming he acquired the nickname Butch. Later, in honour of his friend and mentor Mike Cassidy, he adopted his friend's surname, and thenceforth became known as Butch Cassidy. The rest, as they say, is history. The claim that Cassidy spoke with a broad Lancastrian accent I find hard to believe, after all he was brought up in Utah, but the thought of Paul Newman saying, 'Ey oop lad 'and over t'money oor yawl guduz deed,' gave me some amusement.

Discarding the camping in the park idea, we decided we had no choice but to head up the A6 to Garstang. Thankfully, as we headed out of town we spotted a budget hotel, the sort that once would have been frequented by commercial travellers – basic but clean and pleasant enough – and we booked in with some relief. That evening I made a unilateral decision not to go to the pub. The only premises within walking distance looked dire and I didn't fancy sitting in front of Sky TV, drinking fizzy beer. After some initial sulking as he did not want to go on his own, Mick later conceded I was right. Instead we ate the bread, cheese and olives we had bought earlier for supper and settled down in front of the telly for an hour before getting a jolly good night's sleep.

>>>>>>>>>>>>>>>>>>>>>>>>>>>>>

Stats
Miles: 53
Total miles: 496
Pints of beer (each): 1 (!!!!)
Bandit attacks: 0

>>>>>>>>>>>>>>>>>>>>>>>>>>>>>

DAY
12

PRESTON
≫≫≫≫≫≫≫≫≫≫≫≫ TO ≫≫≫≫≫≫≫≫≫≫≫≫
WINDERMERE

Mick gave me some cause for concern by singing Nana Mouskouri songs as he got ready for breakfast. I was worried this was all getting a bit much and decided if he started on Demis Roussos I would suggest a rest day. Thankfully, he stopped at Nana and so after breakfast (another full English) we set off up the A6. We lasted about five minutes before diving onto minor roads. Now, with a lot of the major industrial cities behind us, we began to feel we were really in the north proper. Only the Lake District and Carlisle separated us from the Scottish border. The landscape was pan-flat, and to the west of the A6 the roads were very quiet. I felt a sense of contentment and freedom as we cycled along, with no sound except the turning of our wheels and the buzzing of spring insects warming up in the morning sunshine.

Suddenly, Mick pointed towards a field, where there was a hare, sitting upright and alert in the sun. Hares suffered a decline in numbers at the beginning of the twentieth century and then, after something of a recovery, they suffered another decline in the 1960s and 1970s from which they have not yet recovered. The reasons for the decline are not clear, but it seems likely that intensification of agriculture and a reduction in countryside diversity are to blame. Hares love hay meadows, 95 per cent of which disappeared in the latter half of the twentieth century in the UK.

Over the past few years, however, I have seen more hares than usual, so I am hopeful their numbers are now increasing. Hare coursing has been illegal in the UK since 2005; whether this is having an effect on numbers I don't know. Anyway, we stopped to watch this one sitting there in the sun when, suddenly, a second hare darted out from the hedge and, to our delight, they started to box. I had always assumed that boxing hares were two males, but apparently not: boxing is part of the spring courtship ritual, with female hares fending off amorous advances from the passionate males. This female was clearly not up for any rumpty tumpty in the grass, and she bopped her suitor a few times before he got the message and sulkily sloped back to his corner of the field. I was impressed with her technique of delivering a smack in the mouth when not in the mood – it beats complaining that you have a headache.

We saw a sign for Glasson Dock and, on a whim, turned left, thinking it sounded interesting. It was. We cycled down flat lanes, the road going nowhere except the dock itself where it performs a big loop around the basin. Glasson sits at the mouth of the River Lune and a dock was opened here in 1787 to save vessels having to navigate the river up to Lancaster. At one time it was the most important dock of the north-west, helping to supply Lancashire during its industrial heyday. Boats were built here as well, one of the most famous being the schooner *Ryelands*, launched in 1887, which later become something of a movie star. In 1949 she became the *Hispaniola* in Disney's *Treasure Island*, and then in 1954 she was *Pequod* in Moby Dick. She became a tourist attraction in Morecambe, where she was known as the *Moby Dick*, before sadly being destroyed by fire in 1972.

A branch of the Lancaster Canal opens out into the marina basin, which was full of sailing yachts, dinghies and the occasional narrowboat. We followed the road down towards the dock, passing the Victoria Inn. The pub is at the end of a small row of terraced houses, which look rather incongruous stuck in the middle of nowhere. Turning left at the pub we came to the controlled lock that separates the marina from the dock itself. Beyond the dock two locks give access to the River Lune and to Morecombe Bay. Entry into the dock from the river is tricky, due to the shallowness of the Lune at low tide, with only a forty-five-minute opportunity before high tide to access the dock.

Crossing the lock we spied a cafe, the delightfully named Lantern O'er Lune. It was a little early, not yet noon, but the place looked inviting and very crowded (which we took to be a good sign) so we decided to stop for an early lunch – despite the fact it was only two hours since we had eaten a full cooked breakfast. I don't normally eat so much, but one thing I had noticed on this ride was that we were almost always hungry. We ordered fish, chips and what I think was pease pudding – it had the same consistency as mushy peas, but was pale yellow rather than the dayglo green we were used to. Or perhaps it was mushy peas au naturel without E102 (yellow) and E133 (blue), commonly used to 'green-up' the dish. I should have asked. It tasted nice anyway, and the fish and chips were fantastic. There were a couple of other cyclists in the cafe and one of them leant over to ask how the ride to John o'Groats was going.

'Fine,' I said, 'but how on earth did you know where we are going?'

'Um, because it's written on your backs,' he said.

Ah yes, forgot about that...

They waved goodbye while we dawdled over a pot of tea. When we emerged blinking in the sunlight half an hour later, we were surprised to see them still outside. The bridge had closed to let a boat into the harbour and they were still waiting to cross. While we were all stood waiting we took the opportunity for a further chat. They told us their two sons had recently been made redundant and they were worried about whether they would be able to find work in the current climate.

'This recession that they keep going on about,' said the woman, 'it's all over the papers now jobs down south are going, but we've had recession up here for years and years already. It hasn't ever gone away.'

Even so, they both insisted on giving us some money for our fund. They also told us about the cycle path along the River Lune, known as the Crook o'Lune, following the track of the old railway line which used to run from Glasson Dock to Lancaster. It turned out to be a fabulous path, nice and smooth and following along the line of the Lune Estuary with lovely views of the River Lune along its length; this is Lancaster's version of Cornwall's Camel Trail. It also forms part of Sustrans National Route 6.

As we entered Lancaster, a different landscape greeted us. Huge derelict buildings towered above as we cycled alongside the river. This was Luneside East, a large piece of contaminated industrial land now owned by the city council. Plans to regenerate the area had stalled and (at the time of writing) it remained a massive eyesore. The rest of the riverside was pleasant, though, and I liked the new Millennium Bridge very much, with its two 'masts' reaching into the sky above the bridge itself, which joins three banks by forming a sort of 'Y' shape. We crossed Ryelands Park and rejoined the A6 for only a few minutes before getting on the towpath of the Lancaster Canal, bound for Carnforth. This was excellent under the wheels, and we spent an enjoyable hour looking at the ducklings and the boats along the way. The Lancaster canal, on the father reaches of the canal system, is very quiet. Indeed, it was only joined to the main network in 2002 with the opening of the 4-mile Millennium Ribble Link near Preston.

At Carnforth we came across the Canal Turn, a delightful canalside pub. The sun was shining and we sat in the garden with a pint of Jennings Bitter, a nice darkish beer, and not too strong at 3.5 per cent. Jennings has been owned by Marston's since 2005 but is still brewed in the Cockermouth brewery. In 2009 the brewery, standing on the confluence of the Rivers Cocker and Derwent, suffered badly in the floods that wrecked the town, and had to temporarily relocate their beer production, but four months later they were back in operation. The national yeast bank in Norwich stores a batch of every British brewery's yeast culture and this was used to restart the beer production after the flood. We got chatting to some older folk who were on an outing and to a chap who had just that week started a new job taking people on boat trips up the canal. There were worse jobs to be had, we thought enviously. We were near the end of the navigable section, beyond which were the Northern Reaches – derelict canal, made unnavigable by the building of the M6. The towpath had also deteriorated to grass and, after a while bumping along, we gave up and got back onto the A6. There is an alternative route, part of Sustrans National Route 6, but it was wiggly-windy and so we decided to make progress on the main road as we were, as usual, not making very good time due to all the stops on the way. The terrain was flat and we plodded along uneventfully up the A6 for an hour before turning left and cycling into the village of Levens. I had been studying my atlas pages and had hatched a plan to avoid the A590, which was a fast and ferocious dual carriageway, by nipping through the village and onto the back road where we hoped to pick up the quieter A5074 Windermere Road into the Lake District.

As we neared the centre of the village we paused to consult the map. A chap, who was just passing at that moment, stopped and asked us where we wanted to go. He was wearing a tartan cap with a red pom-pom, which rang warning bells straight away. I showed him my intended route on the map.

'Oh no,' he said, 'you won't be able to do that; you'll have to get back on the dual carriageway. Now let me see if I can help you.'

He then spent an age peering at the map, trying to work out where Levens was which, as we were right in the middle of the village, I already knew. It was infuriating. He would point at somewhere miles away on the map such as Ambleside and then say,

'No, that's not it; now where's Levens,' spend ages finding it and then point again at the dual carriageway and shake his head.

'That's the only way I'm afraid,' he said sorrowfully.

We thanked him through gritted teeth and cycled on, swiftly finding the route I had originally planned along the 'old road' to the Windermere Road.

I would have appreciated that stretch of flat road much more than I did had I known what was to come. I took the lack of gradient for granted, didn't thank it, barely gave it a thought. An hour later I would have got off my bike and kissed the tarmac had I come across a road as flat. We were heading into the Lake District; the road started to rise and the landscape began to change. Flat fields and fences were replaced by dry stone walls and brown-topped hills but, to our surprise, there were no campsites. As this was a major tourist area I imagined they would be plentiful here, but we didn't pass one. We stopped for a pint at the Brown Horse Inn a few miles outside Windermere and made enquiries.

'Oh yes, just head down that road opposite for 6 or 7 miles or so and you'll find one,' one of the locals told us.

Here we go again. The road being indicated was in the wrong direction for our intended route and 6 or 7 miles, while nothing in a car, was a long detour at the end of a long day on a loaded pushbike, looking for a campsite that might not exist. It would take at least forty-five minutes and I was already struggling. We weakly smiled our thanks and ignored their advice. As we wearily remounted our bikes we received another suggestion.

'There's a backpackers hostel in Windermere,' someone said, 'you could try there.' This sounded more promising than a 6-mile detour, so we got the details and phoned the hostel, which confirmed they had places. 'Is there somewhere for our bikes to be secured?', I asked. The answer was a bit vague: 'Well, you could tie them to a tree outside.'

I hadn't realised that Windermere is in two parts – there is Bowness-on-Windermere, which is at lake level, and Windermere itself, which is up the hill. Needless to say the hostel was up the hill. By the time we had pedalled up it to Windermere proper I was exhausted. We found the hostel but it was clear there was no real place to put our bikes, and the idea of bunks in shared dorms simply didn't appeal. We decided to look for something else.

Mick for some reason thought a B & B that said 'biker friendly' would be a good one to try, even after I pointed out that the sign referred to motorcyclists rather than the pedally sort. You could tell because it had a little picture of someone on a motorbike, presumably for guests who were either international or (more likely, looking at the place) illiterate. Mick was having none of it, however, and marched up to the front door and rang the bell. The door was opened by a chap wearing leather trousers and a vest, which may once have been white, although it was hard to tell. He also sported a considerable beard.

'We're looking for a room for the night, two of us,' said Mick hesitantly.

He had now realised he had made a mistake.

'Come on in,' said the proprietor.

Mick flung a quick desperate look over his shoulder before disappearing inside. Two minutes later he reappeared in the doorway.

'It's twenty-five pounds per person per night,' Mick called out. 'What do you think?'

What did I think? I thought I wouldn't stay there for all the tea in China and India combined, that's what I thought. I knew what Mick was doing, though. Too scared to say he didn't want the room, he was hoping I would get him off the hook. I could tell this by the way he was rolling his eyes and making minute shakes of the head when he thought the owner wasn't looking. Deciding to teach him a lesson for not taking my advice, meanly I called out, 'Well, it's up to you, what do you think?'

'Um, um, dunno, it's up to you,' he said eventually.

After more dithering the owner lost patience.

'I don't fucking believe this!' he said, disappearing back inside and slamming the door.

Mick shuddered.

'You should have seen it,' he said, 'it was disgusting. Worse than the Hotel Rommel.'

'No!' I said, 'It couldn't be.'

'Yes it was. Honestly!'

The Hotel Rommel is in Mersa Matruh, on the Egyptian Mediterranean coast. Mick and I had found ourselves there while travelling to watch a solar eclipse a few years ago. We arrived in the town by bus and, clutching our Lonely Planet Guide, we hailed a taxi.

'Hotel Rommel, please,' we said, having chosen this hotel from our guide as a mid-range establishment with a good write-up. The taxi driver protested.

'No, no,' he said. 'You don't want to go there. I will take you to a better hotel.'

Being seasoned tourists we were wise to this. Oh yes, we thought, and then you will take us to your brother's hotel where we will be charged a fortune.

'No, thank you,' we said firmly. 'Hotel Rommel, please.'

The taxi driver shrugged as if to say 'please yourselves', and dropped us at the hotel right on the edge of town. We got the price at reception, which seemed reasonable, about £7 each, and checked into our room. I would estimate that it had not been dusted since about 1985. A thick layer covered all the surfaces. I made the mistake of turning on the ceiling fan and a thick cloud of dust filled the room. Coughing, I lunged for the off switch. The television was so old you had to change channels by turning a round dial on the front of the set; not that we could pick up any channels on it. Mick went to the bathroom to use the toilet and as he pulled the flush the pipe fell off the wall, spraying water everywhere. He jammed it back on and we looked at each other in dismay.

'Maybe we should have listened to the taxi driver,' said Mick.

The next morning, unwilling to spend more than another second in the place, we decided to skip breakfast and headed for the reception to check out. The chef was sitting in the reception area picking his nose, confirming that skipping breakfast had been the right choice. We realised that we had not seen any other guests during our stay – the entire hotel was empty except for us.

'That will be two hundred US dollars,' said the man behind the desk.

'Two *hundred* dollars?' we said in disbelief.

'Yes, yes, two hundred dollars!'

With that, Mick lost his temper. He banged his fist on the counter.

'Call the police!' he yelled. 'I am being robbed!'

I saw a couple of European passers-by curiously looking into the hotel before scuttling on towards the promenade.

'OK, OK,' said the receptionist, flapping his arms about. 'One moment.'

He picked up the phone and had what was quite clearly a pretend phone conversation.

'OK, OK.' he repeated, putting the phone down.

Then to us: 'Fifty dollars.'

Mick glared at him.

'We will pay you the agreed price,' he said firmly. 'In Egyptian pounds.'

The hotelier bad-temperedly took our payment and we took our leave and checked into a lovely hotel in the centre of town. Since that trip the Hotel Rommel is the standard by which all establishments that we visit are measured.

Leaving the bikers' B & B we scuttled up the road and knocked on a door in a side street that advertised bed and breakfast in the window. By now it was gone nine. The owner said it would cost £40 each, more than we wanted to pay. We demurred, explaining we were on a charity ride, hoping he would reduce his price as it was unlikely he would get another booking that late in the evening in April. Nothing doing.

'You could try next door,' he eventually volunteered.

Next door was a tiny terraced house. We knocked on the door and the owner, a woman who clearly had a good head for business, looked us up and down and gave us a price of £20 each. There was no storage for bikes, however, she said as she had no other residents booked in (just as well, as they would probably have had to share our room), we could put them in the breakfast room. We booked in, went up to our room and immediately got into bed and fell fast asleep.

>>>>>>>>>>>>>>>>>>>>>>>>>>>>

Stats
Miles: 61
Total miles: 557
Pints of beer (each): 2
Scabby B & Bs rejected: 1

>>>>>>>>>>>>>>>>>>>>>>>>>>>>

WINDERMERE

》》》》》》》》》》》》》》 **TO** 》》》》》》》》》》》》》》》

HESKET NEWMARKET

The next morning we were served a good breakfast and having to climb over our bikes to get to the table seemed a small inconvenience well worth putting up with. Mick said he had a proposal for a route today. Now, I am Routes and Mick is Maintenance – this was agreed from the start. But I did not want to appear too dictatorial and it was true that some of my route choices had been questionable. Since leaving Land's End we had cycled over 550 miles and fewer than 50 of them had been on main roads. We had bumped along towpaths and cycle paths, and along tortuous, pot-holed, slurry-covered lanes. Shropshire, with its three unnecessary hills, had been less than ideal, and Runcorn a complete and utter balls-up.

'I know we're taking the scenic route,' said Mick, 'but this is bloody ridiculous. We'll never get there! Here, let me have a go.'

Reluctantly, I handed him the bundle of pages I had torn from the atlas, which I had been using to navigate. He studied the relevant page for a minute or two. 'I know this area pretty well,' he said confidently, 'and the best way to go is along here,' – his finger traced the road from Windermere, along the side of the lake to Ambleside – 'and then up this little road here.'

On the atlas there was a small, innocuous white line connecting the A591 at Ambleside with the A592 Windermere to Patterdale Road at Kirkstone Pass.

'After that it's downhill all the way.'

It seemed harmless enough and, after all, Mick knew the area better than me. I agreed that we would go that way.

The initial section, from Windermere to Ambleside along the A591 was not taxing – after an initial climb it was a downhill coast most of the way. But by the time we got to Ambleside the rain was chucking down, so we dived into a cafe for an hour where we sat huddled next to a radiator, steaming gently. Mercifully, the sun eventually put in an appearance and we set off. At the famous Ambleside Bridge House Mick spotted a bakery and disappeared off to purchase two enormous sticky Bath buns, which were delicious. Ah, the innocent enjoyment of that moment, oblivious of the three hours of agony ahead.

As we turned off the main road at Ambleside the road snaked up out of the town. It looked steep – very steep indeed. I became suspicious when, as the occasional car passed us going the other way, the smell of gently roasting clutch plates wafted down the hill. It suddenly occurred to me that there didn't appear to be much traffic on this road considering we were in a very touristy area. Leaving Ambleside behind, the narrow, winding road, flanked on both sides by dry stone walls, was climbing ever higher. As we struggled to push our heavily loaded bikes up the hill, I said, 'Uh, Mick, how long is it as steep as this?'

'Oh, not far,' was his rather vague reply.

Two miles later we were still struggling upwards.

'Not far now, round this bend and then it's downhill,' he said confidently.

We rounded the bend and the road continued upwards. Mick, now realising he was in big, big trouble, had started to employ distraction techniques.

'Ooh look at that chaffinch, isn't it lovely?' and 'The view is fabulous, isn't it?'

Another mile on and still the hill was going up while the rain was coming down, in horizontal sheets. We sheltered glumly behind a wall for a while, accompanied by a handful of sheep that had evidently had the same idea. I caught what appeared to be a look of empathy in one particularly bedraggled ewe's eye. We were clearly all a bit fed up. By now Mick had become very quiet.

'I may have been thinking of somewhere else,' he muttered.

The road, we discovered later that day in the pub, is known as 'the Struggle'. With a gradient in places of one in four, it rises to 1,500 feet where it meets the slightly less violent route from Troutbeck. It is the Lake District's highest pass that is open to cars. No wonder Wordsworth called it 'this savage pass'. I was feeling pretty savage myself by this point. Much later I also read that President Woodrow Wilson, on a visit to England in 1908, had told his wife that his favourite walk in all of England was the 'three-mile steady almost unbroken ascent' from Ambleside to the top of Kirkstone Pass. He was obviously made of sterner stuff than us, although presumably he wasn't also pushing a loaded bike. At the junction of the two roads is the Kirkstone Pass Inn.

This is 'the inn with altitude', the highest in Cumbria, once known as the Traveller's Rest. An inn has been situated on this spot since the beginning of the sixteenth century, and it must have been as welcome a sight then as it was to us, as we gratefully staggered across the threshold and made for the log fire burning merrily at the end of the room.

It proved to be a bit of an End-to-Enders convention. Two other cyclists in the pub were also doing the journey, although on a different, faster route (no towpaths!) with faster bikes and, it must be admitted, faster legs. Probably fewer pub stops, too. They were on day eight. We discovered that they also came from Bristol and we had a quick comparison of routes, etc. They had, of course, taken the Other Road up the pass. The barman said he had also cycled the End-to-End, but had gone north to south. Like everyone else we spoke to who had taken that route he had battled a headwind all the way.

I was by now feeling slightly mollified by the camaraderie and the coffee, and as we set off on the long downhill run to Glenridding I only felt like subjecting Mick to a lengthy and imaginative form of torture rather than actually killing him. Well wrapped up in hat and gloves, the wind whistled past us as we hurtled down the hill towards Patterdale, leaning forward over the handlebars for minimum drag. A bit too fast, actually, and a bit too scary. I chickened out and partially applied the brakes, while Mick, head down with his coat flapping noisily and cape streaming out behind, careered around the bend and out of sight. I slowed down to admire the view of the lake on the valley floor below, nestled between the green brown fells. When I finally reached the bottom I fully expected to see him in a heap on the road under his bike. Annoyingly, he wasn't. Instead, he was stood nonchalantly on the verge, munching on a banana.

'What took you so long?' he grinned. 'I made forty-five miles an hour.'

Back at lower levels, the sun now kindly put in an appearance as we cycled along. We were now fewer than 500 feet above sea level and the temperature had improved markedly. The road here ran right beside Lake Ullswater, the second-largest in the Lake District. It didn't look very busy though; we could only see a couple of boats on the water and most of them were laid up on one of the small gravel beaches that edge the lake. Partway along the lake is the popular village of Glenridding, which huddles under the imposing bulk of Helvellyn. We stopped at the little gift shop and parked ourselves on the handy picnic tables outside to have our lunch, making huge doorstep sandwiches from provisions we had lugged up with us from Ambleside. I also nipped into the gift shop and treated myself to a little fridge magnet which said 'I've climbed Helvellyn', superimposed over a picture of the fell. I have climbed it, honest, just not on this trip. The previous summer Mick and I had stopped at the campsite here on our way back from a trip to Scotland, with the express purpose of climbing Helvellyn and of walking Striding Edge – a ridge that connects the moor summit with Helvellyn itself. The route starts off OK, along a grassy path, but gradually gets narrower and narrower, culminating in a rocky ridge with breathtaking drop-offs on both sides. It is a notorious spot for accidents and in poor conditions is a very dangerous place indeed. It didn't feel too safe even in good conditions and we finished crossing the ridge on hands and knees, much to the amusement of some younger, but evidently vastly more experienced walkers, who jauntily marched past us. They were, I would guess, aged about ten. It doesn't end there, though, as after the ridge there is an awkward climb up loose scree and rocks before finally reaching the summit – at which point it all suddenly becomes worthwhile. We whooped and ran about on the short, windswept grass, and then admired the spectacular views, before heading down via White Side and Gillside, an altogether more sedate route.

Today we contented ourselves with admiring the fell from the road. I hoped the additional weight of the fridge magnet would not turn out to be the proverbial straw that broke the camel's back.

At Aira Force we turned left, leaving Ullswater behind us. Force comes from the Old Norse word *fors*, meaning waterfall; a reminder that this part of the country was once part of the Danelaw, that area of northern and eastern England subject to Danish rather than Mercian or West Saxon law. The area was marked out following an agreement made between King Alfred the Great and Guthrum, leader of the Danes in around 886, to divide England along a line which ran roughly from London in the south-east to Chester in the north-west – although the boundary was fluid and often disputed. This division of the country explains why southerners think that northern place names sound so terribly, well, northern – foreign, even. As indeed to southerners they are. Places ending in '-thorpe', a hamlet or farmstead (Scunthorpe, Cleethorpes), '-thwaite', a clearing or settlement (Stonethwaite, Branthwaite, Thwaite!) and '-by', a village or town (Whitby, Appleby, Selby) are all Old Norse in origin. The word 'by-law', meaning the local law of the village or town, has the same root. There are plenty of other Old Norse words around here, including *'fell'* (hill), *'beck'* (stream), *'tarn'* (small lake), *'pike'* (peak) and *'gill'* or *'ghyll'* (valley).

Aira Force is probably the most famous waterfall in the Lake District. Mick told me that when he first visited the falls many years ago he was very taken with it.

'This is where I want my ashes to be thrown when I die,' he said. 'I've stipulated it in my will.'

'Yes, well don't expect me to traipse up here with them,' I said. 'I'll just lob you in the Avon instead. Although if that road from Ambleside had gone on much longer I would happily have chucked you down Aira Force *before* you snuffed it! Hey, come to think of it, is there anything in your will for me?'

'Yup,' he said cheerfully. 'I have bequeathed you my unwashed cycling shorts as a memento.'

'You're gross.'

We pressed on up the hill to Matterdale End. As we neared the main road the distinctive shape of Blencathra, also known as Saddleback, dominated the horizon. At Troutbeck (confusingly there are two Troutbecks in this part of Cumbria, must be good fishing hereabouts), we found a path that ran parallel with the A66, until we crossed it onto quiet lanes through to Mungrisdale. The last 10 miles of the day were glorious, flat, quiet roads, with yellow gorse vivid against the backdrop of blue sky. As we crossed Caldbeck Common, fell ponies quietly grazed by the side of the road and we were serenaded by the sound of sheep bleating. The Northern Fells of Carrock Fell and High Pike towered above us on our left, with steep scree slopes slipping down to the road.

The area is designated a Site of Special Scientific Interest; there is little sign now of the mining that took place here for hundreds of years, extracting copper, lead and the rich combination of minerals that can be found here. There was once a saying that 'Caldbeck and the Caldbeck Fells are worth all England else' because of the extensive range of minerals to be found in the area. The area is still popular with mineral collectors, although a permit is now required.

We soon reached our destination for the night – Hesket Newmarket. We had no idea what accommodation was available but we did know there was a fine pub in the village. We decided to call at the pub first and make enquiries. The Old Crown is a special place. It was the first community-owned pub in the country, and is shared by a co-operative of more than 100 local people. Beer is supplied by a microbrewery right behind the premises, which was originally set up simply to supply the pub. This is now the Hesket Newmarket Brewery Co-operative. Most shareholders opt to receive their dividend in liquid form, and I don't blame them.

The brewery owner, Jim Fearnley, first brewed Doris's 90th Birthday Ale in 1988 to celebrate his mother-in-law's birthday. Chris Bonington, who lives down the road at Caldbeck, downed the inaugural pint. The beer became a roaring success, thus immortalising Jim's mother-in-law. It's a lovely, chestnut-coloured beer with a fruity flavour. The brewery also produces Scafell Blonde, a light, golden-coloured beer that uses some lager malts – a good pint for weaning poor lost souls off lager. We found the place to be just as friendly as the other co-operative pub we had come across, back in Grosmont. These two places had much in common, they were welcoming and hospitable, and both shared a determination that the pub should be the centre of the village.

The Old Crown is full of interesting climbing memorabilia: old climbing crampons, pickaxes, ropes and boots, and photos signed by Bonington, Joe Simpson and others. There is also a signed picture of Prince Charles who visited the pub twice, in 2004 and 2007, as part of the Pub is the Hub Initiative, started by HRH in 2001. Pub is the Hub encourages rural pubs to work with local communities, the aim being to help keep the pub open and to provide rural areas with services which would otherwise be lost; they supported the Old Crown in its transition to a co-operative in 2002. I am no royalist, but I could forgive Prince Charles an awful lot if he continues to support pubs like this one.

After enjoying a pint of Doris's, we enquired about local camping facilities. The barman directed us to the farm at the back of the village; there was no answer when we knocked at the farmhouse door but the handwritten sign welcomed campers, so we went into the empty field behind the farmhouse and set up the tent. I nipped over to use the toilet. When I opened the door I stopped in amazement. The room was about 10 feet by 6 feet. Newspaper cuttings, postcards, maps and other snippets of local interest adorned the walls and a pile of magazines and leaflets were stacked up on the table. A bookcase on the left was piled high with games and toys and a couple of sun loungers were set against the opposite wall, together with a table on which rested a visitors' book. In the far corner were a basin and a toilet. I was very taken with it.

We returned to the pub where we tucked into an excellent curry, before repairing to the bar, where we got chatting to some of the other customers. A fellow cyclist, interested in our journey, asked us which route we had taken through the Lake District. We told him we had taken the rather steep one from Ambleside, at which point he seemed suddenly to view us with a different, almost deferential air.

'You took the Struggle?' he asked incredulously. 'With loaded panniers?'

'If that's the road from Ambleside, then yes we did,' we nodded, failing to mention that the only reason we had gone that way was due to a total cock-up on the navigation front.

'Awesome!' he exclaimed, 'Total respect. I won't even take my car that way!'

He called over some of his mates and for the next hour we were feted as cycling heroes and bought more pints of beer. It almost made the agony of the ride worth it. Almost.

>>>>>>>>>>>>>>>>>>>>>>>>>>

Stats
Miles: 35
Total miles: 592
Pints of beer (each): 4
Hills pushed: 1 (the Road from Hell)
Murderous thoughts: 456

>>>>>>>>>>>>>>>>>>>>>>>>>>

HESKET NEWMARKET

>>>>>>>>>>>>>>>>>>>>> **TO** >>>>>>>>>>>>>>>>>>>>

DUMFRIES

The day started well. The sun was shining, the birds were singing. I had felt unwell in the night, with something, which seemed to be a panic attack, or possibly indigestion. I dimly remembered complaining that I couldn't go on. This morning I felt better though, and Mick, although still suffering the effects of a cold, said he, too, was good to go. He did get bored waiting for me to pack and decided to take up t'ai chi to pass the time, striking some idiotic poses on one leg before finally falling over, narrowly missing a cowpat.

Giving up with the t'ai chi, Mick then announced he wished to perform some bike maintenance. As he had opted under our division of labour scheme to undertake all mechanical tasks, I let him get on with it, and finished packing while he fiddled about with the bikes. When he was done we wandered back over to the farmhouse but there was still no answer when I knocked at the door. Presumably they were out doing whatever farming people do in fields in early May, so we pushed the money through the letter box as requested on the sign, hoping there wasn't a dog on the other side of the door waiting to chew up the £5 note.

We headed out of Hesket past the now quiet pub, assuring ourselves that one day we would return. We soon picked up the B5299 to Dalston, where we stopped at the bakery for a couple of currant buns and a quick chat with a woman who had cycled 'End-to-End' some years previously, heading the other way, from John o'Groats to Land's End. She shook her head at the memory.

'It was hard work,' she said. 'The wind was against us all the way.'

Feeling vindicated in our choice of direction, with yet more confirmation that heading north was indeed preferable to heading south, we said farewell.

At Carlisle we had a lovely scrambled egg on toast at a small cafe and we also picked up a miniature bottle of whisky to toast our triumphant crossing of the border. We were in good spirits. I liked what I saw of Carlisle; it has a handsome castle and a very pleasant pedestrianised town centre. It happened to be the first Friday of the month and a farmers' market was being held in the central shopping area, so we took the opportunity to stock up on some provisions.

Following the advice of a friendly local chap, we easily found the back road out of the city. Then it all started to go wrong. A few raindrops came down; I stopped to put my raincoat on and dropped it on the bike chain. Whether it was because he had overcompensated for not using any oil at all for the first week (which I had complained about) I don't know, but Mick had over-generously coated the chain with something called PTFE; horrible, sticky black gunk. For the next week I cursed that oil. It clumped together and spread itself over the rest of the bike. It transferred itself, goodness knows how, onto everything else, the tent, the pannier bags, our clothes, even our bodies. I spent a week with sprocket marks imprinted on my right leg. Its first victim was my coat, which now had black gunk all over the sleeve. Annoyed, I reached into my bar bag to find a tissue and brought out a hand covered in blue ink. My pen had leaked over everything. I cursed loudly.

The road we now found ourselves on was the new one alongside the M6/M74. It is a straight, open road and although it is marked as a B-road the few cars that were travelling on it appeared to think they *were* on the M6, driving at enormous speed and kicking out arcs of spray from their wheels. Then, to cap it all, the rain began really hammering it down. For a while we sheltered under a straggly tree, before deciding that we could well be stood there all day, and there was nothing for it but to keep going. A few miles on we reached the border with Scotland. This was not quite the triumphant crossing we had envisaged. We were drenched, cold and tetchy. (It was just as well we didn't know that drenched and cold was to be a fairly common theme north of the border, or we would have felt even grumpier than we already were.) Nevertheless, we stopped for photos and a tot of whisky, and I tried to look cheerful for the camera, although I was still in a very bad mood about my ruined raincoat. But despite the rain and my grumpiness, it still felt like an achievement to have reached the Scottish border entirely under our own steam. From here we intended to strike out west, heading for Dumfries and then up to Ayrshire, before heading up the west coast of Scotland.

We did not fancy hanging round the wedding capital of the UK with a lot of lovesick tourists, so we skipped Gretna Green and its wedding industry and instead turned left into the town of Gretna itself, whose history seemed more suited to our mood. Gretna had been built from scratch in World War One, as a planned town to house workers at the newly built munitions factory on the shores of the Solway Firth. At the time it was the world's largest munitions factory: it stretched for 9 miles, from Eastriggs to Gretna and beyond and employed 30,000 workers, producing over 800 tons of ammunition per week. Many of the workers were women, attracted by the relatively high wages compared with other work in the area. They were employed in making cordite, mixing nitroglycerine with gun cotton into a paste known as 'Devil's porridge'. The work was dangerous with a high risk of explosion and poisonous fumes. In 1916 Rebecca West wrote an article entitled *The Cordite Makers,* after visiting the factory, in which she describes how the women, dressed in khaki with red hoods, worked twelve-hour shifts in difficult conditions. She relates once incident where the cordite ignited, destroying some of the huts and causing one girl to lose a hand, 'the everyday dangers of the high-explosives factory'. Nothing now survives of the factory, which was dismantled after the war.

Gretna's other rather grim claim to fame is that it is the site of Britain's worst rail disaster. The accident happened on the West Coast Main Line during a change of shift between two signalmen, George Meakin and James Tinsley. The men had an agreement, whereby, if the train was stopping at Quintinshill, Tinsley would ride the train to work rather than walk. This meant he was starting work half an hour late, at 6.30 a.m., rather than 6 a.m., with Meakin covering for him. On the morning of 22 May 1915, Tinsley had ridden the train to work and got off at nearby Quintinshill as usual. Meakin had directed the trains at the junction until that point. While Tinsley was copying his shift details into the log to cover up the fact he had arrived late, both men forgot about the district train, which Meakin had shunted onto the main line. A troop train carrying a Royal Scots Battalion crashed into the back of the train, blocking both lines. Shortly afterwards the express train from Carlisle collided into the wreckage. Two-hundred and twenty-seven people were killed, the majority being soldiers on the troop train, and 246 were injured. Both signalmen were found guilty of involuntary manslaughter, although the disaster was kept a secret until after the end of the World War One for fear of damaging morale.

We were in dire need of a cup of tea but there were no cafes in Gretna that we could find so we cycled on to Eastriggs, where we found a shop that sold a little of everything, including, thank goodness, a cup of tea. We stood inside the shop trying vainly to warm up for a bit before giving up and heading on west, through Annan, with the wind in our faces as we battled along. Avoiding the A75, we took the minor roads to Ruthwell. Just beyond the town we noticed a Scottish flag flying on our left-hand side next to a small rectangular hole in the ground. Intrigued, we stopped to take a closer look. The hole turned out to be Brow Well, a tiny and, up here on the edge of the Solway Firth, somewhat bracing, open-air spa bath. It was here, in July 1796, that Robert Burns came, after his physician and friend Dr Maxwell diagnosed him as suffering from 'flying gout'. It is tempting to mock this now, with our twenty-first-century medical knowledge but flying gout was a common medical term at the time, used to describe conditions of non-specific pain occurring anywhere on the body. In Burns' case, his pains were in his chest and it is now thought more likely that he was suffering from chronic rheumatic heart disease caused from contracting rheumatic fever as a child. The accepted treatment for flying gout was mineral water and sea bathing. So Burns daily immersed himself up to his neck in the chilly waters of the nearby estuary. Unsurprisingly, two weeks of this did nothing to improve his condition, and he returned to his home in Dumfries and never left it again, dying in his bed three days later. He was 37 years old.

Continuing into Dumfries, the sun eventually came out and we watched a couple of lapwings skimming on the breeze. I began to feel more cheerful. Dumfries is a very attractive town, with sturdy red buildings, built along the eastern bank of the River Nith. We headed down towards the river and found ourselves at a pedestrian-only suspension bridge. Up to our right we could see the famous and ancient Devorgilla Bridge, now also pedestrianised, and one of Scotland's oldest. The suspension bridge was built in 1875 and was given a major overhaul in the 1980s. Opposite the bridge an enterprising B & B had put up a sign clearly visible from the opposite bank. We pushed our bikes over the bridge and made a beeline for it. The landlady looked at all our gear and at us, sodden wet. 'Tell you what,' she said, 'I'll give you the downstairs family room and you'll be able to sort out your stuff there'.

The room was huge, with plenty of hot radiators, and we were grateful for the hospitality – especially when the lovely woman also brought us in a bottle of beer on the house. We obviously looked like we needed it. After laying out our stuff to dry we headed into town. Within a few minutes we chanced upon the Globe, tucked down a small, cobbled alleyway off the pedestrianised shopping area. Dating back to 1610, it is claimed to be one of the oldest surviving taverns in Scotland. It is also reputed to have been the favourite drinking *howff* of Burns when he lived in Dumfries. The Globe is also the home of the Burns Howff Club, formed in the pub in 1889 by a group of Burns fans to celebrate the Scottish bard's life and works.

Burns, of course, penned the poem 'Auld Lang Syne', the popularised version of which is now sung drunkenly by revellers across the planet on New Year's Eve. He also wrote 'Ode to a Haggis', which my Scottish friend Frank quotes with great gusto while knifing a haggis every Burns night. I must say I find the alacrity with which he thrusts the knife into the haggis quite unnerving. Haggis, if you have not tried it, is excellent. Needless to say it is not suitable for vegetarians or vegans; it is a dish of sheep's innards – heart, liver and lungs – minced with onion, oatmeal, suet, spices and salt, mixed with stock, and boiled in the animal's stomach for approximately three hours. Yum. It is quite delicious! Lately there has been some nonsense about haggis originating in England, which I think is, quite frankly, a ridiculous notion.

When I was about eight, I was a huge fan of the *Beano*, which ran a comic strip featuring the McTickles and the McHaggises. For some years I was of the firm belief that a haggis was a Scottish animal with legs of unequal length, which meant it could keeps its balance when running around Scottish mountain tops. Worryingly, a recent survey by a fast-food company found that a fifth of Brits still think a haggis is a hilltop-dwelling animal. The *Beano* obviously has a lot to answer for.

The pub was very quiet when we entered and we settled down at one of the tables ready to enjoy our beer. We had been there for about five minutes when the door opened and about two hundred tourists of every imaginable nationality poured in. The few locals present were obviously used to this, and they shuffled to one end of the bar, which had quickly become ten-deep with people waiting to be served. The visitors piled into all the available seats and, just as quickly, there was a massive queue for the toilets. The place was buzzing with the hubbub of people chatting and a couple of tour guides were shouting to make themselves heard above the din. Half an hour later, they were all herded out again, leaving us feeling slightly bemused. The locals shuffled back down the bar and resumed their conversation.

The pub served a fine pint of Criffel Ale from Sulwath Brewers, our first Scottish beer. It was another IPA and a top beer to boot. We tarried for a couple more before heading off to the Jewel in the Crown, an Indian restaurant recommended by the barman that served an excellent curry. Sated, we then wandered back to our B & B for the night.

Stats
Miles: 51
Total miles: 643
Pints of beer (each): 2 beers, plus 1 pint of Kingfisher lager
(which I couldn't finish as I was stuffed fit to burst)
Hilltop haggis spotted: 0

DUMFRIES

 TO

TROON

The day started well with another fine cooked breakfast. On the table there was a bowl full of cereal bars and, while the good lady was out fetching our tea, I took the opportunity to stuff a couple of them in my pocket. When we were packing to leave she said, 'Och, just a wee minute,' and disappeared, coming back moments later with a bag of about ten cereal bars. I could hardly tell her I had already helped myself, so I took them, thanking her, and feeling very small indeed.

'I hope you are ashamed of yourself,' said Mick when we got outside. I was.

We then spent an hour wandering around Dumfries looking for a replacement for the jacket I had covered in oil yesterday – and had since regretfully thrown in the bin, rather than risk it contaminating the rest of my kit with its black goo. I had bought it for next to nothing in a jumble sale, but to have to dispose of it was still annoying. We also stopped to admire the Bard's statue. What with the sightseeing and the shopping it was 11 a.m. by the time we left Dumfries, having checked the route with a local postie. Our plan was to take minor roads through the remote region of Dumfries and Galloway to the coast at Ayrshire. Our first goal was the village of Moniaive, about 20 miles north-west of Dumfries. It was a lovely run – not too hilly – and the weather was finally being kind to us once more. The only thing that slowed us down were the sheep, wandering about in the road, clearly bemused to find themselves sharing it with other life forms.

As we coasted into Moniaive, there was a cycle race going through the village and we looked enviously at the paper-light road bikes whizzing past us as we struggled along with our loaded panniers. We had stumbled into the Drumlanrig Challenge, an annual, hilly 84-mile cycle ride that attracts cyclists from across the UK. These were proper, competent cyclists who didn't grizzle every time they had to climb a hill. People lined the route through the village to cheer them on, and a couple of individuals were wandering among them with buckets collecting donations. We hastily dismounted and got out of the way. The ride was in aid of the development charity Tearfund. On completion of the ride competitors receive a virtual goody bag, containing a virtual T-shirt, a virtual water bottle, virtual energy bar and virtual plasters (in case of a virtual accident). The virtual goody bag comes printed on the back of a real certificate. The real items are sent to countries whose need is greater than ours.

Moniaive is a pretty village with winding streets, flanked by low, whitewashed houses converging on the marketplace. It sits at the point where three glens meet at the end of the remote Cairn Valley and is something of an attraction for artistic types; musicians, artists, writers and designers have made their home there, tempted by the bohemian atmosphere as well as the beauty of the village and its surroundings. Artist James Paterson moved here with his wife in 1884. He was one of the Glasgow Boys, an innovative group of painters who created quite a stir at the end of the nineteenth century and it was at Moniaive that Paterson painted his most famous painting, *The Last Turning*. Paterson's house was later bought by Alex Kapranos, lead singer and guitarist in Franz Ferdinand. Alan Grant of *Judge Dredd* and *Batman* fame also lives here and Joanna Lumley has a place just up the road. The village has a strong community feel, and obviously enjoys any excuse for a party; there is an annual folk festival, beer festival, bluegrass festival, guitar festival and gala day, as well as countless other smaller events though the year. No wonder it has become known as Scotland's Festival Village. We stopped for spaghetti on toast at the fantastic Green Tea House cafe, a wonderful organic cafe near the marketplace, and then stocked up on provisions at the excellent Watson's Grocers. I could see why Moniaive was a desirable place to live.

With our stomachs and pannier bags refilled we were set for the cycle ride over the remote top road to Carsphairn. The road took us through acres and acres of pine forest. Long gradual upward pulls were rewarded with equally long coasts down, and we passed the next two hours very pleasantly. We didn't see a car for miles at a time. We were cycling on the edge of the Galloway Forest Park, which has recently been designated as Europe's first Dark Sky Park. No wonder it felt remote. Well, remote by British standards anyway. Nowhere in Britain is really remote, in the same way as, say, the Australian outback or the Gobi Desert. In Britain you're never more than an hour away from civilisation and, if you're lucky, a nice cup of tea.

It's remote enough for the International Dark-Sky Association though, which has designated the Forest Park as one of the few places in the world dark enough to qualify as an exceptional place for stargazing. (Presumably for stargazing purposes accessibility is also a criteria, there are plenty of darker places on the planet but it would take a special sort of person who would travel across a desert for three days to look at Betelgeuse and Bellatrix frolicking in the night sky.) So far the only other places in the world approved by the International Dark-Sky Association are Natural Bridges National Park, Utah, and Cherry Springs State Park, Pennsylvania.

On a clear night in London it is possible to pick out around 200 stars; in Galloway Forest Park you can see around 7,000. The area has been an unofficial stargazing spot for quite a while. According to *The Times*, a couple of years ago the local police became suspicious when they noticed from car vehicle sensors there were high numbers of people visiting the forest park in the middle of the night. Suspecting nefarious activity, one night they raided a car park by Clatteringshaws Loch in the Park. When they got there they found, not drug dealers or local criminals, but a load of blokes in anoraks and cagoules with their telescopes trained on the Crab Nebula. Afterwards I regretted not setting up camp for the night to do a spot of stargazing ourselves, but we felt we should get some more miles under our belt before stopping for the night – unaware of the tribulations to come.

At Carsphairn we took a break and had a look around the village churchyard. There was a memorial there to the McAdam family and a tablet commemorating John Louden McAdam, the famous road improver who gave his name to Macadam, later developed into tar-bound macadam, or tarmac for short, although McAdam's actual tomb is in Moffat Cemetery. I wondered what he would think of the state of some of the roads we had cycled on over the past few weeks. Turning somersaults in his grave, no doubt. As we travelled up the country we realised many roads were in a dreadful state, and a constant vigilance was vital to avoid falling into holes in the road. What was also noticeable was that it was often the patched up sections that failed most frequently – I considered suggesting to the Department for Transport that they desist from allowing roads to be patched up with a substance that had the appearance and consistency of black blancmange.

From here we were on the A713 and the traffic was faster, though not too heavy, until we turned off near Polnessan. We crossed the border into Ayrshire and the landscape changed from pine forested hills to flat open fields. By now we had cycled about 60 miles and were feeling weary. We decided Stair might be a good place to aim for, for no other reason than a woman in the garage where we stopped for a coffee said she had heard that they did good food at Stair Inn. When we got there we hated it. The feeling was evidently mutual. It was a 'foodie' pub and the bar staff were disdainful and unfriendly, evidently unimpressed with our dinner attire of muddy trousers and oily panniers. We had a swift pint sat outside, huddled on a bench next to the road, and then hightailed it on to Tarbolton, where the guidebook marked a campsite. We detoured for a couple of miles, only to find the campsite was no more and the two pubs in the village were both pretty dire. We decided to cycle on and to stop at a campsite or bed and breakfast, whichever came first.

For more than an hour there was nothing. Finally, on the outskirts of Troon we came across a B & B and knocked on the door. By now we were both looking distinctly grubby and dishevelled. At first I thought there was no one in, as there was no response to our knock. Feeling somewhat desperate by now, I knocked again, more forcefully this time. There was a very long wait. Eventually a woman came to the door, looked at us and said that she was full, which was odd because there were no cars in the car park. We thanked her anyway and headed into the centre of Troon.

Mick suggested a camping spot that he said was brilliant – beautifully flat and with a useful pole for hanging our things on.

'Yeah, looks splendid Mick,' I said, 'but I am not sure whether it is really such a good idea to set up camp on the eighteenth green of the Royal Troon golf course. You know the Scots are crazy for the game; anyone would think they invented it! We'd probably get lashed to a flagstick with a nine-iron stuffed somewhere really painful.'

Mick reluctantly agreed it may not be such a good idea after all, and then pointed out the Scots in fact had invented golf, when a bunch of shepherds, bored out of their brains, decided to use sticks to knock stones into rabbit holes. I thought this unlikely but he swore it was true.

We then spent a long and increasingly frustrating hour looking for somewhere to stay. No doubt there were hundreds of wonderful bed and breakfast establishments hiding around the corner, but we couldn't find them. If pushed, we could have set up camp on the beach but we really, really didn't want to. The wind was whistling in from the sea straight onto the dunes and sand was swirling everywhere. Too tired to cycle, we were now pushing our bikes aimlessly around the town. We passed a swanky hotel. Inside we could see people sat around in huge chintz armchairs and hear the muffled hum of a large number of people enjoying themselves. A bloke in a dinner jacket was stood outside having a smoke and as he opened the door to return to the lovely, warm, inviting lounge, a delicious aroma of roasted lamb wafted out of the door.

'Hold my bike a minute,' said Mick.

'We can't go in there!' I protested, 'that will be a whole week's budget blown in one night!'

Of the two of us, Mick is normally more parsimonious regarding expenditure, whereas I am rather careless with my spending. He was clearly a desperate man.

As I stood outside shivering, I could see him through the large front window, in discussion with an immaculately turned-out receptionist at the front desk. Not a hair was out of place and her Jaeger suit looked fabulous. Mick began gesturing towards the bikes and me, and I realised I must look a mess, splattered as I was with the detritus of the road. In a futile gesture I instinctively tried to smooth down my hair and straighten my clothes. The woman looked at me and then got up from the desk, disappearing into a back room. I sighed, assuming that was the end of the matter but Mick didn't budge. A minute or two later she reappeared, smiling and nodding, and I saw her hand Mick a key.

'Oh my God,' I muttered. 'How much is this going to cost us? Or maybe that's the key to the shed and we are going to kip down in there for the night.' The way I felt now, I would have done so, too.

Mick, it turned out, had indulged in a bit of haggling worthy of a Turkish shopkeeper. The room should have been £200 per person per night, we got it for £85 each. He had pulled out all the stops, using the 'we are doing this for charity' card, as well as the 'my companion is about to collapse with exhaustion' card. Still, the hotel filled an empty room for the night and we got a bargain, although it was still, by far, the most expensive accommodation of the entire trip. The room was huge, decked out in mahogany and with red velvet hanging drapes at the windows. Like a couple of kids we opened all the drawers and cupboards, before having a fight to see who would be first to muddy-up the bathroom. I won that time, although I could tell Mick's efforts were half-hearted. He had, I noted, already located the minibar.

The hotel was full with a large group of very drunk golfers; half of them had come from Dublin and the other half from Inverness. They were enjoying their annual piss-up with some occasional golf thrown in. It was a hell of a party, which was impressive as apparently the previous night they had also been partying hard until 6 a.m., after which they trundled off for a very hungover round of golf, before coming back to the hotel and starting again. Too tired to eat, and in any event the restaurant was closed, we sat in the bar, downing a couple of pints of Northern Light beer from the Orkney Brewery. One of the Dublin contingency, who by now was very drunk, came over and plonked himself down next to us. It was hard to understand exactly what he was saying, but he seemed amiable enough and, after ten minutes or so, he reached into his pocket and slapped £20 on the table for our cause, before staggering off to bed. When I saw him at breakfast the next morning he looked decidedly worse for wear. He gave no indication whatsoever of recognising us and I wondered whether he recalled this magnanimous gesture or whether he had looked in his wallet and thought, 'Feck, oi were robbed last noight!'

On the subject of golf, I am with Mark Twain on this one, when he said that golf 'is a good walk spoiled'. I have tried it and I don't like it. It seems to me to be a silly game. The ball starts miles away from the hole, and the hole is miniscule. There is a rule that says that the ball must be played from where it lies, even if this is under a bush, buried deep in a pile of sand or in a puddle. You have to shout 'FOUR!' as you hit the ball, I don't know why. The game is full of silly words like 'birdie', 'eagle', 'albatross' and 'bogey'. What the fuck are they on about? And silliest of all are the clothes. You have to have absolutely no sense of style and wander around clad in a pink Pringle sweater, yellow checked trousers and white shoes. This is the same for men and women, the only difference being that men will also often adorn their heads with a ridiculous white cap. And these days, even the spoiled walk doesn't happen as people drive everywhere in little carts. The only golf that I think is worth playing is crazy golf, where you have to get the ball up and down little paths, under miniature bridges and through cute little windmills and so forth. This is much more fun. Mick, on the other hand, fancies himself as a bit of a golfer. He says I am an idiot and have no idea what I am talking about. I think he just likes wearing pink.

>>>>>>>>>>>>>>>>>>>>>>>>>>>>

Stats
Miles: 77
Total miles: 720
Pints of beer (each): 3 (bought 4 but fell asleep)
Cereal bars pilfered: 4
Moments of shame: 1

>>>>>>>>>>>>>>>>>>>>>>>>>>>>

DAY
16

TROON

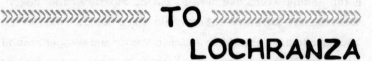

TO

LOCHRANZA

A tourist goes into a butcher's shop in Troon. The butcher is stood with his back to an electric fire. The tourist says: 'Is that your Ayrshire bacon?' And the butcher says: 'No, just warming my hands.'

After a late and copious breakfast, as one would expect in a hotel of this calibre, we set off from Troon, leaving not quite enough time to cycle around the coast to Ardrossan in time for the ferry to Arran. (Most End-to-Enders don't find themselves on the ferry to Arran. It is not exactly the most direct route; a dash though Glasgow or an east-coast route through Edinburgh is quicker. But we (I!), had decided it would be such a shame to miss out the beautiful west coast of Scotland and so we planned to travel up though Arran before catching another ferry back to the mainland and on to Oban and Fort William. We had estimated 10 miles, but in fact it was nearly twenty and the wind was gusting in our faces.

Unusually, Mick was lagging behind. In an effort to encourage him I gave him a chivvy up.

'Come on you low-gear, low-mileage, low-effort, lowlife,' I shouted.

It had the desired effect, as he cycled hard to catch me up (probably to beat me up) but I stayed ahead all the way to Ardrossan. As we turned the corner to head down to the harbour, a tornado-like vortex of wind whirled its way up the street, scooping up discarded newspapers and sweet wrappers, and twirling them in the air like a mad flamenco dancer. I am not at all surprised that Ardrossan has a large wind farm at the back of the town; it probably generates enough power to light up all of Ayrshire.

The harbour area has been transformed since the last time I was here ten years ago. Then the area was semi-derelict, with pubs and shops boarded up, and it had the feel of a place that had abandoned all hope. Now there was a brand new marina and ferry terminal, and many of the dockside buildings had evidently been restored and were being put to new uses; the elegant power station was now a fancy Italian restaurant. We couldn't stop, though; the ferry was in port and we swiftly boarded and took shelter from the wind below deck. Soon we were heading away from the town and across to Brodick. The one-hour ferry trip was very enjoyable, mainly as Arran traders were inviting passengers to sample local produce. Naturally, we availed ourselves of these offerings, merrily tucking into Arran mustard Cheddar sliced onto Arran oatcakes, washed down with Arran malt whisky. We then wandered into the shop and bought an Arran map, a bar of Arran soap and some Arran chocolate. Mick disappeared, so I read the Arran paper for a while and then did the Arran crossword. If we had been on board for much longer, I'd have bought the sodding island.

Crossing the Firth of Clyde, the weather had changed dramatically for the better and the sun shone on our backs as we waited to disembark. We were at the front of the queue, keen to get on land and explore. Unfortunately Mick had forgotten how much weight he was carrying on his bike and, as soon as he started moving, toppled over on the ramp, scattering his belongings. I had been too close behind him and I braked sharply but, alas, it was too late. I collided into the back of him and we both lay on the gangway of the boat in an undignified heap. The other cyclists and foot passengers picked their way past us. When they had gone we collected our gear and crept, shamefaced, off the boat.

'Did anyone see us?' Mick asked anxiously.

'Nooo,' I replied, 'only about three hundred passengers and all of the crew.'

After recovering our composure, we set off in search of the Isle of Arran Brewery and some Arran beer. Using our Arran map we soon found the brewery and visitors' centre shop. We were offered a taste of Red Squirrel, its new brew. Unsurprisingly, it was a dark, reddish-brown brew, with a nuttyish flavour. The launch was delayed, the assistant told us, because it had proved difficult to obtain a photograph of the elusive Arran red squirrel, and the brewery were keen it should be an Arran native that adorned the label. In the very next breath she assured us that if we bought a bottle of beer and sat outside we would be sure to see a red squirrel in the nesting box opposite – practically guaranteed in fact. We stared at the box for ages but no squirrel appeared. We had, we suspected, fallen victim to Arran's superlative sales techniques, but the beer was good and it was a fine place to stop and soak up some rays, so we didn't mind. I even bought an Arran hat. It had 'Arran' emblazoned on it. This island could teach the world a thing or two about marketing.

Red squirrels are in vogue, if not in sight; say 'grey squirrel' in a whisper in Scotland, as these North American interlopers are about as popular here as a fox in a henhouse. Initially kept in zoos, it became fashionable in the late-nineteenth century to release grey squirrels into the wild, presumably because the Victorians thought it would be an interesting thing to do. Larger, and with a wider diet than the reds, the greys are largely blamed for the dramatic fall in numbers of the red that has been driven from its natural habitat. They have also been discovered to carry parapoxvirus or squirrel-pox. The grey squirrels are apparently immune to the disease but it is a killer for the reds.

However, in the case of the disappearing squirrels, we humans are like Billy in the playground, saying to the teacher: 'Please miss, it wasn't me, miss, it was that nasty boy over there, miss, I never did nuffin!' Because we, too, have had a hand in the decline in the red squirrel population. We just don't talk about it much and prefer to point the finger of blame at the little acorn-munching alien. 'It's your fault grey nutkin,' we cry, 'you bushy tailed thug. And we are going to *get* you.'

Long before the grey squirrel had colonised the countryside, we humans were going hell-for-leather for the red squirrel. By the early-twentieth century we had brought out the big guns – literally. Squirrel clubs encouraged members to shoot red squirrels, as they had spread so successfully they were deemed pests and a threat to woodlands. The Highland Squirrel Club alone, between 1903 when it was formed and its demise in 1946, killed more than 100,000 red squirrels. Greys were also in their sights by then, and by the end of 1947 squirrel clubs had also killed more than 100,000 grey squirrels. Now red squirrels are keenly protected, but there is a price on grey nutkin's head. Scotland, home to 75 per cent of the remaining red squirrel population has a massive culling policy for these critters. Any grey squirrels in the area would be wise to keep a very low profile indeed.

We headed north up on the road to the east of the island. The road hugged the coastline and the sun cast dapples of light on the azure sea, warming our faces as we coasted along. Goat Fell towered majestically above us on our left, one of four Corbetts on Arran. We could see the tiny forms of walkers making their way to the summit, possible Corbett baggers keen to strike another off the list. In addition to the Corbetts there are six Marilyns and a Graham on Arran. There are no Munros, however, and Donalds don't venture this far north.

These are the main categories of Scottish mountains, of course. It all started with Hugh Thomas Munro. Born in 1856, he was the eldest son of Sir Campbell Munro, third Baronet of Lindertis. As a boy Hugh liked collecting things: shells, eggs, fossils and the like (egg collecting not being frowned upon then) and, like many boys, he also liked lists. Later on he began collecting mountains. He was co-founder and a keen member of the Scottish Mountaineering Club, and in its journal in 1891 he published a list of all the mountains and summits in Scotland more than 3,000 feet. This was the first time the Scottish mountains had been comprehensively catalogued. Despite the advent of the metric system, which converts 3,000 feet to the more prosaic 914.4 metres, the Munro Tables remain much as Sir Hugh originally listed them, albeit with some revisions over the years. When you consider that during his lifetime Munro climbed all but three of the original 283 mountains, despite being afflicted with arthritis from his thirties onwards, his achievement was remarkable. He died in 1919 after contracting pneumonia whilst volunteering for the French Red Cross in Tarascon, southern France.

Since then many people have completed the Munros in what has now grown into a sport of its own: Munro bagging. Bagging is the activity of collecting the summits of mountains, hills or peaks (not literally obviously, or there would be none left for the rest of us). After Munro, making lists of mountains really took off. Another member of the Scottish Mountaineering Club, John Rooke Corbett provided climbers with a list of Corbetts, summits between 2,500 and 3,000 feet. Peaks between 2,000 and 2,500 feet are named Grahams after Fiona Torbert (née Graham). Donalds are hills in the Scottish Lowlands of more than 2,000 feet; catalogued by Percy Donald, yet another member of the Scottish Mountaineering Club. Marilyns are hills anywhere in Britain with a relative height or prominence of at least 490 feet. Alan Dawson, a prolific hill-lister, coined the name as a humorous reference to the famous Munros. Dawson argued that little hills are often more interesting to climb than then the higher ones, and relative height rather than absolute height was a more useful criterion.

So enthusiasts can now enjoy Corbett bagging, Donald bagging, Graham bagging and Marilyn bagging, as well as Munro bagging, and outside Scotland, Wainwright bagging, Hewitt bagging and Nuttall bagging. That's an awful lot of bagging for one small and not very mountainous country like Britain, if you ask me. Maybe it's just that we British love making lists.

As we cycled farther north we passed a huge erratic boulder, shortly after which the road swung inland and began to rise up.

Within a few short minutes we felt as if we were in a completely different place – in a way I suppose we were. Arran is known as Scotland in miniature because, like Scotland itself, it has both 'lowlands' and 'highlands', and we were now entering the highlands of Arran. The island is bisected by the Highland Boundary Fault, an ancient collision of land masses, which bisects the mainland of Scotland and cuts right across the centre of Arran. Jagged mountains of granite surrounded us, with mists swirling around the peaks.

As we continued up the hill, the temperature dropped markedly and we stopped to dig around in our panniers for our coats, hats and gloves. The contrast with Brodick was breathtaking; it was as if we had, in an instant, been whisked from the shore of Loch Lomond to the Cuillins of Skye. We toiled up the hill and it was with some relief that we finally reached the top and began the downward coast into Lochranza at the northern tip of the island. This end of the island is much quieter than the southern half of Arran, and there's not an awful lot at Lochranza; a small settlement of 200 souls, perched at the end of Loch Ranza that gives the place its name. It does have a campsite, however, situated next to the golf course, and we booked in and pitched our little tent.

We were amused to see sheep grazing on the greens – not a sight you would see at Troon! Apparently red deer can sometimes be seen grazing as well. A game of golf must be interesting – they must have to use sweepers to brush the shit out of the way before taking a putt; it must be like playing curling on grass. Once we had set up camp we strolled down to the Lochranza Hotel. En route we admired the view of the ruined Lochranza Castle, perched on a spit of land right on the edge of the loch itself. The castle is a small tower house, originally built in the twelfth century and used as a royal hunting lodge. It was substantially extended and rebuilt in the sixteenth century, and bought in 1705 by Anne, Duchess of Hamilton and Countess of Arran who had already inherited most of Arran, including Brodick Castle, following the death of her father. The family stopped using the castle later in the eighteenth century and it was left to fall into disrepair. Lately, Historic Scotland has been doing some restoration work, although the castle remains in private hands, which presumably means the taxpayer pays for it on behalf of the owner. Lochranza Hotel was a typically Scottish affair, a large building with an interior dating from the 1970s, as well as 1,000 bottles of malt whisky but no draught beer. The barman said they usually sold Deuchars, but it was off that evening. We settled for a couple of rather expensive bottles of Sunset from Isle of Arran Brewery to wash down our fish and chips, before heading back to the campsite and retiring to our little tent. I drifted off to sleep listening to the rain hammering down on the canvas.

Stats

Miles: 32
Total miles: 752
Pints of beer (each): 2 bottles
Red squirrels sighted: 0
Arran products spotted: 14,983

DAY
17

LOCHRANZA

>>>>>>>>>>>>>>>>>>>>>> **TO** >>>>>>>>>>>>>>>>>>>>>>>

OBAN

We didn't want to do it – we really, really didn't want to – but we just couldn't help it. Resistance was futile. As we landed at Claonaig on the Mull of Kintyre, it settled inside our heads, refusing to do the decent thing and leave us alone. Mick capitulated almost straight away – he would be hopeless under torture, he would sing like a canary. We were hardly off the ferry when he started:

> *Mull of Kintyre,*
> *Oh mist rolling in from the sea,*
> *My desire*
> *Is always to be here*
> *Oh Mull of Kintyre.*

Aaaargh! When the song was released in 1977 it was played on the radio incessantly. It shot to number one in the charts, where it stayed for nine long weeks, selling two million copies and becoming the bestselling single ever in Britain by far up until that time. (This, of course, was in the days when music was bought and sold on tangible bits of round plastic or lengths of tape rather than streamed through the ether.) I was fourteen and emerging from my early teens, which involved such a spectacular lack of musical discernment that I wince even now. The list of shame includes Donny Osmond (and for a mad few months I was even rather keen on little Jimmy and sister Marie), Flintlock (remember them anyone?), David Essex, ABBA, Cliff Richard and many more too painful to mention. I even went to see Cliff Richard in concert at the Bristol Colston Hall. When 'Mull of Kintyre' came out in November of that year I was just discovering a whole new world: punk rock. Overnight my taste in music was transformed. Out went Donny and Marie, in came The Damned, the Sex Pistols and The Clash. Fashion was transformed, too. Out went the peasant skirt with lace trim and the pastel colours. In came a tartan mini-skirt, safety pins and eight-hole Doc Martens.

Dr Marten's boots are iconic. Immortalised in song by Alexei Sayle in an early episode of the classic TV series *The Young Ones*, they were the shoe of choice for everyone from punks to skinheads, anti-Nazi League to neo-fascists. They were invented in Germany by Dr Klaus Märtens, who came up with the idea of air-cushioned soled boots after finding regular army boots too uncomfortable to wear, following a skiing injury he sustained in 1945. The first pair were made in 1947 from discarded rubber picked up on airfields. Märtens went into business with his friend, Dr Herbert Funck producing the boots, which were marketed as an orthopaedic boot. In the early years, 80 per cent of the sales of Dr Martens were to women over forty. Then in the late-1950s Dr Märtens signed an agreement with R. Griggs, a shoe manufacturer based in Northamptonshire to produce the boots in Britain. The first boot was launched on 1 April 1960, and accordingly became known as the 1460. For years this was the only boot they made, eight holes and red with yellow stitching. Now they come in dozens of styles and hundreds of colours, although sadly they are now mostly made in China. I wonder if they would have been as popular if they have been called 'Dr Funcks'.

Anyway, I loved my DMs and my newly spiked-up hair, and in 1977 'Mull of Kintyre' represented everything I had just left behind. I *hated* it. Time is a great healer, however, and that was more than thirty years ago. I have, in recent years, even been known once or twice, to sit through the whole thing, without screaming, 'Get this shite off!' Invariably, this will be at a wedding reception, sometime between midnight and one in the morning, when kids that should have been in bed hours ago have become hyperactive and are running around the dance floor playing touch, and the champagne you drank earlier has worn off, leaving only an excruciating headache. Paul, Linda and the Campbeltown Pipe Band come floating over the disco amplifier system and you decide it really is time to head home to bed.

Now, as we cycled across the top of the mull, I amazed myself by joining Mick in the chorus refrain and we both sang at the top of our voices, 'Oh Mull of Kintyrrrrrre,' in our best Bristolian, scattering sheep in our wake as we dipped up and down on the little road to Kennacraig on the other side of the mull. (Mull, by the way, comes from the Gaelic *Maol,* which means a promontory or 'sticky-out bit'.) Just as well that Paul's gaff is down at the other end of the sticky-out bit, well away from the sound of our singing.

Talking of sticky-out bits, did you know the British Board of Film Classification allegedly used to use the 'Mull of Kintyre Test' to decide whether an image of a man's penis could be shown in a film on general release? Apparently if the winky was so weeny that the angle it made from the vertical (the angle of the dangle) was less than the Mull of Kintyre on a map of Scotland then that was OK. If the angle was greater than the angle of the mull then it was a no-no. The BBFC later denied this, but it's a good story. What the residents of the Mull of Kintyre think about their home being compared to a giant penis I have no idea, and it seemed impolite to enquire. Although, come to think of it, when you look at it on a map it does look a bit like... no, stop it.

Maybe it was Kintyre's revenge for the singing, the penis analogy, or both, but the rain really started to hammer down as we reached the west of the promontory. At Tarbert we went to a cafe and squeezed in along with a hundred other walkers also trying to crowd into the place in an attempt to get some shelter. We all stood there and dripped over the floor forming our own little puddles, until they merged together and formed a lake. I sloshed over to the counter and ordered a slab of cake and a bucket of coffee each.

After a while the ramblers gamely headed off with their hoods up, heads bowed against the wind. Being namby-pamby types, we decided to wait for a while in the hope the rain would ease off.

After about an hour I asked the waitress who was standing pointedly beside our table waiting for us to leave: 'Do you think this is in for long?'

She looked out of the window and up at the sky. 'Och no,' she said, 'it's just a wee bit o' weather. It'll be away again in a week or so.'

I am still not sure if she was serious. We got the message though; we collected our soggy things together and set off once more.

Tarbert Loch Fyne (there are a lot of Tarberts in Scotland, from the Norse *tairbeart* meaning 'drawboat' or 'portage' – a narrow isthmus where boats could be dragged across) was pleasant, even in the rain, with a small harbour lined with neat houses, restaurants and shops. Seafood, as you would expect, was a speciality. It would have been nice to try some, but we had a lot of miles to cover and it was time to get on. On the way up the hill out of Tarbert we passed a trio of men clad in yellow sou'westers, who were clearly not in the least bothered by the rain. They waved to us and, glad of an excuse to get off and push, we pulled over. They were from Glasgow and they told us that, being retired, they often came across here to sail their pride and joy – a 1945 steam tug – on Loch Fyne. As we chatted to them I was irresistibly reminded of Cleggy, Compo and the other one, in *Last of the Summer Wine*. These three were obviously having a fine time, sailing between ports on their beloved launch.

We talked about the pleasure steamers the *Waverley* and the *Balmoral*, both of which regularly run trips both around this part of Scotland and the Bristol Channel down our way.

'The *Waverley* is the last working seagoing paddle steamer in the world!' Scottish Compo enthused. 'You must book a trip on her sometime.'

Mick then told them about a steamer called the SS *Yavari* which he had come across when he had been at Lake Titicaca. She had been built in Britain in kit form and transported across the Andes in 2,766 pieces on the back of mules. Plagued by various problems, including an earthquake, it took six years, rather than the estimated six months, to complete the journey and *Yavari* was finally launched onto the lake in 1870. By the middle of the twentieth century the ship had been abandoned, and it was largely through the efforts of an English expatriate woman by the name of Meriel Larkin that she has been restored to its former glory. The trio were very interested in the tale and if I had not dragged Mick away, I am sure the four of them would be there still, discussing various steam-driven boats, locomotives and such like. Finally we remounted and prepared to head off.

'Hey lassie,' said Scottish Cleggy, 'take some of this to cheer you up along your way.'

He broke a large chunk off a bar of chocolate he had produced from one of the capacious pocket of his sou'wester. I thanked him and popped it in my barbag. Later that day, when the rain had turned monsoon-like, we ate it for pudding, huddled in a bus shelter. (The name, by the way, of the original third character in *Last of the Summer Wine* was Cyril Blamire. You wouldn't have remembered that, would you?)

Unlike England where there are too many routes to choose from, on the west coast of Scotland there are practically none. We now had no choice but to stick to A-roads, although thankfully they were not as busy as, say, Glasgow. We now were headed up the A83 to Ardrishaig. Here we did manage to get off-road for a short while by using the towpath of the Crinan Canal. Designed by John Rennie, and later modified by Thomas Telford, two giants of the canal engineering age, the waterway was opened in 1801 and its 9-mile length saves a round trip of 130 miles around the Mull of Kintyre. The small steamboats, known as Clyde puffers, were once a familiar sight on the canal, bringing up coal from Glasgow, and returning with whisky and other essential items; now the canal is used mainly by yachts and pleasure craft. Passing through the dramatic pine forests of the Knapdale Hills and the boggy peatlands of the Moine Mhor National Nature Reserve, the Crinan has been dubbed 'Britain's most beautiful shortcut' and in dry weather this may well be true. Soaked and cold, viewing the path through lashing rain was probably not the most favourable weather in which to appreciate it. But there were no cars to spray us and the canal path was well laid – no horrible scalpings like the Bridgewater Canal. At Bellanoch we came off the canal and took advantage of the B-road for a while before rejoining the A816 to Kilmartin.

Kilmartin lies in Kilmartin Glen and as we approached from the south along the quiet road, house martins were in abundance, swooping and diving in front of us as we sped along. They were master flyers, skimming just above the ground, before shooting up into the sky and then diving again. We enjoyed sharing the road with them for a few miles. Mick said they were the inspiration for the fixed-wing Spitfire rather than the earlier biplane. I have no idea whether this is true and, if it is, how he knows it. He sounded convincing, though. The sun had finally deigned to put in an appearance and the damp trees glistened in the gentle, late afternoon light. At the junction of the B and A-roads, a field to our left contained the Nether Largie stones – megaliths which are part of a network of prehistoric stones and cairns, and beyond that, Temple Wood, the site of one of the finest Bronze Age stone circles in Scotland. Can you believe there are more than 150 prehistoric sites and 200 other ancient monuments within a 6-mile radius of this small settlement? I found this staggering. No wonder this is one of the most important archaeological sites in Europe.

We found a path just off the road through the woodland and, as we passed through, I had a good feeling about the place. It felt wise, peaceful and somehow *connected*. I said as much to Mick, who said I was starting to sound like an old hippy, and where could he get a cup of tea and something to eat as he was starving.

So we pitched up at Kilmartin House Museum and grabbed a coffee, a sandwich and as much history as we could cram into the half an hour we had available before setting off once more. I was beginning to wish we had set aside two months, or even three for this tour. There was so much to see, it would be lovely to tarry for longer. I also wished it would stop raining. I know this was the wet coast (sorry, west coast) of Scotland and it rains a lot here, but even so.

We followed the coast road up to Oban. The road swept up and down, clinging to the edges of lochs and zigzagging through forests and glens. The wind was coming in from the north-west and this made our progress even slower. Normally, the reward for slogging up a hill is the long coast down the other side – not today. The wind was so strong that cycling downhill was hard work and cycling uphill nigh on impossible. We were soggy. Our bags were soggy. We decided to forget any idea of camping and keep going to Oban.

We rolled into the town at 8 p.m. We had landed on the mainland at 10 a.m. Most of that time had been in the saddle and we were both by now feeling more than a little weary.

We found a street lined with bed and breakfasts and booked into one. It was mediocre but not terrible, which on reflection was my opinion of Oban in general. Sorry, Oban, if this is unfair; it had been a very long day. Having dumped all our wet stuff in the bathroom we went in search of a pub and some grub. Once again, we had cocked-up on the nutrition side of things; it was hours since we had eaten. Too tired to wander around the town, we went into the nearby chippy and ate an enormous portion of fish and chips, before repairing to the first pub we came to, the Tartan

Tavern. The decor was so terrible that, quite frankly, it bordered on criminal, with dark green tartan fabric covering the walls. It did, however, have two very large televisions showing football, which cheered Mick up hugely. Not being a fan, it did little for me, however, and I felt thoroughly fed up. What a stupid thing to be doing, I muttered to myself. All I wanted was to be at home, tucked up into my own warm bed, lying in until noon and then spending all day reading the papers and drinking coffee. Instead, I would be once more risking hypothermia, getting cold, wet, miserable and tired on that stupid bike. As the teams eventually trooped off the pitch ninety minutes later, Mick finally noticed I was a little quiet. He, on the other hand, having supped a couple of pints and enjoyed the game, had now fully regained his *joie de vivre*.

'Wassup?' he said in surprise as he gathered up his empty pint glass to go to the bar for a refill.

'Tired and fed up,' I said sulkily. 'And the beer in here is rubbish.' (It wasn't that bad actually, Old Speckled Hen from Morland Brewery/Greene King, although something local would have been better. But I was in a foul mood by now and wanted to whinge.)

'Aaah, come on Routes,' he said – he had taken to calling me this ever since the Kirkstone Pass debacle – 'you'll be OK in the morning. Tell you what, I'll get you a glass of Talisker' (my favourite malt whisky).

'Ooh OK,' I said rubbing my hands together and cheering up immediately. 'Yes, go on then.'

My mood improved with every subsequent trip to the bar and after an hour or so I felt ready to cycle up Ben Nevis.

Stats
Miles: 64
Total miles: 816
Pints of beer: Me 2, Mick 4
Whiskies: 4
Boring football matches: 1
Annoying songs sung: 1 song, a billion times.

DAY
18

OBAN

 **TO**

INCHREE

The next morning the prospect of cycling up Ben Nevis somehow seemed less attractive. Plus, it was still raining. We hung around in Oban for a couple of hours drinking coffee and pretending to do some shopping, trying to put off the inevitable. We had a look at the huge CalMac ferries in the harbour and gazed from afar at the structure on the hill that dominates the town. When I first saw it I rubbed my eyes and looked again, to check whether I was having some sort of strange vision. What on earth was a colosseum doing stuck on a Scottish hillside?

The colosseum turned out to be a folly built by a local banker, John Stewart McCaig. The project was apparently conceived to assist local stonemasons who struggled to find work in the winter months. This may have been true, however I suspect there may have also been less altruistic motives, as McCaig had originally planned for the colosseum to be filled with statues of himself, his siblings and his parents. It certainly didn't seem to be the most useful of projects and I am not sure whether setting the building at the top of a steep hill was too considerate to the local workforce. Anyway, the modest Mr McCaig died before the project was completed. Presumably none of his family was keen, as the work stopped with him, with only the outer walls completed. I must confess to having no desire whatsoever to climb up and take a closer look at it.

Eventually, we could put it off no longer and we started cycling up the hill out of the town. As we rode past some workmen, fully decked out in our waterproofs, rain dripping off us, they looked at us and laughed. 'Welcome to Scotland!' one of them called out. I did not think it was possible, but if anything the rain was worse today than it had been yesterday – it was coming down in opaque sheets.

We were now on the A85 to Connel, where we joined the A828 by taking an abrupt right turn before swinging left and crossing Connel Bridge, which takes the road across Loch Etive. The bridge was originally built as a single-track railway bridge for the Callander and Oban Railway, carrying the Ballachulish branch line. As road traffic increased, a special service was introduced, whereby a car could be carried across the bridge, loaded onto a wagon and pulled by a charabanc that had been adapted to run on rails. In 1914 the bridge was converted to allow both cars and trains to use it, although not at the same time as the train and vehicles would be close to one another. When the branch line was closed in 1966 the bridge was converted for vehicle use only.

Under the bridge are the Falls of Lora, caused when the tide level in the Firth of Lorn, the body of water between the mainland and the Isle of Mull, drops below the level of the water in Loch Etive. The water then pours out through the narrows under the bridge.

A ledge under the water produces exciting currents and waves, popular with white-water kayakers and with scuba divers of a suicidal disposition. The diver is pulled along by the current in a drift dive and is also pulled down to a depth of up to almost 100 feet. The fact that one section is known as the 'washing machine' is probably all you need to know.

We stopped for a brief rest at the bridge where we stared into the depths below, which were swirling around quite a bit even though it was not yet low tide, then headed on up the coast road. The rain was still hammering down and Mick turned into some kind of Jekyll and Hyde character, one minute swearing loudly and saying he would be getting the train home from Fort William and the next whistling merrily and composing a song to lift our spirits and keep us going. It went something like this (to the tune of 'Over There'):

> *John o'Groats, John o'Groats*
> *The End-to-Enders are coming, the End-to-Enders are*
> *coming*
> *You can rain all you like but we're staying on our bikes*
> *We're going to John o'Groats*
> *You can chuck in the wind but I'm staying with my friend*
> *John o'Groats, John o'Groats*
> *My bike's gone and broke and we're really bloody soaked*
> *But we're going to John o'Groats*

Five miles up the road at Barcaldine we spotted a very new looking cycle path. This, we surmised, was one of the completed sections of the proposed Oban to Fort William cycleway. Initially, the path ran parallel with the road and it was great to be away from traffic for a while. Before long, however, the path crossed the road and headed into the forest on our right-hand side. Mick refused to follow it, worried that it could be a Sustrans meandering route, as they sometimes are, and so we regretfully got back onto the main road. The road hugged the side of Loch Creran and the scenery was beautiful, even in the rain. The road was good quality here with smooth tarmac; John McAdam would have approved of this one. Whether we had the Scottish, the UK or the European government to thank for it I don't know, but we were grateful anyway. Crossing the loch on a boring modern bridge, we headed across country towards Appin.

The rain had finally eased off slightly as we peddled through the village. A mile or so on, the road swung right and began to climb. Looking back from the summit there was a magnificent view of Castle Stalker. Originally built in the fifteenth century, Castle Stalker was originally the stronghold of the Stewarts until 1620 when Duncan, the seventh Stewart chief, in a drunken wager, lost the castle to the Campbells in exchange for a rowing boat. I bet he regretted that one in the morning! It changed hands a couple more times before falling into disrepair in the nineteenth century. In 1965 another Stewart, Lt Col Stewart Allward, bought the castle and spent the next ten years, with help from family and friends, carefully restoring it. Sitting on a little islet just off the shore, it looks the archetypal Scottish castle, and is one of the most photographed in the country. If you are a Monty Python fan you will have seen it – it features as Castle Aaargh in the final scene of the film *Monty Python and the Holy Grail*.

Partway along the road that ran up the side of Loch Linnhe another section of cycle path appeared on our left, so we hopped back on it. The path uses the old Ballachulish branch line and it was very enjoyable, slightly away from the road and travelling through secluded cuttings. We reached Ballachulish Bridge, but before we crossed we stopped for a quick look at the James Stewart Memorial. Tucked away up a flight of steps, just at the southern end of the bridge, and hidden by trees, it's easy to miss if you don't know it's there, despite the Last Clansman Trail signpost. This is the site of the hanging of James Stewart, or James of the Glen, hanged for his alleged involvement in the infamous Appin Murder. It was May 1752, seven years after the defeat of the Jacobites at Culloden. While riding from Appin to Ballachulish through Lettermore Wood, with a group of men, a local factor Colin Campbell was shot dead by a person or persons unknown. On a track just off the A828 there is a cairn erected on the spot where he was killed. Two days later, James Stewart was arrested. He had an alibi stating that he had been several miles away in Acharn on the day of the murder (during his trial at Inverary in September of that year the crown accepted as much), but despite his alibi and a lack of evidence of his involvement in the crime, he was found guilty of being complicit in a conspiracy to kill Colin Campbell. The senior judge in the case was the lord justice general, the Duke of Argyll, otherwise known as Archibald Campbell and Chief of Clan Campbell. Of the fifteen members of the jury, eleven were also Campbells. James Stewart was hanged next to the Ballachulish Ferry, which used to cross the narrows before the building of the bridge. The authorities refused to allow his body to be taken down and it hung there for years, visible to anyone using the busy ferry. Who did commit the murder remains the subject of speculation. The story was immortalised by

Robert Louis Stevenson in the novel *Kidnapped* and continues to cause controversy today.

We crossed Ballachulish Bridge intending to continue on to Fort William. But a couple of miles on, just beyond Onich, we came across the Inchree Activity Centre. The sign outside advertised a bar with a real fire and real ale. In our cold and sodden state the thought of a real fire was too much to resist.

'Shall we just pop in for one pint?' I suggested.

Mick did not need asking twice; he was already cycling up the drive. We lassoed up the bikes and stumbled in. Sure enough, a fire was burning invitingly in the centre of the room. Oh blessed warmth; I hadn't realised how chilled I was. We ordered a couple of pints of Trade Winds from the Cairngorm Brewery. It went down wonderfully. Trade Winds is a fantastic beer and one of my favourites; a pale-golden colour with a lot of wheat and a touch of elderflower. It was so nice that we ordered a couple more. Outside it had started raining again. We were very hungry by now so we asked to see the food menu.

'Sorry, we don't serve food on Tuesdays at this time of year.'

Was it Tuesday? I had no idea what day of the week it was. We must have looked so woebegone that the staff took pity on us.

'I'll see what I can do,' said the woman behind the bar kindly, disappearing off to the kitchen. She came back a few minutes later.

'As long as you're not fussy what you have we can knock you up something,' she said.

I could have kissed her. An hour later we had stuffed ourselves on chicken, new potatoes and vegetables, followed by cake and ice cream. It was getting colder outside and Fort William was only 12 miles down the road, but I really, really didn't want to leave.

'They do accommodation here,' Mick said suddenly.

'Only if you are going canoeing and stuff,' I said. 'And I am *not* going canoeing. I'm wet enough as it is.'

'How do you know?' he retorted. He went to the bar and enquired. The barman said that they had been fully booked with a group but a couple had not turned up.

'We have one chalet room you could have,' he said.

Yessss. Fantastic. We took our stuff round and hung as much as we could in the drying room before returning to the bar where we settled in for the evening. We had a small panic when the barmaid told us we had finished off the Trade Winds, but Red Cuillin from the Isle of Skye Brewery proved an excellent substitute, not unlike Arran's Red Squirrel, with a reddish hue to it. I tapped away on my little notebook while Mick struck up a conversation with another customer – a large American chap wearing a dark suit and tie, who was also working away on his laptop. He said he was in the UK on business.

'Oh,' said Mick. 'What is it that you do?'

'I'm a priest,' he said.

Mick, for once, didn't quite know what to say.

Stats

Miles: 38

Total miles: 854

Pints of beer (each): 4

Vainglorious monuments ignored: 1

Soggy cyclists: 2

Bar staff members almost kissed: 1

INCHREE

≫≫≫≫≫≫≫≫≫≫≫≫≫≫ TO ≫≫≫≫≫≫≫≫≫≫≫≫≫≫

GLEN NEVIS

It only rains twice in Fort William – October to May, and June to September.

What comes after two straight days of rain in Fort William? Monday morning.

What do you call two weeks of rain in Fort William? An Indian summer.

How do the locals predict the weather in Fort William? If you can see Ben Nevis, it's going to rain. If you can't see Ben Nevis, it's raining.

We had expected a cooked breakfast at Inchree, but it turned out to be continental. We had been so excited about booking a room we had not thought to enquire. Nevertheless, there was plenty of it – Mick ate two bowls of cereal, six rounds of toast and stuffed his pockets with cereal bars. He would have eaten the peanut butter had I not stopped him. He's allergic to peanuts but was prepared to risk anaphylactic shock if it meant getting his money's worth.

We had intended this to be a rest day, but having caved in early the previous day after breakfast we retrieved our things from the drying room and set off on the final 12-mile ride into Fort William. Need I bother say it was still raining? It may well be true, as the Scottish Tourist Board claims, that it doesn't always rain in Scotland, and that many places in Scotland are drier than England, but they are all on the east coast. The west coast of Scotland, for all its gorgeous beauty, is undeniably wet. It's the mountains that do it – when the warm air of the Gulf Stream meets the top of them, the air condenses and down comes the wet stuff. And Fort William is the wettest place on the west coast, in an area with some pretty strong competition, because it is right under a large mountain. Well, large by British standards anyway. All of Britain's mountains are pretty tiny in comparison to the world's great mountain ranges. The summit of Everest sits at more than 29,000 feet. Ben Nevis, at 4,408 feet, wouldn't even reach up to Mount Everest's knees and would be barely past its ankles. Even the Lesser Himalayas are higher than the dear old Ben. Alan Dawson observed in *The Relative Hills of Britain* that: 'Many other countries not only have higher mountains, they also have roads, railways, hotels, restaurants, towns and even capital cities that are far higher than any mountain in Britain.'

Ben Nevis still looked pretty big to me, though, and cold – even in May there was snow on the summit, which often stays there all year round. However, despite being the highest mountain in the British Isles, it is nowhere near the most challenging to climb. That accolade would probably go to Sgurr Dearg in the Black Cuillin range, in Skye, which is topped by the Inaccessible Pinnacle or 'In Pin'. It more or less does what it says on the tin, although, like Everest, it gets less inaccessible with every passing year. Everest is so busy these days that there is often a queue to get to the summit.

'After you.'

'No, no, after you.'

Someone at the back yells: 'Keep moving you lot!'

I hear there are plans for a little cafe up there, and possibly a vernacular railway for people who can't be bothered to go the effort of climbing it.

Ben Nevis has a well-laid footpath, which makes the mountain both easy and popular to climb. When we had headed to Scotland the previous summer, our friend Frank (he who kindly drove us to the start of this torturous ride) and who is a keen hillwalker, scoffed at the tourist path and suggested an alternative route which seemed to involve some precipitous climbs and scrambles up Ben's north face. I wasn't keen. It is a fact that, in the northern hemisphere, the north face is always the hardest route. North face of Everest, north face of the Eiger; it's always the worst, the coldest, harshest side of the mountain. The trouble is that what Frank considers an easy climb has Mick and I quaking in our boots. The hills of Scotland are filled with places to which we have given our own epithets: cry-baby-bend, scaredy-cat-ridge, chicken-out-corner, brown-pants-summit (that was a particularly bad day).

So, when we climbed Ben Nevis a couple of years previously, we had stuck to the main route. Despite the numbers of people on the path, we had thoroughly enjoyed our mountain ascent. It still felt pretty special at the top, knowing we were the highest people in the British Isles, if only for a few moments. It was chuffing cold up there, though, and we were very glad of the celebratory nips of whisky we had brought with us to toast our achievement. It took us all day to complete the ascent and descent, and we thought we had done pretty well. Until we heard about Clement Wragge.

Clement Wragge was something of an eccentric. He was born in 1852 and initially studied law at Lincoln's Inn. When he was twenty-two he sailed to Sydney on a windjammer, after which he worked his way across to San Francisco and Salt Lake City where he became rather keen on Mormonism – apparently the polygamy bit appealed to him. He headed back to England in 1878, where he lived until 1883, when, after inheriting a considerable amount of money, he returned to Australia. Down Under he established two observatories, founded the Royal Meteorological Society of Australia, set up a network of weather stations and invented the convention of naming cyclones – giving them the names of unpopular politicians. He could then amuse himself by announcing that so-and-so was currently wandering around aimlessly around the Pacific or so-and-so was once again causing distress. Later, when he retired, he moved to New Zealand, wrote a report on caterpillars and wasps for the government in Rarotonga, and toured extensively through India. When he died at the age of seventy he was working on a publication on the petroglyphs of Easter Island on which, of course, he was an expert.

He is relevant here because, while living in England, he offered his services to the Scottish Meteorological Society, which was drawing up plans to site a mountain observatory on the summit of Ben Nevis. From June until the middle of October 1881, Clement Wragge climbed the mountain every single day. He would set off at 4.30 a.m., take readings on the way up, stay on the summit for two hours before descending again, reaching sea level at 3.30 p.m.

Meanwhile, Mrs Wragge was at the bottom making simultaneous observations, from five o'clock in the morning until six o'clock at night. In the summer of 1882 he was at it again, thankfully his wife, who was now heavily pregnant, was not required, as he used two assistants instead. Although he received a medal from the Scottish Meteorological Society for his efforts, when he applied for the post of superintendant of the observatory when it opened in 1883 he did not get it, despite being the obvious choice. He does not appear to have been the easiest chap to get along with, so perhaps that was the reason.

The observatory was used for twenty years before it closed in 1904. The ruins are still there at the summit, and on top of the tower of the observatory is a shelter for people caught out in inclement weather. A few years ago a group of volunteers were clearing stones and generally having a bit of a tidy-up at the summit when they discovered under a pile of stones – a piano. Honest, no kidding. One of the volunteers was reported as saying: 'We have a constant battle against litter being left on Britain's highest mountain – but this elevates being a litter lout sky high into a completely different category.'

Later, a 64-year-old former Highland Games athlete confessed he had carried the instrument up to the top of Ben Nevis in 1971 where he had played 'Scotland the Brave', much to the enjoyment of some Norwegian tourists who had started dancing. Sounds like everyone had a jolly good time. Apparently he had intended to bring it down from the mountain at a later date but had been unable to find it, although how you lose a 226-lb instrument on the top of a mountain beats me.

We cycled along the road that skirts the bottom of Ben Nevis. There was no prospect of us camping today; we definitely required another drying room. So we passed by the Glen Nevis campsite and made for the youth hostel further up the glen, and right opposite the River Nevis and the foot of the mountain. We did not see many tourists heading up the footpath today. As we stood waiting to book in, a group of half a dozen young walkers staggered into reception – and I thought *we* were wet. They were walking the West Highland Way and had just completed the 16-mile section from Kinlochleven. Foolhardy youths that they were, they had not dressed suitably for Fort William weather and were soaked to the skin and shivering, one or two of them looking like they were verging on hypothermic. The warden, obviously used to this type of thing, fetched some blankets for them to wrap themselves up in. I only just managed to resist the urge to say to them in a mumsy way: 'For goodness sake! You can *see* it's raining. Why on *earth* didn't you wear a coat?'

There were quite a few other cyclists in the hostel. One chap was cycling the four corners of Britain: the Lizard, Land's End, John o'Groats and Cape Wrath. I thought it would be interesting to chat and compare notes. Too late, I realised my mistake. He was disdainful of our amateurish and meandering cycling style.

'Day nineteen?' he said incredulously. 'You should be on your way back by now. I'm on day ten.'

Yeah, yeah, bully for you. Then it was the bikes.

'What are you riding?' he asked.

'Well duh! A bicycle, stupid!' I bit my tongue and said, 'A Dawes.'

'Uh huh, OK, what, a Dawes Galaxy?'

'No, don't think so; not sure what it is, I've had it for years,' I muttered, looking around frantically to see why Mick hadn't rescued me. He was sat at the other end of the room with his head carefully buried behind a newspaper. Traitor.

'Oh really,' he drawled. 'I'm riding a Cannondale Tesoro with Rohloff shifters and derailleur and Schwalbe tyres. It comes with a Knob chainring; I had Dickhead spokes fitted specially, and the saddle is a limited edition from Prickland.'

Or something like that, I had stopped listening properly. He rambled on for a bit and then looked at me. I realised he was expecting me to make a response.

'Sorry, er... didn't quite catch that.'

'I said, what GPS are you using? I've got the latest model, its got Cod enabling connectivity and Triple Three Way P.U.S. technology. It measures altitude, longitude, attitude and fortitude... '

'We don't have a GPS, it's not necessary. I have torn some pages out of an atlas and marked the route with a highlighter pen,' I said, haughtily. 'And so far it has worked perfectly well, we have not got lost at all.'

Mick at this point couldn't help himself and burst out laughing. I glared at him.

We had a mission to complete so we left Cycling Bore caressing his GPS and set off in the rain to trek the 3 miles into Fort William. On the way into town we passed a huge erratic boulder, Samuel's Stone or the Wishing Stone. There are many stories and legends attached to this stone, one of which is that it was placed there to commemorate a victory by a local chieftain. I thought it more likely to have been dropped by a bloody great glacier myself.

We were heading into Fort William in search of pies. Not just any old pies, mind you, these were haggis pies from the multi-prizewinning Nevis 'Say Aye Tae a Pie' Bakery. These pies were worth travelling for. The staff in the pie shop didn't seem to mind us standing in there dripping on the floor while we munched on them.

'It's wet today,' I said conversationally.

'Aye,' said the woman behind the counter.

She didn't elaborate, and it then occurred to me that saying, 'it's wet today' in Fort William was like saying 'it's sunny today' while standing in the middle of the Sahara Desert. A passing camel herder isn't going to look up at the burning sky and reply,

'Well yes it is rather warm, but I've checked the weather forecast and tomorrow looks like it will be cloudy, with maybe a touch of frost in the morning and possibly a shower or two on higher ground.' No, he will look thoroughly unsurprised and say 'aye' in Arabic. The woman in the bakery was right, there was nothing more to be said.

Being English I was used to talking about the weather. As everybody knows, we talk about it an awful lot. When we see a neighbour in the street we wave and say:

'Morning! Lovely day today!' or 'I don't believe it's as cold as it was yesterday!'

In shops, on the bus, when we are stood around the coffee machine at work, in fact, whenever we are required to make small talk, the weather is the subject of choice. We avidly watch the forecasts then complain because they are wrong, we even listen to the shipping forecast for pleasure. English language courses have whole sections devoted to talking about the weather, complete with weather vocabulary lists, and rightly so. It is pretty hard to get along in England unless you can talk about the weather ad infinitum. As Dr Johnson observed: 'When two Englishmen meet, their first talk is of the weather.' The reason, of course, is that it is always doing something unexpected, or something new. The weather changes not even by the day, but by the hour. One minute it's sunny, the next it's hailstones. Blizzards, floods, heatwaves – anything can happen – and that's just in July. When we do get a really extreme weather event (extreme for England anyway), perhaps a dusting of snow or a night when the temperature drops below zero, we get all excited, stock up on bags of sugar and packets of candles, and start talking about the Blitz spirit. Oh yes, we English do like our weather.

When we had feasted on as many haggis pies as we could force down, we waddled across the road to the Grog & Gruel, Fort William's real ale pub. Mick tried the Williams Gold and I tried the Red from the same brewery, based in Alloa. Mick enjoyed his, a golden citrusy beer and I very much liked the Red, a dark, ruby beer with a nutty flavour. We were still freezing cold and wet, though. A couple of chaps sitting near the radiator could see we were in trouble and kindly gave up their seats. We clung to the pipes for a while before heading out into the rain to catch the bus back to the hostel.

Later that evening I was curled up in an armchair in the sitting room when Mick came in. I could tell by his face that something was wrong.

'What is it?' I asked.

'It's my feet,' he said mournfully. 'I think I have trenchfoot. Two of my toenails have fallen off.'

>>>>>>>>>>>>>>>>>>>>>>>>>>>>

Stats
Miles: 12
Total miles: 866
Pints of beer (each): 4
Soakings: A billion
Toenails lost: 2 (both Mick's)

>>>>>>>>>>>>>>>>>>>>>>>>>>>>

DAY
20

GLEN NEVIS
>>>>>>>>>>>>>>>>>>>>>>>> TO >>>>>>>>>>>>>>>>>>>>>>>>
LOCH NESS

*A Scotsman walking through a field sees a man drinking
water from a pool with his hand. The Scotsman shouts:
'Awa ye feel hoor that âs full Oâ coos Sharn.' (Don't
drink the water, it's full of cow shit.) The man shouts
back, 'I'm English, speak English, I don't understand
you!' The Scotsman shouts: 'Use both hands, you'll get
more in!'*

The morning sun burned our skin. We joyfully packed our rain
gear away in our panniers, applied suntan lotion and cycled off
clad only in T-shirts and shorts. We didn't really, I'm joking. It
was still pissing down with rain. To be fair, the day had started
out quite promisingly – it stayed dry for almost ten minutes. But
barely had we left the outskirts of Fort William when the heavens
opened. Out came the wet gear and the eight hours our kit had
spent in the drying room the previous night was once again
completely wasted; it was very soon as wet as when we had put it

in there the night before. We had, by now, got into the routine of wrapping all the stuff in our panniers in double bin-liners to try and keep everything dry, but we were still unable to stop puddles forming in the bottom of our bags. The fact that my faithful little notebook computer was still managing to function in such sodden conditions was something of a miracle.

I had originally planned our route to take us right up the west coast and across the top of Scotland. The mission now was simply to get to the top of Scotland without drowning. We decided to abandon the west coast and head east along the line of the Great Glen towards Inverness. The Great Glen is a major fault line which separates the Grampians from the Northwest Highlands, stretching for 60 miles from Fort William to Inverness and beyond, down through Mull and up through Shetland. The Great Glen is a slip fault, where two land masses are sliding against each other. The rocks along the slip line are prone to erosion and recurrent ice ages have helped carve out the huge valley that travels along the fault.

Scotland is like a liquorice allsort; it is made up of half a dozen different pieces of continent that have become stuck together. The rocks that are found on the islands of Lewis and Harris, and in the north-west of Scotland, are three billion years old, some of the oldest rocks in the world. Around 480 million years ago (give or take a few million years) began a series of collisions between continents that brought the different bits of Scotland together, although at that time 'proto-Scotland' was still part of the same continent as the North American continent of Laurentia, meanwhile England and Wales were miles and miles away in Eastern Avalonia. I am sure many Scots of a nationalist persuasion rather wish it had stayed that way. Unfortunately for them, around 420 million years ago as the Iapetus Ocean closed, Scotland docked at the top of England and it has been stuck there ever since. Then, 60 million years ago, as huge volcanoes erupted down the western side of Scotland, the North Atlantic opened, splitting Scotland and England away from Greenland and North America and we are drifting apart all the time.

If old rocks are your thing then Scotland is a very interesting place indeed. It is therefore not surprising that geology as we know it was invented by a Scot. Although Copernicus, the famous Polish astronomer, recognised 500 years ago that the earth was a planet, the science came into its own after James Hutton, an Edinburgh man born in 1726, picked up some rocks and thought, 'Hmm, I'm pretty sure these are more than 6,000 years old.'

Hutton realised the version of the earth's history provided by biblical scholars was incorrect; he saw that the earth was not static but constantly evolving – that the planet was formed by a continuous cycle in which rocks and soil are compacted into bedrock, which is forced up by volcanic pressure and eventually worn away once more into sediment. This was quite an insight. He became more and more caught up in studying the rocks of Scotland and further afield. He also evidently became saddle-sore, complaining in a letter written while on a field trip to Wales: 'Lord pity the arse that's clagged to a head that will hunt stones.' James, I know exactly what you mean. Lord pity the arse that's clagged to a head that will attempt a 1,000-mile bike ride.

Unfortunately, it seems Hutton's work was difficult to understand; according to Bill Bryson, Hutton's friends encouraged him to expand an earlier paper he had written into a big book, 'in the touching hope that he might somehow stumble onto clarity in a more expansive format'. Luckily his good friend John Playfair was able to elucidate Hutton's thesis and after he published *Illustrations of the Huttonian Theory of the Earth* in 1802, Hutton's work became much more widely known, leading the way for others like Charles Lyell and Charles Darwin, to draw new conclusions from his insight that the world was an ancient and evolving planet.

This morning I was feeling pretty ancient myself and hoped we were in for a not-too-punishing day. Unfortunately, I made an early navigational mistake. We had turned off the road onto the side of the Caledonian Canal. After a few hundred yards it deteriorated into a muddy track before ending up in someone's driveway. I had selected the wrong side of the canal, so we backtracked to the road. I thought of Cycling Bore with his GPS. No doubt he would not have made such a fundamental error, I thought grumpily. We picked up the B8004 instead, which follows the side of the hill facing the Ben Nevis range. It would have been a fantastic view of the mountains had it not been for the rain. I was, by this time, developing a stiff neck from peering out from under my long-peaked cap and hood. My vision was mainly restricted to viewing the road just in front of my front tyre through a narrow slit of about 6 inches wide by 3 inches high. All this majestic scenery was therefore rather wasted.

At Gairlochy locks we met up again with the Caledonian Canal. The canal starts at Loch Linnhe and links the three major lochs of Lochy, Oich and Ness, before finishing up at Inverness. Another effort by Thomas Telford, as well as creating a jolly useful route for boats to travel through Scotland, the canal was conceived as a sort of Victorian job-creation scheme, providing much-needed employment in the Highland region. At the locks there is an option to continue straight on a minor road to Clunes where the Great Glen Way then travels through the forest along the left-hand side of Loch Lochy. However, the path through the forest is not paved and I had read it was not really suitable for touring bikes. We feared that after the amount of rain we had experienced the path would be a quagmire. We decided instead to stick to the road and toiled up the hill to the Commando Monument, which commemorates the commandos who trained near here during World War Two. The monument is in a wonderful situation at the top of the hill overlooking the Ben Nevis range. As we sat there catching our breath, it stopped raining – and started hailstoning instead. The wind was so strong the hailstones came at us horizontally, little ice-bullets, stinging our pink, cold faces.

'Aaargh,' I said raising my arms in front of my face, 'Take cover!'

But there was no cover to be had. We looked enviously at the day-trippers as they ran back to their lovely warm cars and luxury coaches. I seriously considered whether we could hijack one of the cars. We could leap in the back of the car, one each side, press a soggy banana to the driver's head and yell:

'Take us somewhere warm and dry right now or the nodding-dog gets it!'

We didn't hijack any cars. Instead we walked over to the A82 – the main road from Fort William to Inverness. It had no verge or path. We looked at it doubtfully. Four huge lorries hurtled past us, one after the other, swaying alarmingly as they went.

'That's it Routes,' said Mick, 'there's no way I'm cycling down there in this wind, it would be suicidal.'

I had to agree, and we headed back down the road to Gairlochy. It was freezing cold so when we came across a disused church a little way down the road, I suggested we stop and take cover for a bit. Mick refused to come in, saying the place spooked him, and he huddled in the doorway as the rain got heavier. I picked my way inside and stood among the broken pews listening to the rain pattering down on the roof. We had no choice now but to go along the forest path we had eschewed half an hour earlier, and I wondered how we were going to drag our heavily laden road bikes along a muddy cycle track. After a while I ventured out to see how Mick was faring.

'You OK?' I asked tentatively.

'No, I am not OK!' said Mick vehemently. 'This is fucking horrible!'

Thankfully, once we got onto the cycle path the terrain wasn't as bad as we'd feared: the pine forest was so thick that the path was dry and the trees sheltered us from the elements. It was quiet and peaceful in the forest – a welcome relief after the trials of the past hour – and we didn't see another soul. We pushed our bikes some of the way and it gave us chance to appreciate the dramatic geology of the Great Glen. Towering mountains stretched up to our left and the deep, dark waters of Loch Lochy dropped away to our right. We were in the heart of the fault line and it felt humbling. This planet is awesome.

Eventually we emerged from the trees and into farmland as we followed the path to Laggan Locks – two locks that separate Loch Lochy from Laggan Avenue, a section of the canal lined with tall trees – and beyond, Loch Ochy. Opposite the locks was moored the *Eagle Barge*, a 1921 Dutch barge now converted into a cafe/restaurant, which was a very welcome sight.

We hesitated in the doorway, dripping copiously and forming puddles on the floor. Sodden visitors were obviously nothing new, however, and the cafe owner was prepared, pointing us towards a room at the front of the boat where we could take off our wet things. We divested ourselves of coats, hats and gloves, socks and shoes, all of which were soaked through, before padding barefoot to seats in the cafe area. The soup arrived, steaming gently, and by that time so were we. After our meal we lingered at the bar, drinking coffee and chatting to the customers and bar staff. Everyone, as always, was very interested in our expedition, and we collected more sponsor money. I thought how unfair it was to stereotype the Scots as being mean. (Although, have you heard how the Grand Canyon was formed? A Scotsman dropped a coin in a ditch.) Seriously, the generosity of people in Scotland, and indeed throughout our trip, was wonderful. Every time we stopped people would trustingly part with their cash. For all they knew we could be spending it at the next pub, but they gave it to us all the same. I thought this was brilliant. We didn't spend it at the pub, honest. Well, we did, but only because we thought carrying £200 in two-pence pieces would not be a good idea, so we carefully noted all the donations in our little book for totting up and reimbursing at the end.

Fortified after our stop, we decided to have another go at the A82, which looked less ferocious down on this section. It was not too bad – certainly not suicidal – and we soon found ourselves enjoying fabulous scenery as the road squeezed into the valley alongside Loch Oich. At the end of the loch, where another canal section heads off to connect with Loch Ness, we passed a fine little suspension bridge on our left, down a small side road. This turned out to be the Bridge of Oich, not a suspension bridge but a twin-cantilevered bridge, built in 1854 and designed by one James Dredge.

Dredge was a brewer from Bath, and it is thought he designed his first bridge – Victoria Bridge in Bath – as a means of transporting his beer across the River Avon, thus avoiding a long detour around the city centre. I know this bridge, which, unlike the Bridge of Oich, has long been ignored and neglected by the municipal authorities. Anyway, back to Mr Dredge. Things did not go entirely smoothly, it seems, as he was declared bankrupt in 1848, after troubles with a bridge in Weston-super-Mare which was never built, but subsequently he used his patented design for around fifty bridges in England, Scotland and India, including this one. The bridge carried the traffic until 1932, when a new concrete arch bridge was constructed slightly upstream.

Just along the road from the Bridge of Oich, at Aberchalder Swing Bridge, we got back onto the towpath of the canal. The surface was excellent; this section also forms part of the Great Glen Way cycle route, and as we headed east the precipitation was in the form of drizzle rather than driving rain. It is an indication of how bad the conditions had been over the past few days that we now considered misty drizzle to be good weather.

As we entered Fort Augustus, the canal dropped down a flight of five locks before entering Loch Ness. Nessie tourism was in evidence here – next to the lock flight was a model of the monster made from wire and there were plenty of 'Wee Nessies' in the shops next to the canal. In Gaelic, Fort Augustus is known as *Cille Chumein*, after St Cummein who built a church here. The later English name was given to the village after the 1715 Jacobite uprising, when General Wade built one of three forts along the Great Glen here, the other two being at Fort William and Fort George, Inverness. Fort Augustus was named after King George II's younger son, Prince William Augustus, who later became the Duke of Cumberland. In 1746 the prince led the government army at the Battle of Culloden against the Jacobites, the last Jacobite uprising, afterwards earning the epithet Butcher Cumberland for his ruthless conduct in suppressing the Jacobites and destroying the clan system from his headquarters at Fort Augustus. In 1876 a Benedictine Abbey was founded on the site of the fort. It closed in 1998 and the abbey is now a set of luxury apartments.

Situated right next to the canal at the bottom of the flight was the Bothy, so we decided to call in for a quick pint. We had already tried Red Cuillin in Inchree; the Bothy was serving Black Cuillin. The beers are named after the two mountain ranges on the Isle of Skye; the Red Cuillin or Red Hills are a range of rounded, red granite hills. The Black Cuillin are scary-looking mountains, with foreboding jagged peaks of volcanic gabbro and basalt. According to the brewery, Black Cuillin is a 'stout-like beer'. It looked like a stout; it tasted like a stout; but apparently it wasn't a stout. It had a lovely dark, roasted flavour, which I liked. Mick wasn't so keen, he likes the blonde beers, but when I offered to take his off him he said no, he thought he could force it down.

There were a couple of decent local stores in Fort Augustus so we stocked up on food for an evening meal. By now we had been soaked for many hours and tempers were again getting a little frayed. Outside the shop Mick had trouble with his pannier bag. Every time he put it on the bike it fell off. Eventually he completely lost the plot and grabbed the bag. Lifting it to eye level, he glared at it and yelled: 'If you had a face, I would fucking smash it in for you!'

The bag, unsurprisingly, made no response. I shrieked with laughter at this outburst and kept sniggering all the way to Loch Ness Youth Hostel, 10 miles down the road.

We liked the hostel. It had a huge sitting room with fires at each end. Initially the warden tried to place us in a room without heating. Having flirted on the edges of hypothermia several times that day, we objected in the strongest terms, and he quickly capitulated, placing us in a huge family room with piping-hot radiators. We spread out all our stuff in yet another futile attempt to get our things dry and then went down to the kitchen to cook ourselves supper. The hostel appeared to be almost deserted apart from us. The only other residents were an English couple who were house-hunting in the area and while we were eating our respective meals we fell into conversation with them. They asked about our ride and we said it had now degenerated into a linear pub crawl.

'Oh really?' said the woman. 'Drunk-cycling, huh?'

'No,' we said defensively, 'we are always in control of our bikes.'

She looked unconvinced. When they went into the kitchen to wash up Mick leaned over to me and hissed: 'They're coppers. You can tell. They're never off duty are they?'

We spent the rest of the evening relaxing in front of one of the fires, warming our feet, which had turned prune-like due to the prolonged soaking. Mick's trenchfoot, needless to say, had not been improved by the day's antics either. He had lost two more toenails.

>>>>>>>>>>>>>>>>>>>>>>>>>>

Stats
Miles: 49
Total miles: 915
Pints of beer (each): 1
Nessies spotted: 250 (green and furry ones)
Toenails lost: 2 (total 4 – all Mick's)

>>>>>>>>>>>>>>>>>>>>>>>>>>

DAY
21

LOCH NESS

>>>>>>>>>>>>>>>>>>>>>>>>>>>> **TO** >>>>>>>>>>>>>>>>>>>>>>>>>>>>

DORNOCH FIRTH BRIDGE

Breakfast (cereal and toast) was included in the price at the hostel, which at £16 each, we thought was pretty good. As we were eating breakfast the sun shone briefly and we allowed ourselves to hope that today would be dry. The hostel was situated right on the banks of Loch Ness so, after we had finished eating, we went outside where there was a marvellous view across the loch. There was no sign of the monster of course – for the very obvious reason that it doesn't exist. 'Gasp! What's that?' I hear you say. 'Doesn't exist? What about the sightings, the photos, the tea towels, the little furry souvenirs? How can the Loch Ness monster not exist?'

The monster, affectionately known as Nessie, was effectively invented in 1933. Nessie defenders will assert that there are sightings as far back as the seventh century, when Saint Adomnan reported a sighting in *The Life of Saint Columba*. Conveniently, it is rarely mentioned that this sighting of a water beast referred to River Ness, not Loch Ness. Also, it was hardly unusual; early texts are full of stories of mythical beasts, kelpies and other creatures. Practically every Scottish river and loch had a monster of some sort in it. It was only after this monster became famous that Adomnan's text was referred to as proof of the Loch Ness monster's existence.

The story really begins in March 1933, when a local resident of Drumnadrochit, Mrs Mackay, reported to the water bailiff on Loch Ness that she had seen an enormous fish or creature in the loch that she couldn't identify. The bailiff, Alex Campbell, also happened to be a part-time journalist for *The Inverness Courier* and he wrote an article for the newspaper on the sighting of the creature. Being a journo, he beefed up the story to excite his readers' interest. He titled the report *Strange Spectacle in Loch Ness* and in the report 'fish' became 'monster'. Funnily enough, although he worked at the loch, as did his father before him, Alex Campbell had never reported any strange happenings at Loch Ness before this date, although he reported many sightings of the monster in subsequent years – his best sighting being in 1934 at the height of the monster craze.

The story was picked up by the national media, no doubt a welcome change from unremitting gloom about world depression and the rise of fascism, and a number of London journalists headed up to the loch to follow up the story. As it happened, the road alongside Loch Ness had recently been extensively upgraded, making it much easier for tourists to travel around it. Sightings grew along with the media interest and the descriptions became ever more fanciful; a Mr and Mrs Spicer saw 'a most extraordinary animal' crossing the road to the loch; they said it looked like a prehistoric animal and was carrying something in its mouth. Arthur Grant, a veterinary student, claimed a creature walked out in front of his motorcycle. The fact that he was a student, riding his bike home at one o'clock in the morning (had he been in the pub?) does not seem to have detracted from the credibility of his account. Numerous other sightings began to flood in, as people enjoyed their five minutes of fame.

The *Daily Mail* hired Marmaduke Wetherell, a flamboyant actor, film director and self-styled big-game hunter, to go and take a look. Less than two days after arriving at Loch Ness, Wetherell announced he had found tracks of the monster on the shore. Casts were sent to the Natural History Museum for verification. Unfortunately, when the museum examined the tracks found by Wetherell, they announced they belonged to a dried hippopotamus' foot. (Such artefacts were relatively common in the age where big game hunting was admired rather than reviled, being used as umbrella stands, large ashtrays and other, rather revolting, ornaments.) Wetherell was sacked from the *Daily Mail*, although it's not clear whether he was aware the footprints were faked or whether he was victim of a hoax perpetrated by someone else.

A few months later came the publication of the famous 'surgeon's photograph', which purported to show the head and neck of the monster clearly protruding from the waters of the loch. (The surgeon, Robert Wilson, was in fact a gynaecologist, presumably 'surgeon' was felt to be more tasteful.) Sixty years later, Christian Spurling, a keen model maker, confessed that he, his step-brother Ian, and his step-father had created the monster out of a toy submarine and some plastic. His step-father was none other than Marmaduke 'Duke' Wetherell, out for revenge after his public humiliation. They had used Wilson, a friend of a friend, as a front man to add credibility and sent the picture to the *Daily Mail*, Wetherell reportedly saying he would give the paper the monster they wanted.

The hoax photograph created a storm of publicity, the fuss was no doubt much greater than the perpetrators had anticipated. Presumably Wetherell had intended to embarrass the *Daily Mail* by announcing that, like him, they had been taken in by a fake but had decided, because of the furore, to keep quiet. Wilson subsequently refused to have his name associated with the picture or to discuss it further, no doubt for the same reason – it would not have done his career any good to have been associated with what was now a major hoax rather than a small practical joke. In 1975 Wetherell's son Ian admitted to the press that the photograph had been a fake but, curiously, the admission received little attention. Then, in the early 1990s, two Loch Ness researchers, David Martin and Alistair Boyd, followed the trail and uncovered the full story, writing about it in their book *Nessie, the Surgeon's Photograph Exposed*. Despite uncovering the hoax, Boyd continues to believe the monster exists. Of course, Nessie is also pretty good for tourism. Huge numbers of visitors flock to Loch Ness every year, bringing millions of pounds into the local economy. It's hardly surprising therefore that the locals continue to claim there is definitely *something* in the mysterious waters of Loch Ness.

It's a bit of a shame that the loch has become so intertwined with stories of the monster as there is plenty of other interesting stuff about Loch Ness. There's its size for a start. It is 23 miles long, its average depth is 430 feet and at its deepest point it reaches 786 feet. You could put St Paul's Cathedral in Loch Ness and it wouldn't even break the surface. It contains more fresh water than all the lakes in England and Wales combined. That's pretty awesome. It's also pretty old, about 10,000 years, formed when the Great Glen was filled by an enormous glacier, one of the greatest glacial troughs in the British Isles. The glacier found the shattered sides of the fault line easy to erode, resulting now in loch sides, which are extremely steep. It is also, by British standards, geologically active, with frequent minor tremors and earthquakes.

On New Year's Eve 1940, Wellington Bomber N2980, named *R for Robert*, took off from Lossiemouth, on the coast east of Inverness, on a training flight, with eight crew members on board. Flying along the Great Glen they encountered a snowstorm and suffered a loss of power when the starboard engine cut out. Six of the crew bailed out, the rear gunner, Sgt Fensome, was killed when his parachute failed to open. The remaining captain and second pilot landed the plane on Loch Ness and were able to exit the aircraft before it sank below the waters of the loch.

Almost forty years later, Robert Rines, an American lawyer, was trawling the loch looking for evidence of Nessie. He had become convinced of Nessie's existence when, on a holiday to Scotland in 1972, he had looked out of a window and seen the curve of something he couldn't identify, repeatedly breaking the surface of the loch. The 'sighting' spurred Rines, an accomplished inventor, as well as a lawyer, physicist and musician, to develop a high-definition radar and sonar system to assist in the search for Nessie. In 1976, while trawling the loch, Rines discovered the wreck of the bomber, lying at a depth of 230 feet; the aircraft was finally recovered from the waters of the loch in 1985. Incredibly, despite being underwater for 45 years, when they were connected to a battery, the tail lights still worked. After fifteen years and 100,000 volunteer hours of painstaking restoration, the plane is now on display at Brooklands Museum in Weybridge. Of 11,461 Wellington Bombers that were built, *R for Robert* is one of only two that survive. In the meantime, the equipment Rines developed for use in Loch Ness was to be instrumental in locating the wreck of the *Titanic*, in a mile and a half of water, in the North Atlantic in 1985, the same year the bomber was lifted from the depths of the loch.

In the 1950s, Loch Ness was the site of a courageous attempt to break the water-speed record. On September 29, 1952 John Cobb, holder at the time of the world land-speed record, became the fastest person on water, reaching an average speed over a mile of 206 mph in his boat, *Crusader*. Cobb was a shy man and never received the same level of publicity as his contemporary Donald Campbell. However, he was extremely popular with the locals around Loch Ness, taking time to show youngsters from Drumnadrochit around his boat, and refusing to take the boat out on Sundays despite some perfect conditions, out of respect for the religious beliefs of the local people. His wife said that he was a big man, but he was very gentle and very quiet. She said she never saw him angry and didn't think he could be. Crowds had gathered to watch the record-breaking attempt and Cobb's wife watched from the shore. To the horror of the crowd, as the boat slowed down it hit a wave, bounced and disintegrated. John Cobb's body was pulled from the wreckage, which sank to the bottom of the loch. As he did not complete a second run over the measured mile, his record was not permitted to stand. On the road next to the loch is a cairn, placed there as a memorial, by the locals of Glenurquhart. The plaque is by local artist George Bain and includes the Gaelic inscription *'Urram do'n truen Agus do'n iriosal'* ('Honour to the brave and to the humble').

Next to the memorial was a huge waterfall. One consolation of the rain was that we saw some spectacular waterfalls on our route. It was hard to be consoled, however, when within half an hour the heavens opened and we had another torrential downpour. We stood under a tree watching the rain sheeting down for half an hour.

I was not sure how much more water I could take. I was beginning to feel more like a fish than a long-distance cyclist. We plodded on, but we were making slow progress. By one-thirty we had only just made Drumnadrochit, barely 11 miles from the hostel. I was seriously beginning to think John o'Groats was slipping from our grasp.

Drumnadrochit makes the most of its proximity to Loch Ness, so much so that it is known as the Loch Ness Monster Village and is home to both the Loch Ness Centre and Nessie Land Castle Monster Centre but as we did not visit either, I cannot comment on their relative merits. We were more concerned with a problem with my bike. We had foolishly not brought spare brake blocks with us and mine needed replacing.

We went into the tourist information centre to find out whether there was a cycle shop in the town. The woman behind the counter obviously had a lot on her mind, most of which seemed to relate to her good-for-nothing husband and her newly acquired puppy. He sounded like a cad, I must say (the husband not the puppy). Fancy putting newspaper rather than sheets down for the dog to run about on! I agreed that any fool would know the puppy would immediately shred them into a thousand pieces. And did he clear it up? Of course not! I was feeling quite hot under the collar when Mick made an effort to drag the conversation back to something useful.

'Er, is there still a bike shop in Drumna… Drumna… er, around here?' he enquired. The woman remembered herself.

'Och, you dinnae wanna hear aboot all mah complaints,' she said.

I did actually, but Mick felt we really would have to give up if we did not get a move on. Unfortunately, the bike shop was no more, but she helpfully found the details for one in Dingwall. We made a split-second decision to head there rather than Inverness and set off out of the town towards Beauly and Dingwall. The woman in the shop had warned us that there was 'a bit of an up' on the way out. Even worse, our little guidebook mentioned a 'punchy climb'. I have since learned that when any cyclist describes a hill as 'punchy', what they really mean is impossibly steep. I quickly capitulated and started pushing my bike up the hill. Mick tried to use his preferred method of honking up it, but soon gave in as well and dismounted. As we slowly made our way up we suddenly heard a loud crash behind us. A truck coming up the hill had lost its load. Four Portaloos had fallen off the truck and were rolling down the hill. Childishly, we found this highly amusing.

I wasn't laughing for long, though. Mick, still pushing, but walking faster than I, disappeared around the corner. I struggled along behind, my legs aching horribly. Then, as I reached the bend, I got stuck. I simply couldn't move. I was leaning at an angle of 45 degrees gripping the handlebars and trying not to let the bike slide back down the hill. My calf muscles were screaming 'stop!!!' at me and I just stood there for about ten minutes before Mick, realising something was wrong came back down and helped push my bike up the hill. I am sorry to report yet more blubs at this point. Mercifully, at the top there was about 20 miles of downhill and then flat, fast roads. That's the weird thing about cycle touring. One minute you can be having the most dreadful time, soaked to the skin, pushing a heavy bike up fearsome hills, crying, and then half an hour later the sun has come out, the roads are flat and all is wonderful once more. It can be quite wearying, the number of emotions one feels when on a bike.

Anyway, my tears were forgotten as we coasted along. It was probably no accident that as we headed east the weather steadily improved.

Ten miles down the road at Beauly we stopped for a cuppa. The cafe was packed with old ladies having afternoon tea; more fumbling with handbags and purses, and they all gave some money for the cause. We went on through Muir of Ord, got to Dingwall just before closing time and found the bike shop. They were very helpful and pumped extra air in our tyres, which were hopelessly soft. We purchased new brake blocks and then set off on the last 20-mile mission of the day. The A862 clung to the edge of the Cromarty Firth, joining the A9 at the very impressive Cromarty Bridge. A few miles along the road we hopped off the main road again, preferring the quieter coast road. The terrain was completely flat and we sped along, with the firth practically lapping the road, with only a boulder bank separating them.

As we approached Invergordon I was surprised to see a number of oil rigs in the firth. In my southern ignorance I had not realised there were oil rigs in the firth, apparently they are 'resting' here for care and maintenance – a sort of rig recuperation centre. This was a reminder that we were now on the east coast of Scotland, home of the UK oil industry. Or, as the Scottish National Party have it, home of the Scottish oil industry. Oil was discovered in the North Sea in the 1960s and came online in the 1970s. The SNP at this time came up with the slogan, 'It's Scotland's Oil', as an argument for independence and full control over oil revenues. Whether North Sea oil is running out remains a subject of debate, although it seems to be that the stuff has been running out for decades and yet it still keeps coming.

In September 1931, Invergordon was at the centre of one of the very few instances of mutiny by British military personnel, when thousands of sailors went on strike. The global economic situation was dire – America had entered depression following the stock market crash of 1929 and the contraction in credit had been felt in economies across the world. In Britain, unemployment doubled, while exports halved. Revenues plummeted and, faced with a huge budget deficit, the coalition government announced in an emergency budget with swingeing cuts in public expenditure, cuts in benefit payments and public sector pay cuts in an effort to tackle the deficit. (And they say history never repeats itself!) The public sector pay cuts included the pay of able seamen of all classes.

On 15 September 1931, around 1,000 sailors went on strike, causing a panic on the already nervous London Stock Exchange. There was a scramble to sell sterling and, four days later, on 20 September 1931, Britain abandoned the gold standard. The incident has gone down in history as the Invergordon Mutiny.

From Invergordon we passed through a number of small, unexciting settlements: Saltburn, Balintraid, Barbaraville. On the edge of Barbaraville was a large retirement village, with rows and rows of identical little houses set in the middle of nowhere. What on earth would you do in a place like this? Barbaraville has a post box, a bus stop and a telephone box which doesn't accept coins. That's it. Apparently the retirement village itself does also have a small shop and a clubhouse, although we didn't see it.

I have never really understood the concept of moving somewhere when you retire – and in particular somewhere as dead as this. Why on earth would you want to move away from your friends and settle miles away from entertainment, cinemas and theatres? Surely after one retires that's when there is lots more time for all of those things, for hanging out with your mates, taking in a movie and a meal at a local restaurant, and getting pissed without anyone nagging at you. Not for moving to a 'retirement village' in the middle of nowhere with nothing to do and where the entertainment consists of a singalong every Thursday evening and, if you are feeling particularly energetic, a game of snooker. If you move there with your partner or spouse, chances are one of you will peg it within a couple of years, leaving the survivor stuck there all their own. Barbaraville to me looked like somewhere people go to wait to die.

If I moved to Barbaraville I think I would start taking cocaine just to pass the time. I have a friend who vows she is going to start taking drugs when she is in her seventies, as she has always wanted to try them but is worried about getting addicted. She figures that, at that stage, it's not going to matter a whole lot if she sits there, off her face, dribbling into her microwaved dinner. Imagine a whole retirement village all off their heads on drugs!

'I'm afraid the sing-song tonight has been cancelled as Ethel's been baking again. She's eaten half a dozen space cakes and thinks she's a cat. She's sleeping it off now so we'll all meet around the piano at seven o'clock tomorrow evening!'

It was with these musings that I entertained myself as we made our way up the edge of the Cromarty Firth.

Thankfully, there was not even a sniff of a gradient and we sped along, chewing up the miles in a very satisfactory manner, until we coasted into the Royal Burgh of Tain. Tain claims to be the oldest royal burgh in Scotland, dating from 1066 when it was granted a charter by Malcolm III. It must be said there are quite a lot of royal burghs – there were 68 of them in Scotland when they were formally abolished in 1975, although lots of towns continue to use the title. Tain was an attractive town of sandstone buildings and it felt pretty affluent – Scotland's answer to Bath. Consequently, however, we speculated that the bed and breakfast accommodation would probably not be particularly cheap. By now the sun had finally decided to put in a meaningful appearance and so we decided to save some money by camping. In Tain, a local told us there was a campsite a couple of miles up the road. On the way we passed the Glenmorangie whisky distillery and were sorely tempted to visit, but time was against us so we regretfully cycled on. Two miles down the road we reached Dornoch Firth Bridge where there was a campsite with a pub next door. As we got off our bikes three more End-to-Enders rolled into the car park and we naturally fell into conversation about our relative experiences. We were rather crestfallen to discover they had set off from Land's End on the same day we had left Dumfries. We were on day twenty-one. They were on day seven. They planned to reach John o'Groats the following day. Suddenly we felt like slowies rather than the cycling heroes we had thought ourselves to be. But, we reminded ourselves, we were touring, not racing; it was a different thing altogether. They had a support vehicle and back up team; we had our tent and all our gear on our bike. And we cheered up when one of them complained he had seen nothing but tarmac the whole way, and said he would much rather be on our trip.

The landlady did us proud with great food. Mick had surf and turf (steak and prawns), and I had fish and chips. Even the gargantuan appetites we had developed during the course of this trip were not up to finishing the food she put in front of us, although we both made a jolly good effort. Sadly, there was no real ale, but we managed to force down three pints of Tetley's Bitter and some whisky. The others were staying in the pub so we bade them goodnight and made for the door to settle into our tent in the campsite next door. As we were about to leave, the landlady called out: 'If you would like some breakfast, come over at eight in the morning!'

Brilliant. We assured her that we would.

>>>>>>>>>>>>>>>>>>>>>>>>>>>>

Stats
Miles: 63
Total miles: 978
Pints of beer (each): 3
Whiskies (each): 2
Blubs: 1 (mine)
Competent End-to-End cyclists: 3 (not us)

>>>>>>>>>>>>>>>>>>>>>>>>>>>>

DAY
22

DORNOCH FIRTH BRIDGE

>>>>>>>>>>>>>>>>>>>>>>>>>>>> TO >>>>>>>>>>>>>>>>>>>>>>>>>>>>

MELVICH

At quarter to six the next morning, I was awoken by a huge roar just outside the tent. Startled, I screamed out, before realising it was the first train going through. We were fewer than 5 feet away from the main line from Wick to Inverness. It thundered past, leaving us, and the tent, quivering in its wake. The second was not quite as much of a shock and by the third we had blanked them out, didn't even hear them. Well, not quite – but at least my hair had stopped standing on end. We strolled over to the pub for breakfast, which was superb and well worth the fiver each they charged. The speedsters were looking a little tired and grumpy this morning, we thought. We waved them off at eight o'clock before returning to our food, newspapers and endless cups of tea. (We would pay for this later by having to stop at every other field for a pee.)

About an hour later we finally decided we should pack up and get on our way. We had not seen a soul on the campsite since we arrived the previous evening, and we could easily have loaded our bikes and cycled off. Instead, we spent about half an hour trying to find someone to pay. Eventually an old chap appeared, and seemed mildly surprised that we would want to bother.

'I just want to pay for one night's camping,' I explained.

'You wanna pay? Ach well, you were late arriving weren't you, we'll call it a fiver, shall we?'

With the financial transaction completed to everybody's satisfaction, we were ready to tackle the big push up to the top of Scotland. We crossed the bridge that spans the Dornoch Firth and headed up the A9. Or, at least, Mick headed up the A9 – I was having trouble with my bike. Specifically, the wheels did not want to turn; it was like cycling with the brakes on. In fact, I *was* cycling with the brakes on. Mick had replaced the brake blocks the night before and he had managed to fix them so they were pressing onto the rims of my wheel. I called out to him and pulled over. Mick, who was not riding with his brakes on, had managed to cover a considerable distance up the hill and returned down it in a bad temper.

'What is it?' he asked irritably.

'The brake blocks aren't fixed on properly,' I said. 'They are pressing on the rim of the bike.'

He gave them a cursory look.

'They're fine,' he pronounced. 'They just need breaking in, after ten miles or so you won't feel it.'

'TEN MILES!' I exclaimed. 'I'm not cycling ten fucking miles like this!'

'They are FINE!' he yelled.

'They are NOT!' I yelled back.

With that, Mick got on his bike and cycled off back the way we had come.

'Where the hell are you going?' I shouted after him.

'Home!' he yelled over his shoulder, and he disappeared around the corner.

I sat down on the verge. Now what? Mick had the bike tools so even if I wanted to mess about with the brake blocks I couldn't. I was miles from anywhere, with a bike that I couldn't ride. I was tired and thoroughly pissed off. What a damn idiotic thing this was to do, I thought. I was so tired that I couldn't even be bothered to consider what to do next. Which was why I was still sitting there, half an hour later, when Mick returned. He was looking a bit sheepish. It turned out he had got as far as the petrol station where he had stopped for a coffee and a slice of cake – and he didn't even bring me one. Bastard! He later admitted he had committed the male sin of Making a Mistake but had, of course, not wanted to admit it. Twenty minutes later the brakes were fixed and we set off once more.

Once my temper had cooled off, the stretch up the A9 was not as bad as I expected. I had anticipated roaring traffic but, in fact, the road was not too busy and the strange yellow ball in the sky, which we had glimpsed so little of in our tour through Scotland seemed more inclined to stick around for longer today. Soon we were crossing the top of Loch Fleet and then, suddenly, we were on the edge of the North Sea. At about the same time, we reached a personal landmark: our 1,000th mile on this trip. We stopped for a hug and to punch the air for a bit, before taking a quick photo.

I found it difficult to believe we had managed to cycle a thousand miles. We both felt entitled to be more than a little pleased with ourselves. We had just passed a signpost which read 'John o'Groats 76 miles'. Seventy-six miles! Pah, that was nothing!

When we had crossed the border into Scotland I had been pleased, but also aware that Scotland was a lot bigger than we southerners tend to think it is. Now, though, I knew for certain that, save a hideous accident or disaster, we were going to finish this. My heart gave a hop, skip and a jump. This feeling was amazing. See what I mean about the number of emotions you experience on a journey like this? Not an hour before I had been sitting by the side of the road in a thoroughly bad mood, and if a taxi had, at that moment, pulled over, and the driver, leaning out of the window had said: 'Need a lift anywhere, love?' I would, without hesitation, have abandoned my bike, jumped in the cab and cried, 'Yes please, Bristol, and don't stop until you get there!' Now I felt on top of the world, and this was the best, absolutely the best, journey I had ever undertaken in my life.

Congratulations completed, we continued to Golspie, a fair-sized town which, considering the A9 trundles though the middle of it, was not unattractive, with low one or two-storey houses straggling down the main street (imaginatively named Main Street). We called in to the Coffee Bothy, where we fortified ourselves with a cafetière of coffee and the most fabulous flapjacks. The proprietor was a local woman, and she was also a keen walker. I explained our route dilemma: whether to turn off the A9 at Helmsdale and take the minor road to Melvich – no violent hills but remote and committing, or stick to the A9, a shorter route with more options for pulling in for the night, but more traffic and a couple of fearsome hills this side of Wick. She recommended the Melvich option.

Still, we weren't sure. It would mean a total of 75 miles or so and we had already lost time due to the brake blocks debacle. We decided to defer the decision until we got a bit farther up the road. As we were saddling up outside, a chap was sat at one of the tables with his family and he called us over.

'What's BRACE?' he asked. I explained.

'How do I know you are legitimate?' he asked, reasonably enough. I showed him a card with our website address on it, and assured him we were collecting for charity and not for beer money. With that he reached in his pocket and pulled out a £20 note. 'Here you go,' he said.

We thanked him and made sure he saw us conscientiously noting down the amount in our little book, lest he still had doubts about the validity of our cause.

'Not far now,' he observed, as we prepared to depart. 'Can I offer one piece of advice?'

'What's that?'

'Don't stay the night at John o'Groats.'

On up the A9 we went, the road keeping close to the sea, an 18-mile slog through a fairly empty and barren landscape, until we reached the village of Helmsdale, about halfway between Tain and Wick. The Golspie flapjack had long since been burned off in expended calories, so we decided to stop for a spot of lunch. La Mirage looked interesting – it proclaimed itself to be 'The North's Premier Restaurant', although it was not clear what exactly was meant by 'The North'. I come from Bristol for goodness sake, for me The North starts somewhere around Derby or Stoke.

Intriguingly, there was also a sign in the window, which said, 'As seen on TV'. Well, that clinched it. In we went, and stopped in astonishment. We had seen fewer people in the last hour than you could count on one hand, yet the place was packed and waitresses were dashing to and fro, trying to keep up with orders.

Even more astonishing was the decor. Eclectic does not even come close. I can only describe it as Barbara Cartland Goes To Hollywood. It was pure kitsch: neon lights flashed the name of the restaurant and pink feather table lamps stood next to a full-sized mannequin of a New York cop. In a corner, a mannequin's fishnet-stocking-clad legs supported another lamp. The pink walls were festooned with decorations and pictures of celebrities who had visited the restaurant. It turned out the restaurant was indeed a favourite of Barbara Cartland's and, in turn, the restaurant owner, Nancy Sinclair, was quite a big fan of hers, and modelled her appearance on that of the flamboyant writer. Nancy herself, it seems, was quite a character. She started her professional career as a model, working for *Vogue* and others in the 1960s. During these years she also gathered together a group of models who would tour Sutherland giving fashion shows in hotels and halls. In the 1970s Nancy and her son opened La Mirage, which, over the next twenty years, attracted increasing attention both for the quality of the seafood served and the celebrities who made a point of visiting this out-of-the-way restaurant, from Barbara Cartland herself and her daughter Raine, Countess Spencer to Ian Botham, Alex Salmond and Michael Portillo. (Thankfully not all at the same time.) Until her death in 2007, Nancy used to sit in the restaurant, immaculately dressed, supervising proceedings. The present owners had continued to maintain the decor and the superb quality of the food – and long may they continue to do so.

We both had a prawn jacket potato, which was out of this world – a soft, fluffy potato cooked to perfection, piled high with prawns. When we were done, however, we had to make the decision we had put off at Golspie – should we go via Melvich or Wick? We baulked at the thought of a steep hill climb, which we knew we would face on the main A9 road through Wick, and decided to go with the quieter and more gradual incline of the A897 to Melvich.

We set off with more than a little trepidation. This road went up through the Strath of Kildonan, a remote glen with only a handful of houses, for 40 miles or so until our destination, and it was already mid-afternoon. Still, if the worst came to the worst we had our tent so we could simply set up camp. Mick would sulk at not being able to get to a pub, but we would at least have shelter if necessary. It was the right choice. The road up the Strath of Kildonan was beautiful, following the river and with gentle climbs up. Deer leapt across the road in front of us, before making for the hill, obviously suspicious of these strange creatures coming toward them.

At Kildonan we stopped to look at the site of Scotland's one and only gold rush. In 1868, twenty years after the start of the Californian Gold Rush, a local man called Robert Gilchrist discovered gold here. Over the following months more than 3,000 prospectors turned up, coming from as far as the Yukon to seek their fortune in the waters of Kildonan. A temporary settlement sprung up – Baile an Or (Town of Gold) – to accommodate the influx of people hoping to dig a fortune out of the river. For a while the hillsides were covered with people digging for gold, but by the end of the following year little gold was found. At the end of 1869 the Duke of Sutherland stopped issuing new licences. Even today though, a little gold panning takes place on a non-commercial basis. There was a little camp of tents by the water and a few people were trying their luck, so we joined them for a while. We didn't have any pans so we used our hats, sticking them in the water and swishing them about a bit, but sadly no nuggets were forthcoming.

The Sutherlands crop up a lot in the history of the area around here. They were instrumental in the land clearances of the nineteenth century, when thousands of people were evicted from their homes so the land could be used for large-scale sheep farming. The valley we were travelling through was not always deserted, as it is today. In the Strath of Kildonan alone, between 1811 and 1831, the population shrank from 1,574 people to just 257. Many families were pushed to the coastal areas where they were expected to eke out a living from fishing, despite having no experience of this way of life.

Many more highlanders, of course, emigrated around the world and the population of the Highlands has never recovered.

Although listed as an A-road, here it was single width with passing places. Once out of the valley, we saw hardly any cars at all. We had learned by now on these roads not to expect too much from the places marked on the map. Sure enough, Kinbrace turned out to be half a dozen houses at a road junction. We were struck by one house in particular, which, with its brightly painted blue tin walls and red tin roof, would not have looked out of place in Buenos Aires.

As we climbed up, the landscape grew more and more wild and remote. This was flow country – the largest expanse of blanket bog in Europe. It stretched away for miles – a vast flat green-brown landscape, with not a house or a road in sight except the one we were on. It was so quiet; the only sounds we could hear were the occasional call of a bird and the blowing of the wind as we pedalled along. At Forsinard, the RSPB has a visitors' centre, Forsinard Flows, which is housed in the railway station building. I wished I was better at identifying birds; the geese I could recognise and we could hear cuckoos all along the route. Mick is better than me and he identified a couple of merlin and some hen harriers. The rabbits I could identify – we saw about a trillion of them, including one ginger and white little bunny. The ride was a delight.

We were, however, a bit disappointed by the ride 'down' from Fornisard to Melvich. The profile in our guidebook promised a steady down slope; in fact it was nothing of the sort, it was down, then up, then flat – all into the wind. We were by now getting a little weary and it was getting late by the time we got to the junction with the A836, which crosses the top of Scotland. We turned left and headed into Melvich. We came to a pub, the Halladale Inn, which had a camping field and shower block. Despite it being only half past eight, the landlord did not seem keen to serve us food, and within ten minutes we saw his wife hastily disappearing out to walk the dogs.

The landlord was evidently not keen on selling us beer, either, complaining he would have made more money out of us had we ordered a cup of coffee each. We stole a surreptitious look at each other. Another complaining landlord! The beer was not brilliant; it was a keg beer of some sort. When we settled down with our drinks, the landlord, having no other customers, decided to plonk himself down next to us. After an hour or so, it was something of a relief to call it a night and crawl into our little tent.

>>>>>>>>>>>>>>>>>>>>>>>>>>>>

Stats
Miles: 73
Total miles: 1,051
Pints of beer (each): 2 (rubbish ones)
Gold nuggets found: 0
Miserable landlords: 1

>>>>>>>>>>>>>>>>>>>>>>>>>>>>

DAY
23

MELVICH

>>>>>>>>>>>>>>>>>>>>> TO >>>>>>>>>>>>>>>>>>>>>
JOHN O'GROATS

We were preparing ourselves for the final push across the top
of Scotland to John o'Groats. As we packed up our tent, we got
chatting with the only other campers on the site – a couple in a
touring van. They had just arrived back from Orkney. 'Orkney
is different, it's not like the mainland at all,' one of them said.
'It's more' – she paused, searching for the right word – 'it's more
sophisticated. You should go,' she said, 'if you have the time.'

I told her we should have about a week free after we had
completed the trip to John o'Groats.

'Oh you should definitely go over to Orkney then,' she said. 'Go
to the Pickaquoy campsite in Kirkwall, it's fabulous.'

This sounded like a good idea so I wrote the name down for
reference.

As we set off from Melvich, memories of howling wind and
lashing rain faded. The sun was out and as we cycled along we
were in high spirits, singing our John o'Groats song. We were
now only about 38 miles from our destination. The newsagent's

at Reay had a coffee machine, so we had a small pit stop at the little table behind the petrol pumps. The landscape was changing from moor to pastureland and the sheep all had six legs, so I knew we were getting close to Dounreay nuclear power station. The power station is now a nuclear storage facility, having been decommissioned in the 1990s and to say it's an eyesore is something of an understatement. The 'golf ball', which once housed Britain's experimental fast-breeder reactor, is said to have an important place in Scotland's heritage. For the life, of me I cannot see why. Apparently after decommissioning the public were asked to send in ideas for what to do with it. Suggestions included converting the ball into a museum or hotel. Maybe it's just me, but the idea of staying in a hotel in the middle of a radioactive no-go area simply doesn't appeal. And a museum? A museum of what? Mutant insects? Glow-in-the-dark pottery? Radioactive art?

The nuclear facility has been dogged by reports of incompetence. In 2006, a nearby beach was fenced off after pieces of plutonium fuel rods were found there. In 2007, the UK Atomic Energy Authority admitted illegally dumping nuclear fuel waste into a landfill site and allowing irradiated nuclear fuel to be discharged into the Pentland Firth. Earlier, in 1998, there had been a big fuss when a lot of highly enriched uranium– enough to make a dozen atomic bombs – had gone missing. Ten years later it was announced the uranium had been found, apparently it had turned up in some waste bins. So that's alright then. Oh well, at least they found it. Mick asked if I fancied a swim. He said we could probably dispense with our dayglo jackets afterwards. I declined.

After Dounreay, the landscape was flat and fairly featureless for a good few miles, broken up only by the occasional array of wind turbines on the horizon or small group of houses, huddled by the side of the road. At Bridge of Forss there was a welcome change in the scenery, as the road curved round and over the River Forss. Next to the bridge was an attractive Constablesque scene, with an old mill on either side of the river and steps and a path leading down. We spent a pleasant half-hour here looking for trout, before heading on our way.

We coasted into Thurso, which, as it was Sunday, was pretty much shut. We liked it, though, with its wide streets and attractive buildings, and the Pentland Hotel was open for Sunday lunch. As we pulled up outside we saw our speedster friends from Dornoch Bridge who were just booking into the hotel having finished the ride the day before. Eight days start to finish! They waved to us.

'Congratulations!' said one of them, shaking Mick's hand.

'Erm, we haven't got there yet,' said Mick, sheepishly. 'We're still on our way.'

They both laughed heartily at this, before strolling off to the bar, and no doubt a well-earned bath and long sleep. I looked after them enviously before remounting the bike. Still, only 18 miles to go – we were almost there!

But – this being a journey of back roads and detours – it seemed fitting we should take one final detour before the finish... and so, at Dunnet, we swung left onto the road up to the promontory of Dunnet Head, the northernmost point on the British mainland. Well, it was only 5 miles each way and it seemed a shame not to; who knew when we would be passing this way again? (In fact, it turned out to be exactly six days later, but we were not to know that at the time.) The road snaked to the headland where there were glorious views across the Pentland

Firth to the Isle of Stroma, beyond which lay the island of Hoy and the rest of Orkney. Stroma, at the turn of the twentieth century, had a population of more than 370 people. Over the next sixty years more and more people left for work on the mainland. In 1955, there were still around 80 islanders, but over the next few years the school, the church and the shop closed and the last families departed the island less than ten years later. Stroma is now uninhabited and used for grazing sheep. There was something terribly poignant about all the ruined empty houses and farmsteads dotted across the island.

We got back from our detour and passed a signpost telling us that we still had 17 miles to go. It must be psychological because it was not that hilly – although a stiff breeze was against us – but those 17 miles felt as though they were some of the hardest of the whole journey.

'I'm finished,' I wailed. 'I can't go on!'

'You ain't finished, soldier!' yelled Mick, morphing into the colour-sergeant-major in the film Zulu. 'You ain't dead till I tell you you're dead! Keep cycling!'

It worked. I laughed and kept cycling. One thing we had noticed on our journey though, was the inaccuracy of the signposts – not just in Scotland but throughout our trip. One minute the sign to the next village would say 17 miles and the next one would say 16, and the next 19, and so on. It was as though a couple of blokes had gone out and said: 'Well, Bert, I reckon it's about sixteen miles to the next village.'

'Sixteen miles?' says Bert. 'Never. It's not an inch over thirteen miles, that.'

'Do you reckon? Ah well, let's split the difference and call it fourteen and a half miles then.'

'Aye, OK, stick the sign up, then we can get off home.'

For all I know, that is how it happened.

We passed the entrance to the Castle of Mey, which the Queen Mother bought in 1952. She had been visiting a friend in the area – not long after the death of her husband George VI – when she came across it (it was then known as Barrogill Castle). At the time it was semi-derelict and allegedly the family that owned it lived in one room, with sheep occupying the rest. She bought and restored it, and used it as a holiday home, visiting it frequently up until her death in 2002, although she ceased to own it in 1996 when it was gifted to a charitable trust. It is said that under the Queen Mother's ownership money was not wasted on decor or gadgets. According to Ashe Windham, the Queen Mother's equerry at the castle, on one occasion he mentioned the upstairs curtains were falling to bits. The QM replied that she thought that they would last a few more years yet. Windham said that of an evening they would sit around an ancient video machine and rented TV set, watching old episodes of *Fawlty Towers* and *Yes, Minister*. I found this curious, after all the QM was known for her lavish parties and extravagance, not to mention enormous overdraft, but maybe it was the case that, as she allegedly said to her decorator when he suggested reupholstering an armchair, she was too old to bother with that sort of thing.

We were now close to our destination and were feeling very upbeat. Mick was whistling 'Going Home', the theme tune from *Local Hero*. To get to John o'Groats there is a left turn off the A836 at the Seaview Hotel and then it is a gentle downward run into the village. At the corner we stopped. The sign said 'John o'Groats ¼ mile'.

Mick and I looked at each other. 'We've done it Routes,' he said.

I nodded, feeling a bit choked. This journey had been so hard at times. Some nights I had been so tired that I thought there would be no way I would be able to get back in the saddle the next morning. It had pushed me to the limit. It felt such an achievement to have made it.

'Come on,' Mick said, 'let's cycle down together.' So, cycling side by side, with Mick grinning from ear to ear and me wiping snot from my nose onto my sleeve, we arrived at John o'Groats.

And then we got lost. Or at least, we couldn't find the official finish line. I had seen photos of it and knew that, like its counterpart at Land's End, it was painted on the road with 'start' on one side and 'finish' on the other. But we simply could not find it and no one seemed to know what we were talking about. We asked a tour guide waiting for a cycling team coming in, thinking he would be sure to know. He didn't.

'It ends here,' he said, pointing at the small roundabout in the middle of the road.

'No, it certainly does not!' we thought.

We found a couple standing by the pier and asked them, they too looked blank. It was gone six o'clock, the official photographer had gone home and both the shop and the cafe were now closed. The place was rapidly becoming deserted. We took some photos by the ferry wall, but it wasn't the same. Then, finally, just as we were about to give up, we discovered it. We had wandered up to look at the old John o'Groats' Hotel that was derelict and surrounded by security fencing. In front of the old entrance, surrounded by weeds, was the official finish line, painted onto the crumbling tarmac. We crossed the line together and gave ourselves a big pat on the back.

As we were congratulating each other a couple approached us. By now we were the only people about. They were, like us, in their mid-forties.

'Would you like us to take your picture?' the woman asked.

'Oh, yes please,' I said gratefully.

She duly took some snaps of us crossing the finish line. As she handed back the camera she asked casually, 'So, where are you planning to go from here?'

We explained that we would be crossing to Orkney for a few days before cycling back down to catch a plane from Inverness.

'Why don't you stay with us on your way back?' she said. 'We live just a few miles down the road towards Wick.'

The chap with her nodded enthusiastically.

'Yes, we would love it,' he said. 'Here, take our number and promise you will come and stay.'

We fidgeted uncomfortably. We had barely exchanged a few sentences with these people. Why were they asking us to stay with them? We're Brits for God's sake, we need to get to know you for about five years before inviting you to tea. But then the woman gave Mick a long, lingering smile and it finally dawned on me. Well, I suppose there is not a lot to do for entertainment in these parts. We took their number and said goodbye.

'I suppose we could call in on the way back down,' said Mick.

'Not a chance,' I said.

John o'Groats receives around 112,000 visitors per year and it's said the average length of stay is about fifteen minutes. I wondered what people managed do here for as long as that. There was the signpost, I suppose. You could spend two minutes there taking photos. Two minutes to admire the view and another minute to bemoan the state of the derelict John o'Groats House Hotel. The hotel is built next to the site of Jan de Groot's house. De Groot, of course, is the eponymous Dutch ferryman who, in the fifteenth century, ran a ferry from here to Orkney. He is buried in nearby Canisbay. The hotel itself was built in 1875 and is now owned by Heritage Great Britain, which also owns the Land's End visitors' attraction and the Snowdon Mountain Railway, among other things. It's a magnificent gothic building, which would look fantastic if it were restored. There are ambitious and somewhat controversial plans to redevelop John o'Groats, however, this is not the first time plans have been announced and then shelved. OK, that's five minutes. How on earth do people manage to stay as long as fifteen minutes? Lonely Planet famously slated John o'Groats as a 'seedy tourist trap' remarking that 'if John was a person, he'd be a second-hand car salesman or a gerrymandering politician'. I think it's worse than that. If John was a person, he'd be a down-and-out, a vagrant with trousers held up with string, who dimly recalls more prosperous times and harbours vague hopes of better things to come.

Not surprisingly, another piece of advice from our cyclist friends was that we should, on no account, arrange to stay in John o'Groats.

'Cross the line, sign the book and get out of there,' they had advised, having completed the journey a couple of years previously and done precisely that. We also remembered the advice from the man in Golspie and now we could see what they meant.

However, we needed to be in John o'Groats for the ferry at eight-thirty the next morning. Following the suggestion of the couple in Melvich, we were intending to catch the ferry to

Orkney and, given our current state of exhaustion, neither of us was terribly keen on cycling off somewhere and then coming back. Ignoring our friends' advice, we decided to stay in John o'Groats. There was a campsite but we had heard the showers were hopeless and freezing cold, and we wanted a proper bed for the night. So we wandered up to the local hotel, which was full, but they had rooms at their guesthouse over the road. The decor was interesting – peeling period wallpaper from the 1960s and the shower was also a period piece. We got a bit raggy when we discovered the long-life milk was off, and I stalked over the road to the hotel for a jug of the fresh stuff. After a shower and change of clothes we repaired to the bar in the hotel. They had no proper beer on draught, of course. I asked the barmaid which bottled beer they had and she pointed to some bottles of Kronenbourg. Oh dear. Finally, at the back of the shelf she managed to find a few bottles of Orkney Ale gathering dust and we polished them off with an Arran single malt. Then our food arrived. The hotel claimed it served the 'finest succulent food, delicately prepared by our experienced local chef'. The pie was cold and the carrots were clearly from the freezer. We were less than impressed. Still, despite the hotel's shortcomings we felt very pleased with ourselves. We had cycled the length of the country and had clocked up 1,097 miles. We spent the next hour reminiscing about the journey.

'I've wanted to do this trip for the past twenty years,' said Mick. 'It's such a classic. But I didn't want to go on my own and I couldn't find anyone idiotic enough to do it with me.'

'Thanks,' I said.

In truth we were both chuffed to bits. Mick had fulfilled a long-held dream and I had proved to myself that I wasn't a total quitter. And, despite the fact that we were slow and had taken twice as long as most to complete the ride, we now considered ourselves 'proper cyclists'. 'Not that many people,' Mick pointed out 'can say they have seen the entire length of Britain from a bicycle.'

We then proceeded to quiz each other.

'What was your favourite bit?' I asked.

'All of it,' he said promptly.

'You can't choose all of it!' I said, laughing. 'Pick a favourite bit.'

'OK... cycling through the Marches; the hares boxing; the bottom bit of Arran; getting here today... '

'OK, OK, that'll do!'

'Alright, your turn', said Mick.

'The Wye Valley; the view from the Stiperstones and realising there were no more hills for days; the down bits of the Lake District. Worst bit?' I asked.

'The haunted church at Gairlochy. Yours?'

'The brake blocks row,' I said.

'I knew you'd say that! Best pub?'

'Angel at Grosmont. You?'

'Crown at Hesket Newmarket.'

'Best pint?'

This question caused considerable discussion. It was a tricky one; there were so many excellent ones to choose from. In the end, Mick plumped for Proper Job from St Austell, which we'd had in Padstow. I went for Trade Winds from the Cairngorm Brewery, which we'd sampled at Inchree.

'I do blame you, though, for putting a hex on the weather.'

'What do you mean?' asked Mick.

'Your statement,' I said pointing accusingly at him, 'on day one – that we would have no more than four days rain on the entire trip!'

'I know, I got that wrong, didn't I?' said Mick ruefully.

In fact, when we added it up, we had had ten wet days and thirteen dry ones. Seven of the ten wet days had been in Scotland; six of those seven wet days had been on the west coast.

'Hah, so it wasn't *my* fault,' said Mick. 'It was *yours* for taking us on your foolish scenic route. If we'd gone through Edinburgh as I suggested, then we *would* have only had four wet days.'

'Oh, shut up and get us another beer!' I said.

Stats
Miles: 45
Total miles so far: 1,096
Pints of beer (each): 3 bottles
Tasty meals: 0
Offers from swingers: 1
Mutual pats on back: 10,645,230

DAY 24

JOHN O'GROATS
>>>>>>>>>>>>>>>>>>>>>> TO >>>>>>>>>>>>>>>>>>>>>>
KIRKWALL

Breakfast did not improve our impression of the Seaview Hotel. We were served a measly portion of 'full Scottish breakfast', which included the worst sausage I have ever tasted – it would probably qualify as vegetarian, as it appeared to consist entirely of rusk, accompanied by a dayglo orange drink, optimistically described as 'juice'. I went straight for the tea – hopefully they couldn't mess that up.

There were quite a few End-to-Enders in the hotel and Mick, in an effort to strike up a conversation, asked one of them how long he had taken to cycle from Land's End.

'Ten days' he replied proudly.

'Oh, not bad,' said Mick. This comment, where we come from, translates literally as 'not bad', i.e. good. The chap did not take it in this spirit, however, understanding it to be something of a slight or a put down.

'Not bad?' he repeated incredulously. 'How long did you take then?'

'Um, twenty-three days,' said Mick.

'Oh, really?' said the cyclist. '*Not bad* yourself, then.'

He stalked off towards the cereal bar – he was probably very tired, we thought, charitably. But we didn't try to start a conversation with anyone else after that. Instead we spent some more time congratulating ourselves on our achievement – over 1,000 miles in twenty-three days was not that bad for two middle-aged, out-of-condition cyclists, we thought with satisfaction.

My thoughts turned to what we would do next. I had calculated that three days should be ample for the ride south to Inverness, via Wick, a distance of about 115 miles. This left us with four days to visit Orkney. Mick had been non-committal about the proposal. 'I don't care where we go,' he said, 'as long as it's got a shower and a decent pint. I think I've earned them.'

When we had resentfully settled the undeservedly large bill for the hotel, we headed for the jetty, where the boat to Orkney was waiting, and hoisted our bikes on board.

Soon we were steaming away from the mainland, across the Pentland Firth to Orkney. I relaxed on deck, enjoying the warmth of the sun on my face and breathing in the fresh, salty air. Mick stood against the rails, peering out to sea, hoping for a glimpse of a minke whale or an orca, both of which can be seen in these waters. As we passed Stroma, the sea swirled alarmingly around the boat. The Pentland Firth, the piece of water that squeezes between the Scottish mainland and the southernmost islands of Orkney, has a fearsome reputation, with some of the fastest currents in the world, reportedly reaching up to 12 knots (18 mph for landlubbers). No wonder there are plans to harness some of the colossal energy that these flows generate.

As we drew near to Orkney, with the island of Hoy on our left, it was a shame that the impressive sea stack known as the Old

Man of Hoy was hidden from view coming this way. We came in to dock at the busy metropolis of Burwick, at the bottom of the southernmost island, South Ronaldsay. Well, it had a toilet. Which, on closer inspection, proved to be closed. Unfortunately, therefore, our first act on landing on Orkney was to pee furtively behind the toilet block. Rather ignominious, but couldn't be helped – needs must and all that. Apart from the toilet and the car park there was nothing much else at Burwick as far as we could see.

We asked for directions to Kirkwall from the coach driver who was busy loading every other passenger from the ferry except us onto his vehicle.

'There's only one road,' he said, pointing north. 'Kirkwall's that way. It's a long way, though.'

'How far?' we asked.

'About twenty miles north from here,' he said.

We laughed.

'Oh, ho,' we scoffed. 'Twenty miles? That's nothing, we've cycled here from Land's End.'

The coach driver, who was now grabbing a last chance for a smoke before driving his charges up to Kirkwall, was suitably impressed. We swelled with pride. We were ace cyclists once more – at least in this man's eyes. Farther up the road, as we paused for a photo by the Welcome to Orkney sign, the coach went by. We guessed by the number of passengers that waved to us, that the driver had passed on the tale of our feat and we waved jovially back. Luckily, they were not there to see us cycle around the corner, swear loudly at the sight of the hill in front of us and promptly get off and push.

We stopped at St Margaret's Hope, known locally as the Hope or the Hup, for a break. Who Margaret was isn't certain. It could refer to Margaret, the wife of Malcolm III, who died in 1093 and was canonised in 1250; or Margaret could refer to Margaret, daughter of King Erik of Norway, who was despatched in 1290, aged seven, from Bergen, bound for Scotland where she was due to marry the young Edward, heir to the English throne. Storms blew the ship off course and they eventually landed at St Margaret's Hope where the poor child died, apparently of seasickness. She was the last of the House of Dunkeld, the dynasty that had ruled Scotland since 1058. If Margaret had survived then the crowns of England and Scotland would have been united 300 years earlier than they actually were, and Scottish history would have been very different.

We found a little cafe where, over a cup of coffee and some superlative cheesecake, the owner told us, in a lovely lilting accent, that she was Orcadian but that many of the 20,000 on Orkney were incomers.

'I call them two-season tourists,' she said. 'They don't stay. They come for a holiday in the summer and then move here, but the winter soon sees them off.'

She laughed.

'The incomers can't do the winters,' she said. 'The wind drives them out. It's always windy. And it's often dark by two in the afternoon. They can't stand it.'

I could see that winter on Orkney would be quite a different prospect to two weeks in the summer. And we had already experienced the wind that had been gusting around us ever since we arrived. It is so windy that there are practically no trees on Orkney, even the vegetation hunkers down up here. It is said that women on Orkney have two hairstyles: a 'wind from the south' style or 'wind from the north' style.

The main town, Kirkwall, where we were headed, is on the Mainland, the largest of the seventy or so islands and skerries that make up Orkney, although only sixteen of them are inhabited. Between us and the Mainland lay the islands of Burray, Glims Holm and Lamb Holm. Crossing between islands was not a problem, however, as there is a causeway that links them all, as a result of an incident at the start of the World War Two.

In 1939, HMS *Royal Oak* was moored in Scapa Flow, the natural harbour in the centre of the Orkney Islands. On 14 October, barely a month after war had been declared, *U-Boat U47*, under the command of Gunther Prien, silently entered the harbour and torpedoed the *Royal Oak* before exiting the way it had come in. There was a huge explosion and the ship sank within minutes. More than 800 of the 1,200-man crew were killed, 120 of them boys under the age of eighteen. In Germany, Prien acquired the nickname Der Stier von Scapa Flow or the Bull of Scapa Flow. The attack badly shook the British who had considered the Flow to be impregnable. Within a month, Churchill had visited Orkney and ordered the construction of four permanent barriers to block the eastern entrance into Scapa Flow. The construction took four and a half years and the barriers were completed in September 1944, with rather unfortunate timing – they were finally officially opened on 12 May 1945, two weeks after Hitler committed suicide and four days after VE Day. It does mean, however, that the southern islands of Orkney are now linked to the Mainland by one road that crosses the four Churchill Barriers.

From South Ronaldsay we crossed Barrier No. 4 to Burray. Along the eastern side of Burray is Bu Sands, a lovely long and sandy beach backed by sand dunes where we stopped for a while and took our hot and smelly feet out for an airing.

A group of schoolchildren were having an al fresco lesson on the beach, I wondered whether the stultifying health and safety requirements that afflicted schools in England were less draconian here. In Bristol it is barely possible to take children for a walk in the local park without months of form filling, police checks, and other ridiculous and pointless bureaucracy.

Barrier No. 3, across Weddel Sound, links Burray with the small island of Glims Holm. In the water just next to the causeway is the arresting sight of the brown upturned hull of *The Reginald*, a schooner that was sunk as a blockship in the sound in 1915. To our left we could see the hulls of other wrecks just protruding from the water.

As we crossed the island of Lamb Holm, we came upon a statue of St George fashioned out of concrete. Behind the statue, and set back some way, was an odd-looking structure. Painted white and red, topped with a bell and decorated with a carving of the head of Christ, it looks exactly like a Mediterranean church, and we wondered how it came to be built all the way up here. Viewed sideways on, it is even more surprising as it then becomes obvious that the front is a facade and the building is actually two Nissen huts joined together.

The chapel was built by Italian prisoners of war, 550 of whom were held at a camp here, having been captured in North Africa in 1942, with a further 800 housed in camps on Burray. The prisoners were moved here to work on building those barriers that Churchill had ordered. This was a bit dodgy, as using prisoners of war for work connected to the war effort was banned by the Geneva Conventions. Churchill claimed that the main purpose of the barriers was improvement to communications to the southern Orkney Islands, rather than for the war effort and, after some complaints, the prisoners agreed to carry out the work.

The Italian prisoners were an imaginative lot it seems. Deprived of entertainment, and no doubt needing some distraction to get them through the long nights of an Orcadian winter, they set about making their own. They created elaborate theatre sets and performed operettas, and they constructed a bowling alley made of concrete, as well as a concrete billiard table, complete with concrete balls.

Being Catholic, many prisoners also wanted a church and after making representations, the camp commandant and the prisoner's chaplain agreed the prisoners should have one. The prisoners decorated it and what a superb job they made of it, creating a stunningly beautiful interior.

Most amazing of all is the painting, created by Domenico Chiocchetti. Chiocchetti painted the walls and ceiling with *trompe l'oeil* brickwork and frescoes. Behind the altar he painted a beautiful Madonna and child. The baby Jesus is holding an olive branch and one of two cherubs below the Madonna is placing a sword in a sheath. Both images were intended to symbolise peace. The other cherub is holding a shield with the heraldic badge of Moena, Chiocchetti's home town. He became so involved with his work that even after the camp was disbanded he stayed behind for some weeks to complete it.

Over the years some of the prisoners of war have returned to Orkney. One of them, Bruno Volpi, on a visit in 1992, explained that 'in spite of being trapped in a barbed wire camp, down in spirit, physically and morally deprived of many things', they could still find 'something inside that could be set free'.

The chapel is one of the most visited monuments on Orkney, a remarkable symbol of hope and reconciliation.

Next door to the Italian chapel was the Orkney Wine Shop, run by Emile, a Dutchman who moved to Orkney a decade ago. He started making fruit wine as a hobby and the business has grown from there. He told us that he never uses preservatives or sulphites in his wine, sulphites being commonly used by commercial wine producers to halt the fermentation process. Instead, fermentation is allowed to stop naturally, thereby producing wine that is stronger in alcohol content than usual and is also completely free of additives. A double plus! We had an enjoyable hour trying all the wines that were available, some of them twice, just to make sure. We bought a case and asked him to send them on to Bristol as we felt that carrying twelve bottles of wine might slow us up even more. From Lamb Holm we crossed the final barrier, Barrier No. 1, to the Mainland and peddled the last few miles to the little town that is Orkney's capital.

Kirkwall, from the Norse Kirkjuvagr meaning Church Bay, feels as much a Scandinavian town as a Scottish one. Narrow streets snake away from the harbour, lined with grey houses with small windows; like the vegetation, the buildings look like they are used to lying low to avoid the weather. Many places were flying the new Orkney flag, a blue and yellow cross on a red background. The flag was introduced in 2007, but not without controversy, the previous 'unofficial' St Magnus flag of a red cross on a yellow background was deemed by the Lord Lyon, King of Arms in Scotland as being too similar to the old arms of the Kingdom of Ulster. The St Magnus flag was therefore not included in the options when Orcadians voted for a choice of flag design. The new flag is very reminiscent of Scandinavian flags. I suppose it's not so surprising, Kirkwall is nearer to Bergen than Edinburgh and centuries of Viking rule have left its mark. Once Orkney had been a base for people with very scary names to launch attacks on Scotland and northern England – people like Sigurd the Mighty,

Eric Bloodaxe and Thorfinn Skullsplitter, 7th Viking Earl of Orkney. No one knows whose skull was split to earn this epithet, but I bet it hurt.

We remembered the advice we had received in Melvich and looked for the Pickaquoy Centre. We soon found it, and were immediately impressed.

The complex includes a large campsite, leisure centre, cafebar, a cinema and a concert hall. It was by far the best camping facility we had come across. I thought ruefully of the campsite at John o'Groats that we had spurned. Why couldn't it have been more like this one? We immediately decided to make Pickaquoy our base for a few days and booked in at the reception, before going down to the adjacent campsite to pitch our tent. A ladies' hockey match was in progress on the all-weather pitch, I didn't see why we had to put our tent right next to the fence, but Mick said something about the hedge sheltering us from the wind and so I reluctantly agreed. I then couldn't get him to concentrate on the job in hand of unpacking and setting up the tent, he kept saying he needed a rest after all that cycling. He cracked open a bottle of beer and sat down on the grass, facing the hockey pitch.

'Why don't you go and check out the washroom facilities?' he suggested.

Gaining entry to the wash block was a challenge, there was a complicated code system on the door, but once inside I was immediately impressed. The brand-new building included kitchens, washing machines and dryers, a large lounge and rows of lovely hot showers.

When I had showered and dragged Mick away from the hockey match, we wandered down to the harbour. It was eight in the evening and in May there was still plenty of light. We came upon a bar called Helgi's, which had a Nordic theme, a beautiful Orkney slate floor and an unusual menu. I wondered what Rabbie Burns would have made of haggis lasagne, but it was very nice, especially when washed down with some excellent Scapa Special beer from the Highland Brewing Company. The brewery is based in Swannay, right at the top of the mainland, and the beer was fabulous: a golden pale ale with a malty flavour – it really was quite delicious. It was the first decent draught pint we had found since the pint of Black Cuillin, the- stout-that-wasn't-a-stout in Fort Augustus, four days and more than 200 miles away. We sat for a couple of hours over the good food and beer, reminiscing about our journey. This was more like it!

>>>>>>>>>>>>>>>>>>>>>>>>>>>>

Stats
Miles: 26
Total miles: 1,122
Pints of beer (each): 3
Islands visited: 5
Stroppy tired cyclists: 1 (not us)

>>>>>>>>>>>>>>>>>>>>>>>>>>>>

KIRKWALL

〉〉〉〉〉〉〉〉〉〉〉〉〉〉〉〉〉〉〉〉〉〉〉〉〉〉

By now our clothes were in a pretty disgusting state. Apart from the occasional rinsing-out of cycling shorts, none of our clothes had been washed properly since we left Bristol twenty days ago, unless you count the regular dousings with Scottish rain. So we allocated today as a rest, recuperation and wash day, making use of the washing machine and dryer on site. After a morning of laundry and leisurely ablutions, we bought some food for lunch in one of the nearby supermarkets and then devoted the afternoon to sightseeing around Kirkwall. We took a look first at St Magnus Cathedral, which stands on the main street, dominating the surrounding buildings. I liked this one very much. It is constructed in a lovely pink sandstone, which gives it warmth, and is beautifully elegant. The new stained-glass window, designed by Crear McCartney and installed in 1987 to commemorate 850 years of the cathedral, was stunning.

The cathedral was founded in 1137 by Earl Rögnvald, in memory of his uncle Magnus who had been joint ruler of Orkney in the twelfth century, when Orkney was part of the Scandinavian empire. Magnus had a sort of job-share arrangement with his cousin, Earl Hakon. Their respective followers did not exactly get along and so, in around 1117, Hakon got his cook to kill Magnus with a blow to the head with his axe, a favourite Viking technique. When Rögnvald claimed his half share twenty years later, he began work on the 'church of stone' in memory of his murdered uncle, interring Magnus' remains in one of the columns of the cathedral. In 1919, during renovation work in the cathedral, a wooden box was found containing human bones, including a skull with very obvious injuries (i.e., a bloody big hole in it). It is likely that these are the bones of poor Magnus.

Here's a piece of trivia for you: in 1997 St Magnus Cathedral was the setting for the last ever episode of *Mastermind*, hosted by Magnus Magnusson. When I was a kid in the mid-1970s, Sunday nights were synonymous with *Mastermind*. My mum would wheel in plates of sandwiches and cakes on her gold hostess trolley, and we would all settle in front of the telly to watch it. I loved the dramatic theme tune and the dreaded black chair, spot-lit in the middle of the room. Bill Wright, the producer, drew on his experiences of being interrogated as a prisoner of war to create the programme, and whilst Magnus was a rather kindly interrogator, it was entertaining watching the contestants quake as they made their way to the chair.

In the specialist knowledge rounds, of course, we didn't have a chance. They would always be on really obscure topics: World War Two campaigns in north Italy, the life cycle and habits of the honeybee, the postal history of Southern Africa (I'm not making these up!). We wouldn't have a clue what any of the answers were. The entertainment came in enjoying watching the contestants crack up after a row of wrong answers, as they became gibbering wrecks, lisping 'pass' to every subsequent question.

Then came the general knowledge rounds. This time we at least had a hope of answering a question. Occasionally one of us would think we knew the answer and would triumphantly shout it out, only to look crestfallen when proved to be completely wrong. If we collectively answered two questions correctly in an episode we considered we were doing extremely well. Amongst the real contestants, this round sorted out those who could swot up on a subject from those who genuinely knew a lot of random stuff. Occasionally someone who had done really badly in the specialist round would sparkle with confidence as they answered every question correctly in the general knowledge round but, more often than not, the experience of complete and utter collapse in confidence in round one would result in another dreadful performance in round two, before the crushing embarrassment of the final results being read out. It was brilliant.

After we had finished with the cathedral we stuck our heads into The Orkney Museum. After an hour, Mick was still studying some ancient artefacts in detail and I was starting to feel bored. I left him to it and had a wander around some of the shops. Orkney has a highly developed art and craft industry, and I enjoyed looking at some of the work produced by local artists. Silver jewellery appeared to be a speciality, with local designers producing some really exquisite pieces. There was a plethora of other local work, too: knitwear, ceramics, furniture and textiles, including the Orkney chair, a high-backed design made from wood and straw. Many of the pieces took inspiration from Orkney's Nordic heritage and from the sea and shores of the islands.

When Mick had finally had his fill of ancient artefacts, we wandered up the hill to the Highland Park Distillery. The collection of old grey slate buildings that make up the distillery is attractive, with the towers topped by the distinctive distillery pagodas. The distillery is said to have been founded by Magnus (Mansie) Eunson in 1798. Like many people on Orkney, he had more than one job, being a butcher and a beadle by day and a smuggler by night, illegally distilling whisky at his bothy on the common land above Kirkwall. The story is that Mansie was known for his sense of humour and his ability to get himself out of the stickiest of situations. One day, hearing that customs officials were on their way, he covered the illegal barrels of whisky with a white cloth. When the officials came to the house they were greeted by a group of people gathered around what appeared to be a coffin, holding prayer books and wailing, while Mansie knelt at the head with a bible in his hand. One of the attendants whispered 'smallpox' to the officials, who thereupon left the house pretty sharpish, without discovering the barrels underneath the 'coffin'.

There were only four of us on the distillery tour, the other two were a couple from Shropshire. When we told them we were from Bristol they said, 'Gosh, that's quite a drive, we thought we had a driven a long way but that's even further.'

Hurrah! We had another chance to show off!

'Oh,' we said nonchalantly, 'we didn't drive, we cycled.'

'What, from Bristol?' was the (as we had hoped) amazed response.

'No,' (airily) 'from Land's End.'

'What??? You are kidding!'

We basked in the glory for a while, before the tour guide dragged us back to the topic in hand. We enjoyed the tour very much, although we were not persuaded to buy a bottle of the 45-year-old special edition at £900 a bottle. Maybe next time. Instead we enjoyed a sip of the 12-year-old malt which was included in the ticket price.

Returning to the town, we decided to try the bar at one of the hotels. We asked for two pints of Red McGregor from Orkney Brewery. The barmaid pulled a pint and then said she was sorry, there was only enough in the barrel for another half a pint, which she served me, evidently the dregs of the barrel. She charged us £5 as the bar priced half a pint at £1.90; a pint cost £3.10. I may have only scraped O level maths grade C, but even I know that half of £3.10 is not £1.90. I resented being charged a premium for only having a half, especially as it was not my choice. *And* it was beer that should not have been given away let alone sold at a premium price. To cap it all there was a very drunk exile from Bristol at the bar.

'What am I doing here?' he boomed, answering a non-existent question. 'I'll tell you what I'm doing here! I cycled here and then my bloody chain broke!'

We smiled through gritted teeth, complained about the beer, got our money back, and repaired to our usual haunt of Helgi's on the harbour front. Later, I mentioned to Mick that I would like to try a seafood restaurant while we were in Orkney. Mick said he knew just the place. When he showed me the restaurant he had in mind I was slightly less enthusiastic. It had 'fish and chips' in red flashing neon letters on the window. It was good, though, the chips weren't greasy and I have never had a haggis burger before.

After we had eaten we wandered back to the campsite, walking round the Peedie Sea, a body of water behind the breakwater, which looks like an oversized boating lake. We crawled into our sleeping bags and, as usual, I had barely laid my head on my blow-up pillow before I was asleep. One thing that had not been an issue on this trip was insomnia.

≫≫≫≫≫≫≫≫≫≫≫≫≫≫≫≫≫

Stats
Miles: 0
Total miles: 1,117
Pints of beer (each): 3
Undrinkable pints of beer: 1½
Haggis burgers: 1

≫≫≫≫≫≫≫≫≫≫≫≫≫≫≫≫≫

AROUND ORKNEY

》》》》》》》》》》》》》》》》》》》》》》

Sometimes, as Mick pointed out later, I just don't know when enough is enough. The day had been planned as another day of rest and recuperation – but, no, I had to go and plan a 40-mile round-trip around West Mainland. It was noticeably colder and much windier than the previous day, and within half a mile of leaving the campsite I soon realised shorts and a T-shirt was hopelessly optimistic attire, and quickly donned every item of clothing in my pannier. On the upside, all that was then left in the bag were two salmon rolls and a banana – a welcome reduction in weight after lugging all our gear up the country.

We headed out of Kirkwall towards Scapa village, where a long stretch of pink-and-white sand separated the road from the waters of Scapa Bay. We had optimistically assumed we would be able to get a cuppa along the way but we passed nothing but small hamlets until Stromness, where we headed purposefully for the nearest cafe before exploring the town. With its straggling streets and grey buildings crowding round the harbour, Stromness felt like a hardier cousin of St Ives. The St Ives comparison was reinforced when we came across the new Pier Arts Centre, which occupied a very modern and striking building on the main street, and which houses a permanent collection of work by the St Ives School. Behind the main street, which runs parallel to the harbour, smaller streets and lanes, with curious names such as Khyber Pass and Hellihole Road, crept up the hillside of Brinkies Brae, the granite hill behind the town.

There were plenty of blue plaques indicating houses of interest. One marked the birthplace of Eliza Fraser, who married Captain James Fraser. In 1836 they had left Sydney bound for Singapore on a brig named *The Stirling Castle* when they were shipwrecked on a reef. They managed to get in lifeboats to K'Gari, a sand island (the largest sand island in the world, in fact). James Fraser died, according to Eliza, he was speared by one of the aborigines who took them prisoner. Other accounts tell a different story, and state the native people were, in fact, trying to help the hapless Europeans. In any event, when Eliza got back to Britain a year later she gained huge publicity, sympathy and money from her increasingly lurid accounts of her ordeal – and the island they had landed on was renamed Fraser Island. Down the road from Eliza Fraser's place was Mrs Humphrey's House, which during 1835–36 had apparently been a temporary hospital for 'scurvy-ridden whale men who had been trapped in the ice for months'. Conditions were obviously pretty harsh back then.

Many of the houses in Kirkwall have a low-slung, Scandinavian look to them. Slightly unnervingly, a few of the houses also had whalebones nailed above windows and doorframes, another reminder of the importance of whaling to the town's history. Whaling fleets often recruited from the local population, finding the Orkney men to be hard-working and able to adapt to the harsh conditions of northern Canada, and the Hudson Bay

Company recruited most of their labour here before crossing to North America.

Stromness has a namesake, Stromness whaling station, established in 1912 at South Georgia in the Falkland Islands, taking its name from the Orcadian town. It was the southern Stromness that Ernest Shackleton and two of his men staggered into with matted hair and tattered clothes, having crossed the inhospitable island following the shipwreck of *Endurance*. Eventually, three months later, all the shipwrecked men were rescued from Elephant Island, after waiting for 105 days for help to arrive. It was a feat of the utmost endurance and the fact everyone was saved helped turn Shackleton's epic rescue mission into the stuff of legend.

Back in Orkney's Stromness, we were reminded of another story of endurance when we came across Raes Close. At the bottom of the road is a plaque, which reads: 'The Orcadian Arctic explorer John Rae, in 1854, discovered Rae Strait (the last link in the Northwest Passage) and the tragic fate of the Franklin Expedition'. Like Shackleton's, Franklin's expedition is a tale of hardship and endurance in horrendous conditions, not in the icy seas near the South Pole however, but in the equally treacherous ice of the north. This one did not have such a happy ending, though.

Sir John Franklin had set off from Orkney on 19 May 1845 in command of two ships, *Terror* and *Erebus*, on an expedition to find the Northwest Passage. They became trapped in the ice for two full winters. Then they disappeared.

In 1854, John Rae, an Orcadian from Clestrain, just across the bay from Stromness, was given some information by local Inuit about the fate of the expedition while surveying the area for the Hudson Bay Company. They told him they had come across a party of white men who had died of starvation. Rae also reported the Inuit had told him that in the last stages of starvation the surviving crew had resorted to cannibalism, a suggestion which was greeted with outrage back in Britain. Forensic examination of bones discovered more recently shows the Inuit reports of cannibalism were correct and a recent theory is that lead in the newly introduced canned food or in the ship's water system was a factor in the disaster, poisoning and fatally weakening the crew. In the 1980s three crew members who died early in the expedition were exhumed and examined. Due to the extreme icy conditions the bodies were perfectly preserved, with skin, hair, eyes and teeth all intact. The National Maritime Museum in London has various artefacts from the doomed expedition, including a sea boot found at the poignantly named Starvation Cove – the farthest point that men from the expedition reached. Nowadays things are very different, of course. TV crews follow Ben Fogle and James Cracknell across the Antarctic, and tour companies offer trips to the Arctic. Expeditions certainly aren't what they used to be.

We left Stromness and continued heading north. On a whim we took a left turn and headed down the coast road to Yesnaby. The road terminated at a small car park where there were the remains of some World War Two observation posts. Leaving the bikes and walking south along the clifftops, we were rewarded with the most dramatic scenery. Magnificent cliffs made up of layer upon layer of golden sandstone plunged into the sea, repeatedly pummelled by waves crashing in from the Atlantic, and guillemots whistled shrilly from the far cliffs. Farther along was 'the Castle', an impressive sea stack which is often used as a practice run for climbers preparing to tackle the Old Man of Hoy, an even more impressive sea stack. We could see the Old Man in the distance, just sticking out from the cliffs.

By now the wind was beginning to pick up. This was relative as it never really stops here. I had mistimed the day – we weren't going to make the next destination, the Neolithic site of Scara Brae, it would be closed by the time we got there. I suggested heading north anyway as I wanted a picture of Mick stood next to the road sign for Twatt, a small settlement a few miles farther on. (Twatt is from Old Norse and means 'a parcel of land'). Mick did not think this a good reason to add a further 20 miles to our journey (he said something quite rude which I won't repeat), so instead we headed south-east back to Kirkwall. We were on what was, even for Orkney, a minor road, with a loch to either side of us – to our left, the Loch of Harray and on our right, the Loch of Stenness. Suddenly, on our right, on slightly higher ground, we saw the Ring of Brodgar, a huge Neolithic circle of standing stones. We pulled into the car park and followed the path up to the ring itself, which had no entry fee or obvious restrictions.

Stonehenge, which I would classify as one of the most disappointing attractions in the country, could learn something here. Managed by English Heritage, Stonehenge costs an eye-watering £7.50 per adult to visit. You pay at the 'visitors' centre', put up in 1968 as a temporary measure. You then traipse under the busy road where you follow a roped-off walkway around the edge of the stones, which you look at, from a distance, barely closer than if you had just stood at the perimeter fence and saved yourself a few quid. You try and feel impressed when actually you are rather bored. It's no wonder that Stonehenge regularly figures top of the list of the country's most disappointing attractions. Locally, the lesser-visited Avebury, and the practically ignored Stanton Drew stone circles are much more satisfying places to visit. At Stonehenge the long talked about visitors' centre and re-routing of the roads never happens, despite having been discussed for the past forty years. Just lately the government has announced the latest plan for a £25 million visitors' centre at Stonehenge has been axed and senior druid King Arthur Pendragon, who has long campaigned for better care to be taken of the site, expressed his concern that Stonehenge should not become reliant on commercial funding.

'I don't want to see Americans going back in 2012 with T-shirts saying, "I've been to McDonald's, Stonehenge",' he said. Remembering my dismay when I saw, opposite the Great Sphinx at Giza, a branch of Pizza Hut, I am inclined to agree with Mr Pendragon. However, there is no doubt that Stonehenge could do with some improvements to the visitor experience.

Back in Orkney, all was peaceful and quiet. It was gone seven now and there was no one else, except us, wandering among the stones. The stones stood like sentries, silhouetted against the evening sky, while behind them the water of the loch glistened. Twenty-seven stones are apparently still standing, although I confess I didn't count them. It is thought they were erected between 2500 and 2000 BC – for what purpose, nobody really knows.

Mick, having no soul, was unmoved. 'I can feel the energy, the power, the mysticism!' he mocked.

We carried on down the road for about a mile, crossing a causeway across the bottom of the lochs to another group of megaliths, the Standing Stones of Stenness, comprising four huge stones, although it is thought there were once twelve. The area, known as the Heart of Neolithic Orkney is a UNESCO World Heritage Site, and is one of the most important Neolithic sites in western Europe. Until 1814, there was a significant megalith, just to the north of the Standing Stones of Stenness, known as the Odin Stone. It was thought to be around 3,000 years old, and was believed to be the site of ancient ceremonies on Orkney. Large numbers of people used to visit the stones and the farmer, an incomer or 'ferrylouper' by the name of Captain W. Mackay, objected to people coming onto his land. He proceeded to destroy the Odin stone by pulling it down and breaking it up with hammers. Outraged, the locals tried twice to burn his house down, but he managed to topple one of the Stenness Stones and destroy another, before a court order finally stopped him.

The cycle back to Kirkwall was difficult. The wind was really whipping in from the east now, making it difficult to make progress. Suddenly I realised how very tired I was. We took a breather in a bus shelter where Mick expressed his opinion of my touring route by screwing up the map and throwing it away.

'OK,' I conceded. 'Tomorrow we will *definitely* rest.'

That evening as we sat in the bar at Helgi's with a pint of our usual Scapa Special Mick said he was putting his foot down. 'No more,' he said firmly, 'I mean it.'

I looked at him aghast. 'No more?' I said. 'But we've only had one pint!'

'No, you idiot! No cycling tomorrow. I've had enough. Oh and by the way.'

'What?'

'It's your round.'

Stats
Miles: 46
Total miles: 1,168
Pints of beer (each): 4
Ruined maps: 1
Stroppy, tired cyclists: 2 (us)

REST DAY

》》》》》》》》》》》》》》》》》》》》》》》》》

Having decided we would definitely do nothing today (and after consuming rather too many beers in Helgi's last night) I didn't wake up until gone ten, when the shrieks from the playing field finally penetrated my alcohol-induced stupor. Mick was still giving it zeds, snoring away contentedly, so I crept out of the tent and, after some luxurious ablutions in the wash block, I wandered up to the cafe at the leisure centre next door.

Relaxing in an armchair with my third pot of tea and a newspaper, I reflected that Mick had been right to insist he was not doing anything today. My problem is I'm always worried I'll miss something, that when we get home someone will say: 'Oh didn't you see such-and-such, it's the best thing in Scotland.'

It dawned on me that Mick and I had come to Orkney with completely different ideas of what we would do here. I had switched into full sightseeing mode, whereas Mick just wanted to sit around for a few days in a place that wasn't John o'Groats.

I now realised he was right; I was so awfully tired that I would not in my present condition be able to do justice to anywhere we might visit. Today you could have plonked me at the most amazing place in the world; Tutankhamun's tomb, a beach on Bora Bora, the temple at Angkor Wat, and I would have yawned and said something like: 'Yeah well, when you've seen one temple you've seen them all, if you don't mind I'm just off for a little nap.'

As Alain de Botton observed in *The Art of Travel*, our mood colours our perception of the places we visit and we cannot help but allow our inner mind to impinge on the experience. If we are tired the place seems to pall, and if we are vexed the place we are in seems to lose its shine. And no matter what we do, we cannot but help bring ourselves with us when we travel, with all our worries, anxieties and niggles. That is why travelling is never as 'pure' as we think it will be. After a disappointing trip to Barbados, Botton comments: 'I had inadvertently brought myself with me to the island.'

In my case I had inadvertently brought myself on an 1,100-mile cycle ride, when I should have brought someone who was at least ten years younger, ten times fitter and much less grumpy when confronted with a hill.

Mick finally appeared, yawning and rubbing his eyes. We lounged around in the cafe at the leisure centre for another hour or so, reading some more papers, before walking the short distance into the centre of Kirkwall. Once there, we whiled away another couple of hours in the old town hall, opposite the cathedral, which had now been converted into a community cafe and offered excellent-value meals.

'Now this,' said Mick, after he had eaten, leaning back into the sofa with his hands behind his head and legs outstretched in front of him, 'this is a *proper* rest day.'

'Another pot of tea?' I said.

Stats
Miles cycled: 0
Total miles: 1,168
Pints of beer (each): 2
Cups of coffee: 5
Cups of tea: 10
Papers read: 4

DAY 28

KIRKWALL

>>>>>>>>>>>>>>>>>>>>>>> TO >>>>>>>>>>>>>>>>>>>>>>>

ST MARGARET'S HOPE

Today was my birthday, so I treated myself to a bit of a lie-in. We only had to get ourselves back to St Margaret's Hope today, where we planned to stay in a bed and breakfast, before heading back to South Ronaldsay to catch the ferry to John o'Groats and start heading home.

We struggled against the wind down the Mainland. At St Mary's, at the bottom of the Mainland and just before the causeway over to the next island of Lamb Holm, the road swung east and we came to a complete stop. It was impossible to cycle, so we pushed the bikes for a while, heads down against the blasts. It took us a good few hours to get back to St Margaret's Hope and I arrived sporting a 'wind from the south' hairstyle.

I thought it a little odd that Mick suggested I take a look around the village while he went on to the cafe; when I got there I realised that he had, with the connivance of the cafe owner, loaded up a huge slice of her superlative cheesecake with as many candles as the cake would hold. The two of them then proceeded to sing a memorable rendition of 'Happy Birthday'. Mick, now in full showing-off mode, then announced his intention to take me out for a meal at the Creel that evening. The cafe owner, who had evidently sized him up pretty well from our two brief visits, laughed.

'You can't afford that, boy,' she said, 'that's too rich for you.'

The Creel was one of the best, if not the best, restaurant on Orkney, renowned for its superb seafood. Mick took up the challenge.

'You wanna bet? I'm off to book it right now.'

We did go to the Creel, and the seafood was superb; queen scallops followed by monkfish and squid casserole, washed down with a superb bottle of wine. Whether Mick was secretly crying when he got the bill, I don't know, as I had discreetly stepped outside to avoid causing him any embarrassment, and I know he would have gallantly refused any offer of mine to help him out with the bill. Wouldn't he? Anyway, it was a fantastic birthday. Tomorrow we would be leaving Orkney and heading home and tonight's celebration was the perfect finish to our travels up the country.

>>>>>>>>>>>>>>>>>>>>>>>>>>>>

Stats
Miles: 18
Total miles: 1,186
Pints of beer (each): 0
Expensive bottles of wine: 1
Slices of birthday cheesecake: 1

>>>>>>>>>>>>>>>>>>>>>>>>>>>>

DAY
29

ST MARGARET'S HOPE
TO
THURSO

At breakfast I mentioned to our host at the B & B that we were intending to head back down to Burwick to catch the ferry back to John o'Groats.

'Och, the ferry will not be out today,' she said. 'It's graying right up.'

She turned to ask her brother.

'Is the ferry running today, Robert?' she asked him.

Robert expressed his doubts but kindly got on the phone to the ferry company who confirmed the John o'Groats ferry was indeed suspended due to bad weather.

We were dismayed until he explained we could take the new catamaran from the Hope back to the Scottish mainland. We were eternally grateful for their advice; we would not have been best pleased had we cycled to the other end of the island to wait for a non-existent ferry.

As we headed down to the quay we were sidetracked by a sign which said 'Coffee Morning' – and suddenly found ourselves in the midst of a Liberal Democrat fundraising event. I asked whether the MP had come out of the expenses scandal unscathed.

'Oh, yes,' said the woman at the cake counter, 'Our MP has not had his nose in the trough. Unlike some of them,' she added scornfully.

Mick, however, definitely had his nose in the trough. While she had been talking to me he had taken the opportunity to surreptitiously fill his pockets with home-made cakes and biscuits.

We left the Lib Dems and cycled around the harbour to the ferry terminal, where a very fancy red and white catamaran was waiting. MV *Pentalina* was a brand new craft operated by Pentland Ferries. She had recently been brought to Orkney from the Philippines to replace the aging *Pentalina-B*. The bed and breakfast owner had remarked that unlike NorthLink and Caledonian-MacBrayne Ferries, which receive millions of pounds in state subsidies, Pentland Ferries receives no public funding at all, having to finance the ferries and any dock improvements at the St Gills terminal themselves. This was understandably an issue of some resentment for the residents here.

We embarked, trying not to be too concerned about the lashing down of vehicles that was taking place on the car deck as we pushed our bikes past. One of the crew came and took our bikes away, and tied them firmly to one of the rails. As we crossed the Pentland Firth the boat lifted and fell in the swell, up and down, up and down. I didn't feel at all well and was already regretting having consumed quite so many stolen cakes. Meanwhile, Mick had turned an interesting shade of green. I looked around the lounge, but the other passengers seemed unconcerned that we would surely all be floundering at the bottom of the sea in a matter of moments. They read the paper or dozed a little, blissfully unconcerned and apparently not experiencing the turmoil that at that moment was taking place in my intestines. We didn't sink of course and as the boat was so fast the journey took little more than forty-five minutes. We staggered off the boat at the other end and sat on the dockside for a while to compose ourselves.

We had docked at Gills Bay, which is only about 4 miles west of John o'Groats. We decided to cycle back there to claim a refund for our return ticket on the ferry that had not run. Fourteen quid each was not an amount to be easily forsaken, after all that's four pints of beer each. We would then head down the coast to Wick and on to Inverness. It would also give us a chance to see John o'Groats when it was open, just in case we hadn't given it a fair chance the first time.

When we got there I went to the ferry ticket office to get our refund while Mick went off to use the toilet. He came back in a bad mood. Apparently there was a twenty pence charge to use the toilet, which he didn't have as I had all the money. He had told the attendant that if he was refused entry to the toilet he would have no choice but to urinate on the wall, as he was desperate. The attendant had let him use the facilities free of charge, although he was far from happy about it.

We went into the gift shop where I bought yet another fridge magnet, this time with a little map of the country on it. A red line ran from Land's End to John o'Groats and underneath it said '875 miles'.

'Huh,' said Mick when he saw it. 'Not with your navigation it's not.'

I decided a dignified silence would be the best response to this cutting remark, although that didn't stop me poking him hard in the ribs.

We stopped for a coffee in the unremarkable cafe and signed the End-to-End book at the back. We also tried, by standing just outside the cordon, to take a photograph by the 'official signpost' without paying the exorbitant fee of £9, thus attracting the ire of the photographer.

'You're not allowed to take photographs by the signpost!' he bellowed.

'Then move your signpost,' retorted Mick. 'It's spoiling my view.'

By then we had had enough. It was time to leave John o'Groats.

We had only cycled to the crossroads on the edge of the village when we realised that heading south into the prevailing wind would be no easier here on the Scottish mainland than it was on Orkney. Maximum effort resulted in a travelling speed of about half a mile per hour. At this rate we wouldn't reach Inverness for a month and our flight left in three days' time. Suddenly I didn't feel quite so smug about booking bargain flights from Inverness rather than the train from Thurso. What were we going to do? I remembered something I had read on the Internet while researching this trip, about a cycle bus that ran a daily service up and down the west coast of Scotland from Durness and Cape Wrath to Inverness. Their website had shown a picture of a trailer on the back of the bus which would carry your bicycle. I took a split-second decision to head west rather than south, that way we would be cycling with the wind behind us, or at least not directly against us. It was 100 miles in the wrong direction and I had no idea whether we would be able to catch a bus when we got there but decided to hope for the best. Mick didn't seem bothered by this last-minute change of plan. I wondered whether he secretly hoped we would miss our flight so that we could cycle all the way home again.

As we set off down the road to Thurso, the third time now that we had traversed this particular section of tarmac, a lone cyclist was battling the wind coming the other way. As he passed us he called out, 'Are you Ellie?'

What on earth? We were in about as remote an area as it is possible to be, miles from home. How could he possibly have known who I was?

'I've been reading your blog,' he said. 'I guessed it was you.'

The blue plastic capes, I think, may have given it away. He turned to Mick and said, 'How's your trenchfoot mate? Lost any more toenails?' Mick mumbled something in reply about his feet being much better now. After the cyclist had gone on his way, Mick gave me a hard stare: 'What,' he said, 'have you been writing in that damn blog?'

Actually, by this stage, my cape had more or less disintegrated. It now consisted of a few shreds of plastic, which flew out in all directions as I cycled along. I couldn't understand it. Mick's was still in perfect condition, yet mine was wrecked. Why? It was the same with our panniers, mine were covered in dirt and filth, and yet his were perfectly clean, the same as they had been the day we set out from Land's End. It wasn't fair. Mick says that some people are naturally scruffy and I am one of them, whereas he is naturally debonair and stylish. I resolved to push him into the next dirty puddle we came to and to slash up his cape when he was asleep as punishment for his smugness.

We traipsed back through Mey, Dunnett and Castletown to Thurso, where we decided to stop for the night. The tourist information office was closed, but there were some phone numbers for bed and breakfasts on the door. We phoned a few with no joy, then trudged around the streets, knocking on doors (not any doors, obviously, only ones with B & B signs in the window), before one kindly woman said she had no vacancies, but her daughter, Kay, who ran another establishment up the road, said she could fit us in.

Once we had taken a welcome shower, we headed back out into the bright lights of Thurso. There didn't seem a *huge* amount to do here on a Thursday night; there was the Newmarket Bar, but everyone in there was about twenty-five years younger than me so I didn't fancy it. We wandered along the river and headed up to the railway station, wanting to have a look at Britain's most northerly station – the one we should have been using had we managed to book onto the rail network all those weeks ago.

By now we were starving so we decided to make for the Pentland Hotel for some food. We had a fine steak dinner, accompanied by a couple of pints of keg beer, as that was all that was available. An early night seemed like a good idea, under the circumstances, so we plodded back up the hill to the B & B. It was drizzling and chilly for the middle of May and up there, on the top of Scotland, we felt a long way from home.

>>>>>>>>>>>>>>>>>>>>>>>>>>>>

Stats
Miles: 27
Total miles: 1,213
Pints of beer (each): 2
Scary boat crossings: 1
Stolen Lib-Dem cakes: 6 (Mick)

>>>>>>>>>>>>>>>>>>>>>>>>>>>>

DAY
30

THURSO
>>>>>>>>>>>>>>>>>>>>> TO >>>>>>>>>>>>>>>>>>>>>
TONGUE

At breakfast, Kay's husband Michael chatted amiably to us about our tour, the local economy and the area. He worked at Dounreay, he told us, and although the site was still a huge local employer – a fifth of the local population worked at the plant – they expected that number to decrease considerably as the power station was decommissioned. The hope was, he told us, that as the jobs at Dounreay disappeared, new ones would emerge in sustainable energy projects.

'We get a lot of weather up here,' he said, 'it would be crazy not to harness it.'

I agreed wholeheartedly that there was indeed a lot of weather up here.

We told him we were headed west towards Tongue and Loch Eriboll and he laughed at our rubbishy English pronunciation.

'A *lock*,' he said, 'is a device in a door which you open with a key. A *loch* is a Scottish lake.'

We practised this for a while: 'Lochhhhhhh, lochhhhhhhhh,' until breakfast arrived and shut us up. After breakfast we paid another visit to the Pentland Hotel to avail ourselves of their Internet service. It was with some relief that I was able to confirm we could indeed catch the cycle bus from Durness to Inverness. All we had to do was get ourselves to Durness on the north-east tip of Scotland. We were now on a mission to get west without delay. As we left Thurso another touring cyclist, who was travelling the same way, joined us. Aged about seventy, he only stayed with us for about a mile, before realising we were hopelessly slow, and he soon pedalled on ahead.

We travelled back through the same series of small settlements we had passed a few days earlier; Bridge of Forss, Reay and Melvich. Just the other side of Melvich we came to the Melvich Hotel. The hotel was evidently undergoing some refurbishment, but the bar was open, so we decided to call in for a quick drink. A football match was showing on the TV and the dozen or so (male) locals were all gathered around it. Mick assured me that Hibernian-Celtic was an unmissable game, so we ended up staying for the rest of the match before I could drag him out of the bar.

From Melvich the scenery became more attractive, with bright-yellow gorse and broom lining the road, which undulated gently across the top of Scotland. Beyond the gorse and tufted grass was the blue water of the Pentland Firth, white-tipped waves hinting at the choppiness of the sea. The road was top quality and a sign informed us the work had been part-funded by the European Union. On the other side of the road, the brown peat moors stretched away to the mountains in the distance. There was so much space. Space for the land and sky to stretch out and really make itself comfortable, no squishing into corners as it does in cities. I felt my spirit expand along with the landscape, and took a deep breath of fresh air and contentment.

We came to Bettyhill, another village created at the time of the Highland Clearances. It derives its name from Elizabeth Sutherland, who had a village built here to house some of the thousands of people who had been cleared off the land by her and her husband. Between 1811 and 1821, some 15,000 people were cleared from the Sutherland estates and one witness reported counting some 250 crofts on fire from one vantage point in Strathnaver, the valley that stretched south from Bettyhill.

On our right, as we came into the village, was a camping and caravan park, where we spotted the cyclist who had left us behind at Thurso. He had already set up camp, cooked and was eating his lunch as we passed. He gave us a wave and we gave a slightly abashed wave back. I tried to convey, with complicated gestures, that it was Mick's fault we had taken so long and that it wasn't me that was slow. I could tell, however, that it was lost in translation, as he threw me a puzzled, almost pitying look, before returning to his lunch. After Bettyhill the road swung south, following the course of the River Naver for a while, before turning west again towards Tongue Bay. The road stretched away into the distance, a silver-grey ribbon weaving through the landscape. On either side of the road peaty tarns glistened silver in the afternoon sunlight, turning deep blue as we passed them.

It was gone six when we arrived in Tongue. It was a matter of some regret that the village shop was closed as we had been hoping to purchase some classic 'I Love Tongue' stickers for our friends. We followed the signs for the youth hostel via a hairpin right-hand bend to the bottom of the village. We swung into the drive of the youth hostel, where my bike promptly skidded on the layer of gravel and I fell off, giving me the opportunity to say, as I picked myself up and dusted down, that it had been 'a slip of the Tongue'. After I had picked out the pieces of gravel embedded in my knees and elbows, we booked in. The youth hostel was very well set up and smartly decorated, although there was the usual 'make your own bed and be out of the hostel between 11 a.m. and 5 p.m.' routine. There were, however, home-made cakes on offer, baked by the warden, which were excellent. The location of the hostel is the best part though, set in an old hunting lodge right next to the Kyle of Tongue, where the sea reaches a pointed finger 10 miles inland.

In the evening we wandered back up the hill to the village. There were two hotels – the Ben Loyal Hotel and the Tongue Hotel. We decided to try the Ben Loyal Hotel first. We stopped to admire the view from the car park of the impressive mountain which rose behind the village, before strolling into the bar area. We appeared to be the only customers that evening. Mick ordered a pint of Sheepshaggers from the Cairngorm Brewery, I had a pint of Nessie's Monster Mash from the same stable. I thought the labels a bit silly but as Cairngorm also brewed the superlative Trade Winds we decided to give them the benefit of the doubt. Both were OK, although I preferred the Nessie. As we were the only customers, and the landlord appeared to have time on his hands, I started a conversation.

'What's the name of the big mountain behind the village?' I asked. 'It looks magnificent.'

The landlord gave me a look, which I couldn't quite fathom.

'It's called Ben Loyal,' he replied.

Of course it was. The conversation faltered after that and I looked around for something to distract me.

On the wall was a photograph of petrol head Jeremy Clarkson and some newspaper clippings from 2004. Clarkson apparently was very taken with the scenery of northern Scotland, which he was able to view from a helicopter while being winched from the summit of a nearby Scottish mountain. (Although widely reported at the time as being Ben Tongue, the mountain in question was in fact the one next door – Cnoc an Fhreiceadain.) What was Clarkson doing being winched from a mountain? Unlike most sensible people who walk and take in the scenery, Clarkson had driven his 4x4 up it, churning up peat bogs and heather as he went. Unsurprisingly, encouraging people to charge around the countryside and up mountains in off-road vehicles was a stunt that was not universally welcomed.

Clarkson wasn't the first to attempt driving up a Scottish mountain as a publicity stunt, however; this is accredited to one Henry Alexander Jnr. In 1911 Alexander, aged twenty-two, drove his dad's 20-horsepower Model T Ford to the top of Ben Nevis.

'Um, Dad, can I borrow the car?'

'Of course son, but go careful with it.'

'Duh, of course I will! It's not like I'm gonna take it up a *mountain* or something.'

It took several days to get up and down – with no helicopter assistance, of course, and he was reputed to have enjoyed the experience so much that in 1928 he did it all over again.

After a couple of pints in the Ben Loyal we tried the public bar of the Tongue Hotel, the Brass Tap, where a few locals were watching the football. It was a friendly enough place and a couple of the chaps at the bar asked us where we were headed. We explained we were on our way to Durness.

'Ach, it's a lovely run,' said one of them. 'Ye'll get a surprise as you get to Loch Eriboll though.' We asked him what he meant but he just smiled. 'You'll see,' he said.

>>>>>>>>>>>>>>>>>>>>>>>>>>>>

Stats
Miles: 47
Total miles: 1,260
Pints of beer (each): 3, plus 1 bottle
Boring football matches: 2
Humorously named Scottish villages: 1

>>>>>>>>>>>>>>>>>>>>>>>>>>>>

DAY
31

TONGUE

≫≫≫≫≫≫≫≫≫≫≫≫ **TO** ≫≫≫≫≫≫≫≫≫≫≫≫

INVERNESS

A bright, sunny morning greeted us as we set off across the causeway, which stretches across the Kyle of Tongue. The causeway was built in 1971, making the journey to the far west of Scotland much easier. Until 1828, Tongue's communication with the outside world was by sea, until the ubiquitous Thomas Telford completed the road south from Tongue to Lairg, soon followed by roads east to Thurso and west to Durness. The causeway finally did away with the passenger ferry that used to cross the Kyle and also afforded magnificent views as we crossed. Pink-tinged sand flats flanked the blue water to our left, home to innumerable sea birds and on our right, the entrance to the Kyle was a regular haunt of otters, seals, porpoise, dolphins and whales. I had no idea this part of Scotland was so beautiful; I almost felt like weeping with the sheer joy of being here. I probably would have done except Mick would have said, 'For *God's sake*, what's the matter *now*?'

Incredibly peaceful now, a few hundred years ago the Kyle of Tongue was the site of a significant skirmish between Bonnie

Prince Charlie's Jacobites and government troops. In March 1746 the ship *Hazard*, which had been captured from the English and renamed *Le Prince Charles Stewart*, left France for Inverness, carrying firearms and £13,000 of gold from Louis XV destined for Bonnie Prince Charlie – in support of his campaign to remove George II from the Scottish throne. However, the ship was attacked by King George's fleet in the Moray Firth and scarpered north around Duncansby Head, with the navy frigate *Sheerness* in pursuit. *Sheerness* was the faster of the two and in desperation *Le Prince Charles Stewart*, on the advice of local pilots, turned into the Kyle of Tongue. Having a shallower draught than *Sheerness*, the Jacobites hoped to be able to sail far enough into the kyle to evade the guns of the navy frigate. Unfortunately the ship ran aground on one of the sand banks. After five hours of bombardment, what was left of the crew decided to make for the shore, and get the arms and gold out overland. They headed down the side of the kyle but at the head were intercepted by Lord Reay's militia and captured. The government troops recovered some, but not all, of the gold, which, it was said the Jacobites hid along the side of the kyle, and finally, just before being captured, threw the remainder in Loch Hakel at the top of the kyle. When word of the capture reached Bonnie Prince Charlie he sent 1,500 men north to try and retrieve the booty but they were defeated en route, thus leaving him 1,500 troops short at the Battle of Culloden the following month. It is said that occasionally a gold coin turns up, embedded in the hooves of cattle grazing by the side of the loch.

By now we had been on our bikes pretty much all day every day for a month, and it was beginning to feel almost as natural to be in the saddle as it was out. After the incident on the first morning when the chain came off, the trip had been remarkably hassle-free with regard to mishaps. The only problems had been the upside-down brake blocks and overdoing the oil, neither of which were the bike's fault. Before setting off I had avidly read other people's blog accounts of cycling End-to-End and they seemed to be littered with tales of punctures, broken spokes, snapped chains, buckled rims and countless other disasters. We had crashed our way along towpaths, rocky cycle paths, a couple of fields and countless bumpy roads with appalling potholes, and had no major problems at all. I can only assume it was beginner's luck.

Continuing west across the top of Scotland, the road took us across 14 miles of the Moine or A'Mhoine, a huge, flat and wild expanse of heather and peat moor, dotted with dark, boggy pools. After my embarrassing moment in the hotel the previous evening, I now recognised the distinctive four peaks of Ben Loyal rising out of the landscape, the view of which had accompanied us for some miles. Although at 2,506 feet, Ben Loyal only just qualifies as a Corbett; what it lacks in height it makes up for in majesty, which is no doubt why it is known as the 'queen of Scottish mountains'. Beyond Ben Loyal rose the steep peak of Ben Hope, Scotland's most northerly Munro.

No one lives here – the only building is the now derelict Moine House, set back on an old road, which passed slightly south of the one on which we were travelling. Built as a halfway house, it was intended to offer shelter to travellers crossing the moor; it was the only building we saw across the whole of the Moine. Yet, although deserted, this area is known across the world, famous for its Thrust. The Highlands Controversy was one of the major scientific arguments of the time. Key to the debate was the layer of rocks along the western side of the Moine where great wedges of older rocks have been thrust over younger Cambrian ones. This was long before plate tectonics had even been dreamed of and the two most prominent geologists of the day, Roderick Murchison and Archibald Geikie, maintained that the rocks must have been laid down in the order that they were found. Charles Lapworth had trained as a teacher but was a keen amateur geologist. He proved to be pretty good at it, and was eventually appointed as the first professor of geology at Birmingham University. He thought Murchison and Geikie were wrong, and that the complex layering of rock at the Moine was due to folding – older rocks having been heaved up and over younger rocks millions of years ago. Benjamin Peach and John Horne were sent to the area by the British Geological Survey to examine the rocks and try to resolve the controversy. Peach was intuitive and insightful, but was easily distracted; when out for the day he filled his notebooks with paintings and sketches of the wildlife around him, rather than documenting his discoveries. Luckily, Horne was a methodical sort of chap and was meticulous about writing up notes.

Even so, it was not until 1907, some twenty-four years after their field trip, that they finally published their findings. Peach and Horne concluded that the rocks were indeed stacked in the wrong order, and that the cause of this must have been movements in the earth's crust. The resulting book, *The North-West Highlands Memoir*, is one of the most revered geological texts of all time and the Moine Thrust remains one of the most famous geological features on Earth.

As we approached Loch Eriboll we suddenly understood what the chap in the bar in Tongue had meant. The road unexpectedly tipped downwards, even at bike speed it felt like we were falling off the end of the road, and below was a spectacular view of the loch. Loch Eriboll is vast – a mile wide, 10 miles long and, in places, 360 feet deep. There was no causeway or ferry this time so our only option was to cycle the single-track road around it. Immediately below us was a distinctive feature, a long piece of land connected to the shore by a narrow shingle beach. Known as Ard Neakie, this used to be the terminus for a ferry that would cross the loch to Portnancon on the other side, until the 1930s.

Somewhat disconcertingly, a rather large number of battleships appeared to be stationed in the waters of the loch. We later discovered we had arrived in the middle of a military exercise, which are not uncommon here. In World War Two Loch Eriboll was used as a base for naval vessels and, at the end of World War Two, thirty-three German U-boats surrendered here as part of Operation Deadlight, although the event was heavily censored at the time. It was nicknamed Loch 'Orrible by servicemen stationed here, I suppose it is a bit remote and it gets its fair share of weather here, too, but today it looked glorious and not 'orrible at all.

We cycled down the eastern side to the foot of the loch beyond which the mountain of Foinaven and its surrounding peaks stretched away to the south. Foinaven was the subject of some attention a few years ago when an Ordnance Survey map showed the main peak of Ganu Mor to be 2,999 feet, only a foot away from being a coveted Munro. Munro baggers got very excited about this and arguments raged for a decade as to whether it was or whether it wasn't. Finally in 2007 the Munro Society commissioned a major survey using the latest satellite-positioning equipment. Foinaven was declared to be 2,988 feet high, a full 12 feet short of the required height, and everybody calmed down again.

On the Grand National racecourse at Aintree, between the fences Becher's Brook and Canal Turn, is a small fence known as Foinavon. Foinavon was a horse, named after the Scottish mountain, that was entered in the 1967 Grand National (albeit with slightly different spelling). His prospects were not brilliant; in fact his owner was so unenthusiastic about his chances that he was not even at the race. At the start of the race the odds of Foinavon winning were 100–1. By the twenty-third fence Foinavon was lagging behind. Up in front a loose horse suddenly veered across the course in front of the fence causing a huge pile up of horses and riders. Foinavon, coming up from behind, swerved to avoid the melee and jumped gracefully over fence twenty-three, while other riders were still struggling to remount and jump the fence. Foinavon romped home and thousands of punters wished they had put more than a shilling each way on the rank outsider.

We headed up the other side of the loch. At Laid village, a tiny hamlet halfway up the other side of the loch, we got very excited when we saw a sign for a cafe. By now small pleasures loomed large and up here it was foolish to pass up the chance of a cup of tea; it could be miles before another opportunity arose. We pulled over and went in. The proprietor had evidently been working hard baking all morning and offered a range of delicious-looking home-made cakes for sale.

'What would you like?' I asked Mick, having made my selection – a huge slice of carrot cake. He looked at the array of cakes and pondered for a moment before saying to the chap behind the counter, 'Have you got any Kit Kats?'

'No,' the man replied dryly, 'I don't make Kit Kats.'

'Oh, OK.' Pause. 'Mars Bars?'

'No.'

'Oh well,' said Mick, trying not to look disappointed. 'I'll have carrot cake, then.'

Not long after leaving the cafe we had our first and last close shave with a vehicle, when a white van roared past us on the narrow road forcing us to dive, with our bikes, onto the verge. Within seconds the van had disappeared up the road, leaving a cloud of dust behind it. This was one of the quietest roads in the entire country and we had escaped being squashed by millimetres. Mick shook his fist and swore loudly. I wondered whether the cafe owner had sent out a hit man; it seemed a coincidence.

Apart from the van, we had been amazed by the courtesy shown towards cyclists in Scotland. Used to the mutual enmity that often characterises the driver–cyclist relationship in cities, imagine our surprise when drivers not only thanked us for pulling in, they pulled over to let us go first! We cycled passed them smiling and waving, and the occupants of the waiting car smiled and waved back – it was wonderful.

At the entrance to the loch the road swung west once more, past beautiful, quiet, deserted beaches, as it wriggled its way along the coast towards Durness. The sea looked inviting, although, this being northern Scotland, I was not taken in. I had made that mistake once before, at Applecross on the west coast, where I had gleefully charged into the sea on a hot summer day, only to about turn and run, shrieking, straight out again. I had no intention of dipping even a toe in the water without a full wetsuit including boots.

We passed a lay-by set back off the road.

'That would make a good campervan spot,' said Mick. I groaned. He had been making this comment at least five times a day whenever we passed anywhere remotely suitable for parking his campervan.

'Yes, it would,' I replied automatically.

Mick had a number of other stock phrases, which he employed with wearying regularity:

1. *'One day this will all flood.'*
   He would announce this whenever he saw any piece of flat land. The Somerset Levels, the Shropshire Plain, practically all of Cheshire and the west side of Lancashire were, according to Mick, set to disappear underwater in the very near future.

2. *'Just around this corner and it's downhill after that.'*
   This statement was more wishful thinking than rooted in any kind of knowledge of the local landscape. After The Struggle at Ambleside I stopped taking any notice of this one.

3. *'My lungs are burning – is that normal?'*
   Whenever we had to cycle uphill.

4. *'It's looking brighter over there.'*
   Whenever it was raining, in an attempt to cheer us up.

5. *'Is it too early for a pint?'*
   Every time we passed a pub.

On the whole, Mick and I had managed to get along pretty well, the brake block row aside. I am fairly sure I would not have finished the ride had I been on my own; when my spirits were flagging then a chivvy-up or a sing-song helped no end. And if I had been doing this on my own, I doubt I would have had the chance to sample as many beers.

Just before Durness we came to Smoo Cave. Sir Walter Scott visited here in 1814, reaching the cave in a rowing boat from Loch Eriboll. Judging by his diary he didn't like it much: 'When we reached the extremity of this passage, we found it declined suddenly to a horrible gulf, or well, filled with dark water, and of great depth, over which the rock closed'; and 'Imagination can figure few deaths more horrible than to be sucked under these rocks into some unfathomable abyss...'

Undeterred by Scott's account, I was keen to take a look. Smoo Cave is unique within the UK in being half sea cave and half limestone karst; the entrance cavern was formed by the action of the sea and the rear of the cave by underground stream water. It is also the largest cave entrance in the UK, measuring more than 50 feet high and 100 feet wide. Inside the chamber was a sign advertising trips into the back of the cave by boat. Mick was whimpering something about claustrophobia but I took no notice and booked us up.

Eventually, about eight of us clambered into a little dinghy and bobbed into the cave. Above us, light streamed in from a large hole in the roof, through which the waters of Allt Smoo, glittering in the sunshine, cascaded noisily into the pool below. It was incredibly beautiful. Above the cave a wooden walkway allows you to view the waterfall from the top as well, so after alighting from our little boat we climbed back up to the road and spent some time peering into the cave from above.

The bus back to Inverness left Smoo Cave at quarter past three. As it was now two o'clock and we were getting peckish we decided to see if we could find something to eat. We set off towards the village and soon came across the village hall, which is nearer Smoo than Durness. As luck would have it, we had arrived during the Cape Wrath Challenge, a week of very hilly, masochistic running races around the north-west corner of Scotland. Today's race had finished with refreshments in the hall and, although they were now packing up, two of the ladies on the food stall very kindly made us some cheese sandwiches, which they sold to us for a few pennies.

The gardens were landscaped with the help of BBC TV's *Beechgrove Garden* and include the John Lennon Memorial Garden. Lennon apparently spent many happy childhood summers in Durness with his cousin Stanley Parkes, whose family owned a croft here. Lennon returned to Durness in 1969 with Yoko Ono, his son Julian and her daughter Kyoko, for a family holiday. Wanting to get away from it all, John dispensed with their chauffeur and drove the family there himself in a white Austin Maxi. Unfortunately, although John had many talents, driving wasn't one of them. He had poor eyesight and little road sense, and wasn't used to driving. On the single-track road near Loch Eriboll, maybe somewhere close to the site of our brush with the white van, they met a car coming the other way. John panicked and drove the car off the road, resulting in both he and Yoko needing stitches at the Lawson Memorial Hospital in Golspie. According to Parkes, after the accident, Yoko had the Austin Maxi shipped to their mansion in Ascot and mounted in the garden on a concrete plinth, as a reminder of their mortality.

I remember the Maxi (not that particular one, but the model); we used to have one when I was a teenager. I must say the last thing I would want to do with it is mount it on a plinth. It was a terrible car, even by British Leyland standards – an ugly thing shaped like a box on wheels. Why my dad chose to buy one painted shit-brown I have no idea, but it was the 1970s, when the entire population seemed to have been struck by a collective attack of bad taste. The Maxi did, however, have one great feature from my point of view – the number of people you could crowd into it. After parties I would, on behalf of my dad, magnanimously offer a lift home to half the guests.

'Is there enough room?' they would ask.

'Oh yes,' I replied confidently. 'We've got a Maxi.'

One evening my poor, long-suffering dad, turned up to collect me from a friend's house and found a throng of youngsters standing around on the pavement.

'Are they waiting for a bus?' asked my dad innocently.

'Um, no, I said we could give them a lift,' I replied.

He got a bit panicky when someone went round and opened the rear tailgate.

'No one gets in the boot!' he yelled.

'Relax, man,' said the spotty youth, whom at the time I thought super-cool. 'I was just slinging my guitar in.'

I am horror-struck now by my selfishness; it didn't even occur to me that my dad might not want to spend the early hours of the morning driving my mates around Bristol. But if he objected, he never said so.

We were ready and waiting for the bus when it arrived from Inverness. The cycle bus was operated by Tim Dearman Coaches and we thought it a superb idea. A trailer is attached to the back of the bus and can accommodate eleven bikes. The driver told us that, although it is advisable to book in advance, they have never left anyone stranded (although on one or two occasions they have had to load bikes into the coach as well). We sat down in the seats with relief. We would be travelling the west coast of Scotland after all, albeit not quite in the manner originally intended.

The scenery was superlative, and I felt a twinge of regret that we had been unable to execute our original plan of cycling up this way. We stopped at numerous settlements, occasionally detouring out to the coast to places like Kinlochbervie, where there is a massive fish-handling depot, and the attractive village of Lochinver, before stopping for a three-second comfort break at Ullapool. We made a crazy dash to the toilet and leapt back onto the bus, which then trundled onto Inverness, depositing us at the bus station four and a half hours after our departure from Durness. Tim Dearman retired in April 2011, but D&E Coaches is now running the same service. As far as I know this is the only bus of its type in the country, but I would very much like to see more of them.

We weren't too sure what to do about accommodation in Inverness. Our helpful bus driver confirmed there was a municipal campsite not too far from the centre of town, so we headed for that. On the way, as we headed down Kenneth Street, we passed numerous bed and breakfast establishments. I was amused at the signs outside advertising facilities designed to tempt the weary traveller: colour TV; tea and coffee; central heating in all rooms. And on some signs – unbelievably – hot and cold water! Hot *and* cold water! Well I never! Inverness rocks, doesn't it?

Despite the temptations of a bed and breakfast with hot *and* cold water, we pressed on to the campsite at the Bught, which was a reasonable enough site. One of the poles snapped when we were putting up the tent, so some makeshift repairs were necessary, but we managed to get the thing up (although it did look slightly lopsided and I was glad that the weather was set to be fair for a couple of days). Once camp had been set up, we headed into town in search of a pint of beer. It was twenty years since I had last been to Inverness. I'm not sure whether the place had changed dramatically in the intervening years or whether my memory was playing tricks on me, maybe a bit of both. I remembered an elegant town, with old granite buildings and a fine river. The river was still there, and as pleasant as ever, but the town itself looked tired, and the streets full of pound shops and empty retail units. I found it rather depressing. And there was no sign of a decent pint.

Finding a pub serving a well-kept pint in a strange town is often not easy. Finding one north of the Scottish border is more problematic, simply because real ale is not as widespread as it is down south, although the situation is improving each year. We found it slightly embarrassing going into various pubs, looking at the pumps offering keg beer and then shuffling out again, so we developed an elaborate role play which we dubbed 'Looking for Kenny'. One of us would stick our noses around the door, hoping from this vantage point to be able to see the bar and what beer was on offer. If there was no cask beer available the 'looker' would call out to the other one:

'No, Kenny's not here, now where did he say he would meet us?' after which we would quietly withdraw and go on to the next pub. Occasionally we could not see the bar from the doorway and would go into the pub, casting glances left and right, whilst taking in the pumps at the same time.

'Nope, Kenny's not here,' we would say in a resigned tone, heading for the door. 'Thanks anyway!' we would say to the bartender to ensure that they didn't take offence at our failure to purchase a drink.

'Kenny' was not at the first half a dozen or so pubs we tried; indeed, we began to wonder whether he had deserted Inverness altogether, when we came across the Castle Tavern, which was a real ale drinker's paradise. We cheered up immediately and, as this was our last night, we proceeded to indulge in our own little beer festival. The first offering was from the Isle of Skye Brewery (brewers of the two Cuillin beers), Flora MacDonald's – a house beer brewed especially for the pub. It was a nice copper-coloured beer, which went down a treat as the first pint. Mick went for a second, while I tried Texas from the Houston Brewing Company, a darker ruby beer. Someone at the bar mentioned Blackfriars, another real ale pub – suddenly from there being no beer at all, we were spoilt for choice.

We headed down the road to Blackfriars, where I had Orkney Best from the Highland Brewing Company and Mick went for Ossian from the Inveralmond Brewery, both excellent golden beers. And to think that before we set off on this trip we thought all we would be able to get north of the border would be a pint of McEwan's! At this point we should have called it a night, but I really wanted to try a glass of Beinn Dearg Ale from An Teallach Brewery. After all, it was our last night and I was unlikely to come across this beer back in England. I asked for a half of 'Been Durrg' and could tell by the way the barman's mouth twitched that my pronunciation was a little off. The beer was excellent though, a nice, sweetish beer, and a fine one to finish on before walking the not inconsiderable distance back to the campsite.

After the evening's entertainment I had completely forgotten the delicate condition of the tent, which was only staying up through force of habit and sheer goodwill. For some reason the entrance seemed to move as I aimed for it, and I bumped my head on the top of the tent. It fell down. We crawled in as best we could and went to sleep. Maybe it was just as well this was the last night of the trip.

>>>>>>>>>>>>>>>>>>>>>>>>>>>>>>>>>

Stats
Miles: 24
Total miles: 1,284
Pints of beer (each): 5½, maybe 6½
Bus journeys: 1 (100 miles)
Assassination attempts: 1

>>>>>>>>>>>>>>>>>>>>>>>>>>>>>>>>>

GOING HOME

>>>>>>>>>>>>>>>>>>>>>>>>>>>>>>>

Before catching our flight, we had to get to the airport, which was about 8 miles east of the city along the coast of the Moray Firth. The main road didn't look too inviting, so we took a quieter, although slightly hillier, road further inland. This was the B9006 or Culloden Road. After passing through the village of Culloden we came to Drumossie Moor, which is now more commonly known as Culloden Moor. We checked our watches and decided we had just enough time to call into the new visitors' centre, which had come into view on our right-hand side. Culloden Moor is, of course, the site of the last battle to be fought on British soil, or at least the last one up until the time of writing. We didn't have time to go up the moor itself, so we contented ourselves by mooching around the visitors' centre. It had an excellent gift shop, with the chance to purchase everything a tourist visiting Scotland could desire. I bought some souvenirs for the family. Mick was unable to resist buying a joke tam-o'-shanter complete with ginger hair. He said he wanted to cheer himself up as he was feeling rather glum at the prospect of returning home.

It did feel a bit strange. We had been on the road for a month and it had given both of us a sense of freedom. Now we were going home and back to our usual routines. I'm not sure whether the desire to move around isn't hardwired into our brains somewhere; after all, it's not that long, in evolutionary terms, since human beings have taken to settling in one place. In quite a lot of cultures they still don't. But return home we must.

Return home! The flight! We had done it again. We had become so caught up with the moment that we had forgotten we were on a schedule. We hastily remounted our bikes and hightailed it to the airport. Relieved, we discovered we still had half an hour before we had to board our plane, time which we needed in order to execute our flight action plan. Our elected airline, in common with most today, wouldn't take cycles in the hold unless suitably packaged, so the previous day we had visited a DIY store and purchased a lot of clear plastic, some tape, a pair of scissors and a screwdriver. We now proceeded to deflate the tyres on the bikes, loosen and turn the handlebars, and wrap them up in the plastic. To save paying for several pieces of luggage we also had the bright idea of wrapping all the pannier bags in one piece of plastic and booking it on as one outsize item. We took up quite a lot of room on the concourse sorting all this out, while other passengers stepped round us, and it also took a lot longer than we thought. It was with some relief that, slightly hot and bothered now, we finally booked everything onto the flight and took our seats on the plane.

We didn't feel quite so smug when we arrived at Bristol. We had been a bit stingy with the tape, so the plastic wrapping around our panniers had fallen apart, causing all the contents to spill out. Luckily, the staff were very helpful and retrieved all the composite parts for us. When our bikes were offloaded, after everyone else had collected their luggage from the carousel and gone home, we realised, to our dismay, that the bicycle pump we had faithfully carried with us on the journey in case of punctures, had a fitting that was the wrong size and we were unable to reinflate the tyres.

I marvelled at our incompetence. Mick said less of the 'our' as it had been my responsibility to buy a lightweight pump. I retorted that he should have checked it before we left, as he was Maintenance. The recriminations continued for some minutes, after which I phoned my sister, who gallantly drove out to the airport with another pump.

Once the bikes had been sorted we waved her goodbye again and cycled into Bristol from the airport. Mick was still wearing his tam-o'-shanter, with fake ginger hair splaying out from under the tartan cap, and was garnering quizzical looks from passing motorists. It was early evening and, as we coasted alongside the harbour into the centre of town, we passed waterfront pubs and bars, their tables thronged with people enjoying the late-spring sunshine. As we passed them, Mick looked at me.

'Is it,' he said, 'too early for a pint?'

>>>>>>>>>>>>>>>>>>>>>>>>>>>

Stats
Miles: 28
Total miles: 1,312
Wonderful cycling trips: 1 (each)!

>>>>>>>>>>>>>>>>>>>>>>>>>>>

BEER INDEX

FIFTY OF THE BEST BEERS OF THE TRIP:

1. Tinners
   Brewery: St Austell Brewery, St Austell, Cornwall
   Pub: Tinners Arms, Zennor, Cornwall

2. Eden Ale
   Brewery: Sharp's Brewery, Rock, Cornwall (parent
   company Molson Coors)
   Pub: Perranporth Inn, Perranporth, Cornwall

3. Proper Job IPA
   Brewery: St Austell Brewery, St Austell, Cornwall.
   Pub: Shipwrights Inn, Padstow, Cornwall

4. Otter Ale
   Brewery: Otter Brewery, Honiton, Devon
   Pub: Three Little Pigs, Crediton, Devon

5. Red Rock
   Brewery: Red Rock Brewery, Bishopsteignton, Devon
   Pub: Silverton Inn, Silverton, Devon

6. Dobs Best Bitter
   Brewery: Exe Valley Brewery, Silverton, Devon
   Pub: Lamb Inn, Silverton, Devon

7. Yellowhammer
   Brewery: O'Hanlon's Brewing Company, Whimple near
   Exeter, Devon
   Pub: The Three Tuns, Silverton, Devon

8. Summerset
   Brewery: Yeovil Ales, Yeovil, Somerset
   Pub: New Inn, Wedmore, Somerset

9. Gorge Best Bitter
   Brewery: Cheddar Ales, Cheddar, Somerset
   Pub: Riverside Inn, Cheddar, Somerset

10. Brigstow Bitter
    Brewery: Arbor Ales, Kingswood, Bristol
    Pub: Cornubia, Redcliffe, Bristol

11. Wye Valley Bitter
    Brewery: Wye Valley Brewery, Stoke Lacy, Herefordshire
    Pub: The Bell, Skenfrith, Monmouthshire

12. Cwrw Hâf
    Brewery: Tomos Watkin, Swansea, Wales (Hurns Brewing Company)
    Pub: The Angel Inn, Grosmont, Monmouthshire

13. .410
    Brewery: Golden Valley Ales, Peterchurch, Herefordshire
    Pub: The Angel Inn, Grosmont, Monmouthshire

14. Butty Bach
    Brewery: Wye Valley Brewery, Stoke Lacy, Herefordshire
    Pub: The Angel Inn, Grosmont, Monmouthshire

15. Twisted Spire
    Brewery: Hobsons Brewery, Newhouse Farm, Worcestershire
    Pub: The Baron at Bucknell, Worcestershire

16. Hobsons Best Bitter
    Brewery: Hobsons Brewery, Newhouse Farm, Worcestershire
    Pub: Hundred House Inn, Purslow, Shropshire

17. Big Nev's
    Brewery: Six Bells Brewery, Bishop's Castle, Shropshire
    Pub: The Six Bells Brewery & Pub, Bishop's Castle, Shropshire

18. Goldings
    Brewery: Six Bells Brewery, Bishop's Castle, Shropshire
    Pub: The Six Bells Brewery & Pub, Bishop's Castle, Shropshire

19. Cloud Nine
    Brewery: Six Bells Brewery, Bishop's Castle, Shropshire
    Pub: The Six Bells Brewery & Pub, Bishop's Castle, Shropshire

20. Marathon Ale
    Brewery: Six Bells Brewery, Bishop's Castle, Shropshire
    Pub: The Six Bells Brewery & Pub, Bishop's Castle, Shropshire

21. Solstice
    Brewery: The Three Tuns (John Roberts Brewing Co),
    Bishop's Castle, Shropshire
    Pub: The Three Tuns, Bishop's Castle, Shropshire

22. Mojo
    Brewery: Monty's Brewery, Montgomery, Powys
    Pub: The Horseshoe Inn, Bridges, Ratlinghope

23. Hobgoblin
    Brewery: Wychwood Brewery, Witney, Oxfordshire (parent
    company Marston's)
    Pub: The Carrier's Inn, Hatchmere, Cheshire

24. Owzat!
    Brewery: Slater's Ales, Stafford, Staffordshire
    Pub: The Original Farmer's Arms, Eccleston, Lancashire

25. Jennings Bitter
    Brewery: Jennings Brewery, Cockermouth, Cumbria
    (parent company Marston's)
    Pub: The Canal Turn, Carnforth, Cumbria

26. Bluebird Bitter
    Brewery: Coniston Brewing Company, Coniston, Cumbria
    Pub: The Brown Horse Inn, Winster, Windermere, Cumbria

27. Doris's 90th Birthday Ale
    Brewery: Hesket Newmarket Brewery, Hesket Newmarket, Cumbria
    Pub: Old Crown, Hesket Newmarket, Cumbria

28. Haystacks
    Brewery: Hesket Newmarket Brewery, Hesket Newmarket, Cumbria
    Pub: Old Crown, Hesket Newmarket, Cumbria

29. Scafell Blonde
    Brewery: Hesket Newmarket Brewery, Hesket Newmarket, Cumbria
    Pub: Old Crown, Hesket Newmarket, Cumbria

30. Skiddaw
    Brewery: Hesket Newmarket Brewery, Hesket Newmarket, Cumbria
    Pub: Old Crown, Hesket Newmarket

31. Criffel
    Brewery: Sulwath Brewers, Castle Douglas, Dumfries and Galloway
    Pub: The Globe Inn, Dumfries

BEER INDEX

32. Northern Light
Brewery: The Orkney Brewery, Sandwick, Orkney (parent company Sinclair Breweries)
Pub: South Beach Hotel, Troon, Ayrshire

33. Arran Red Squirrel (bottled)
Brewery: Isle of Arran Brewery, Brodick, Isle of Arran
Pub: Brewery shop

34. Arran Sunset (bottled)
Brewery: Isle of Arran Brewery, Brodick, Isle of Arran
Pub: Lochranza Hotel, Lochranza, Isle of Arran

35. Old Speckled Hen
Brewery: Morland Brewery, Bury St Edmunds, Suffolk (parent company Greene King)
Pub: The Tartan Tavern, Oban, Argyll

36. Trade Winds
Brewery: Cairngorm Brewery Company, Aviemore, Inverness-shire
Pub: The Inchree Centre, Onich

37. Red Cuillin
Brewery: Isle of Skye Brewing Company, Uig, Isle of Skye
Pub: The Inchree Centre, Onich, Fort William

38. Williams Gold
Brewery: Williams Brothers Brewing Company, Alloa, Clackmananshire
Pub: The Grog & Gruel, Fort William, Inverness-shire

39. Williams Red
    Brewery: Williams Brothers Brewing Company, Alloa, Clackmananshire
    Pub: The Grog and Gruel, Fort William, Inverness-shire

40. Black Cuillin
    Brewery: Isle of Skye Brewing Company, Uig, Isle of Skye
    Pub: The Bothy, Fort Augustus, Inverness-shire

41. Dark Island (bottle)
    Brewery: The Orkney Brewery, Sandwick, Orkney (parent company Sinclair Breweries)
    Pub: The Seaview Hotel, John o'Groats

42. Scapa Special
    Brewery: The Highland Brewing Company, Swannay, Orkney
    Pub: Helgi's, Kirkwall, Orkney

43. Schiehallion (bottled)
    Brewery: Harviestoun Brewery, Alva, Clackmannanshire
    Pub: Melvich Hotel, Melvich, Caithness

44. Sheepshaggers Gold
    Brewery: Cairngorm Brewery Company, Aviemore, Inverness-shire
    Pub: The Ben Loyal Hotel, Tongue, Sutherland

45. Nessie's Monster Mash
    Brewery: Cairngorm Brewery Company, Aviemore,
    Inverness-shire
    Pub: The Ben Loyal Hotel, Tongue, Sutherland

46. Flora MacDonald's
    Brewery: Isle of Skye Brewing Company, Uig, Isle of Skye
    Pub: Castle Tavern, Inverness

47. Texas
    Brewery: Houston Brewing Company, Houston,
    Renfrewshire
    Pub: Castle Tavern, Inverness

48. Orkney Best
    Brewery: The Highland Brewing Company, Swannay, Orkney
    Pub: Blackfriars, Inverness

49. Ossian
    Brewery: The Inveralmond Brewery, Perth
    Pub: Blackfriars, Inverness

50. Beinn Dearg Ale
    Brewery: An Teallach Ale Company, Dundonnell,
    Wester Ross
    Pub: Blackfriars, Inverness

ACKNOWLEDGEMENTS

With thanks to Richard Bennett, Katie Hayes, Frank Band, Asim Ilyas and Yvonne Parks for your advice and support. Thanks also to all the people at Summersdale, especially Chris Turton, for so ably editing this book. Thanks to Billy Muir for your very useful advice. A big thank you to everyone who sponsored us and encouraged us along the route. Finally, thanks to Mick for talking me into doing this ride in the first place.

ARE WE NEARLY THERE YET?

A Family's 8,000 Car
Journey Around Britain

Ben Hatch

ISBN: 978 1 84953 155 9

£8.99

Paperback

They were bored, broke, burned out and turning 40. So when Ben and his wife Dinah were approached to write a guidebook about family travel, they embraced the open road, ignoring friends' warnings: 'One of you will come back chopped up in a bin bag in the roof box.'

Featuring deadly puff adders, Billie Piper's pyjamas and a friend of Hitler's, it's a story about love, death, falling out, moving on and growing up, and 8,000 misguided miles in a Vauxhall Astra.

'A voyage of pain, argument, baby wipes, discovery and utter delight... Never travel in a car with children without this book by your side...'   TERRY WOGAN

'A funny, touching cross-country jaunt that's as much about being a kid as it is about being a grown-up (And thank God someone else did it so you don't have to...)'   DANNY WALLACE

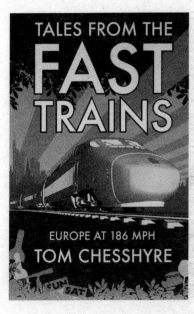

TALES FROM THE FAST TRAINS
Europe at 186 mph

Tom Chesshyre

ISBN: 978 1 84953 151 1

£8.99

Paperback

Tired of airport security queues, delays and all those extra taxes and charges, Tom Chesshyre embarks on a series of high-speed adventures across the Continent on its fast trains instead. He discovers the hidden delights of mysterious Luxembourg, super-trendy Rotterdam, much-maligned Frankfurt and lovely lakeside Lausanne, via a pop concert in Lille.

It's 186 mph all the way – well, apart from a power cut in the Channel Tunnel on the way to Antwerp. What fun can you have at the ends of the lines? Jump on board and find out...

'If you've "done" Paris and Bruges and are wondering, "Where next?", then this may be a quiet revelation'   ANDREW MARR

'splendid twenty-first-century railway adventure. At last, this IS the age of the train'   SIMON CALDER

Have you enjoyed this book?

If so, why not write a review on your favourite website?
Thanks very much for buying this Summersdale book.

www.summersdale.com